God and the Financial Crisis

God and the Financial Crisis:

Essays on Faith, Economics, and Politics in the Wake of the Great Recession

Edited by

Gary D. Badcock

Cambridge Scholars Publishing

God and the Financial Crisis: Essays on Faith, Economics, and Politics in the Wake of the Great Recession

Edited by Gary D. Badcock

This book first published 2016

Cambridge Scholars Publishing

Lady Stephenson Library, Newcastle upon Tyne, NE6 2PA, UK

British Library Cataloguing in Publication Data
A catalogue record for this book is available from the British Library

ISBN (10): 1-4438-8596-7
ISBN (13): 978-1-4438-8596-6

TABLE OF CONTENTS

PREFACE

This collection is drawn from a series of Conference events and special papers contributed over the period 2011–14, hosted by the Centre for Public Theology at Huron University College in London, Ontario.

The goal of the Centre for Public Theology is to facilitate research on issues of broad public concern, bringing academic theology into dialogue with other academic disciplines and with the public at large. This interdisciplinary approach is aimed both at encouraging a movement in theology beyond what has become the ghetto-world of conventional religion in the contemporary West, and at making useful contributions to scholarly thinking about pressing issues in public life. Our recent projects have included work on subjects such as the Afghanistan war, out of which a previous collection was published by Cambridge Scholars.[1]

This new volume represents the main outcome of a somewhat larger overall project on the financial crisis of 2008, and the ensuing "Great Recession." The chapters herein have been written by people from a variety of disciplinary backgrounds, walks of life, political persuasions, and theological traditions—all sharing a general conviction, however, that questions of money, together with contemporary problems of poverty, inequality, and economic stability, are too important *not* to be made the subject of theological analysis and critique. The contributions range over themes as diverse as the actual events in the banks leading up to the crash of 2008, to the nature of religion, business ethics, economic growth and global development, idolatry and its contemporary expressions, and, not least, what has lately come to be known as "quantitative easing for people instead of banks."

A recurring theme in what follows is that religious ideals and assumptions have profound cultural importance, including in the sphere of economic life—and that such ideals and assumptions are found pervasively in the contemporary West. They appear, however, not only in specialized, overtly religious institutions such as the churches, but also in

---

[1] Gary D. Badcock and Darren C. Marks, eds., *War, Human Dignity and Nation Building: Theological Perspectives on Canada's Role in Afghanistan* (Newcastle upon Tyne: Cambridge Scholars, 2010).

those quasi-religious, customary, and mainly unquestioned assumptions that govern individual and collective life well beyond the specialized world of institutional religion. What this volume suggests is that mainstream patterns of economic and social experience in the modern West are governed by such customary beliefs (such as our "belief" in free individuals who make choices in an abstractly free market) and practices (such as the consumerism which is embraced as the meaning of life), which is to say that they can be illuminated by appeal to the categories of religion, and possibly that they can best be understood in this way.

As editor, I would like to thank my recent Centre for Public Theology Research Assistants, the Rev. Malith Kur and Mr. Tristan Paule, for their work in helping to prepare this collection for publication. In the planning phase also, a number of people lent a hand. Particular thanks goes to Mrs. Sharon Lindenburger, whose skills were so invaluable, and to Mr. Andrew Labenek, whose willingness to contribute concretely amid a hectic schedule was much appreciated. Thanks also to my colleague in the Centre for Public Theology, Dr. Darren C. Marks, for his friendship and collaboration, and to the former Dean of Theology at Huron University College, the Rev. Dr. Bill Danaher, for his support. Finally, special gratitude is due to the contributors to this volume, who have been exceedingly patient as publication was delayed by life's circumstances.

I would like also to acknowledge the support of the Social Sciences and Humanities Research Council of Canada, whose Aids to Small Universities grant made the Centre for Public Theology at Huron University College possible—and with it, the publication of this volume.

Gary D. Badcock

CONTRIBUTORS

Gary D. Badcock is the Peache Professor of Divinity at Huron University College, Western University.

Frederick Bird is Research Professor in Political Science at the University of Waterloo, and Distinguished Professor Emeritus, Concordia University.

Bill Blaikie, a United Church of Canada Minister and a retired Canadian socialist politician, is Director of the Knowles-Woodsworth Centre for Theology and Public Policy at the University of Winnipeg.

George H. Crowell was a student of Reinhold Neibuhr and taught Social Ethics in the Religious Studies Department, University of Windsor, 1968-1996.

Robert H. Nelson is Professor of Environmental Policy in the School of Public Policy at the University of Maryland.

Suzanne M. Wilson is Director of the Office for Systemic Justice for the Canadian Federation of the Sisters of St. Joseph.

CHAPTER ONE

A FAILURE OF THE "GODS?": A THEOLOGICAL RESPONSE TO THE FINANCIAL CRISIS

GARY D. BADCOCK[1]

An Age of Ideology

We live, I wish to suggest, in a peculiar age of ideology and dogmatism. Contrary to the commonly-held view that what surrounds us is a sea of relativism, ours can instead be regarded in a number of ways as an age of certainties that are unquestioningly assumed, obeyed, and even forcefully imposed, effectively as articles of faith. Our dogmatism is nowhere more evident than in the world of politics and economics (though similar things might well be said of multiple spheres).[2] In politics, the power of our dogmas became plain for all to see in, for instance, the invasion of Iraq in 2003, which supposedly was to be welcomed by its people as salvation, but which has turned out to be anything but that; or in the election in 2008 of a man who was presented almost as the 'saviour of the world,' Barack Obama—raising for himself, of course, a series of unrealizable expectations that would come back to haunt him, and those who supported him. William Cavanaugh has memorably referred to the cultural assumptions underlying such views as "state soteriology:" the claim, endemic in mo-

---

[1] Gary D. Badcock is the Peache Professor of Divinity at Huron University College, Western University.

[2] A generation ago, the polymath Michael Polanyi argued against the then-dominant scientific positivism, maintaining that its efforts to escape the tradition-bound limits of "faith" were futile, since everything from academic mores to language itself to the very publications upon which science depends are rooted in socially-mediated concepts and practices that become unintelligible once faith is removed from the system. The "tacit" knowledge assumed by science, Polanyi shows, constitutes one of the modern forms of dogmatism.

dernity and certainly deeply characteristic of that paradigmatic Enlightenment democracy, the United States, that humanity can be redeemed from brokenness through the state.[3] The absurdity of assuming that anything other than mixed gains can be made in the political order ought to be apparent to anyone who has lived in, with, and under one, but under the influence of this particular dogma it is difficult to stop people from assuming that society is perfectible.

That we live in an age of ideology is, however, even more evident in the unquestioning assumptions made in the discourse of human rights, which are asserted in law even though no explanation can be offered within the terms of our present worldview for whence and why they exist, other than the sheer fact of their declaration as self-evident (which does not really make them so). It is evident among the politically correct who generally, as is well known, can brook no contradiction, and whom one often and paradoxically fears to confront on pain of persecution, exclusion, or professional dismissal.[4] And it is evident, not least, in the world of economics—where, as the French sociologist Pierre Bourdieu frequently put it, a neoliberal utopianism founded on the dogmatic abstraction of "a pure and perfect market" has reigned supreme for most of our adult lives.[5]

Now, of course, it does not follow from any of this that dogmatism is necessarily or always a bad thing. The ancient word "dogma," though having pejorative associations in contemporary usage, simply means a "teaching" (or sometimes a "law" or "decree" when used in a more legal sense). We continue today to rely on the equivalents of the ancient "dogmas," though less in religion than in the secular sphere: the line we are fed, that the chemicals in pre-packaged food are safe to consume, for instance, or that a vaccination is safe to receive, are rather akin to "decrees" delivered by the regulatory bodies hearkening to a lab-coated "priesthood," and we act upon their judgments mostly on the basis of their authority, which in turn cannot function except on the basis of public trust. On the whole, the

---

[3] William T. Cavanaugh, "The City: Beyond Secular Parodies," in John Milbank, Catherine Pickstock and Graham Ward, eds., *Radical Orthodoxy* (New York: Routledge, 1999).

[4] A useful illustration is the reaction seen a few years ago to former Archbishop of Canterbury George Carey's claim that opponents of gay marriage in the United Kingdom are being publicly vilified much as the Jews were in the early days of Nazism—the reaction being as important and interesting for present purposes as Carey's initial observation.

[5] Pierre Bourdieu, "The essence of neoliberalism," *Le Monde Diplomatique*, English Edition, Dec. 8, 1998, http://www.mondediplo.com/1998/12/08bourdieu .

existence of such a nexus of authority and of fiduciary trust in so much of life is a good thing, and we cannot do without it, even if it is true that the dynamic can also lead to damage.

In the world of economics, however, the neoliberalism of the past thirty years, involving at its heart financial deregulation and the globalization of financial markets, together with a commitment to free trade and the subordination of collective national and especially labour interests to the maximization of profit, has presented itself as the only "realistic" description of economic reality. The logic of neoliberalism has, of course, been applied in some contexts more consistently than in others, and it is significant that those economies in which it has been most consistently followed were among those most obviously crippled by the meltdown that began in 2008. The truth of the matter, however, is that the kind of macroeconomic theory on which it relied was always a kind of *faith*, and indeed, how far this faith went is apparent in the light of the Lehman failure and the banking crisis that ensued. It is highly significant that almost none of the economists in neoliberal favour saw the crisis coming, and in fact most major economic figures of the decade (such as Ben Bernanke, Chairman of the Federal Reserve, the central bank of the United States) actually believed at the time that a financial crisis was theoretically impossible. The macroeconomic struggles of the past were over: the classical view of free markets had triumphed; in broad terms, the conviction was that free markets can cheerfully be left free to regulate themselves. The market, so the mantra went, is naturally self-regulating and self-correcting; thus, merely if we leave it alone, "all shall be well."

Such was, and is, the free market faith. It is perhaps understandable, in the light of the revolutions of 1989, the collapse of the Soviet Union, the rise of "capitalist" China—or of a quasi-mercantilist China at any rate—that leading representatives of the "free world" should have thought their victory so complete. The now-classic literary expression of this particular form of fiduciary *hubris* was the 1989 essay of Francis Fukuyama, "The End of History?" which presented the outcome of the Cold War literally as the pinnacle of human socio-political development.[6] Fukuyama is, of course, widely ridiculed for this little piece, particularly in the light of 9/11 and all that ensued, but it is no stretch to conclude that he read the times in

[6] Francis Fukuyama, "The End of History?" *The National Interest*, Summer 1989. The essay was followed by a somewhat less triumphalist reworking of the theme in Fukuyama, *The End of History and the Last Man* (New York: Free Press, 1992).

a way that proved prophetic in the economic sphere at least—or so, at any rate, until very recently.

The tides of faith ebb and flow in any fiduciary system. What we can say in retrospect today is that these free market convictions, which first motivated and which then sustained the dominant economic policies of the past three decades, is today at a much lower ebb—among some, it is at its lowest ebb, arguably, since the aftermath of the Great Depression. True, the abstraction of the pure and perfect market may not be dead, but it is certainly a wounded creature, and indeed, in many centres of economic policy-making, it is fascinating to see that the figure of Doctor John Maynard Keynes has appeared again at the infirmary door, after thirty years of exile, ready to soothe the market's ills. Even the "neocon" Harper government in Canada implemented clearly Keynesian economic strategies on a monumental scale in the wake of the 2008 crash, occasioning howls of protest from a vocal segment of its supporters. The world of mammon is not quite as simple as it seemed just a few years ago.

It is, then, not only the markets that crashed. For what has also taken place is a crisis of confidence in one of the leading ideas of our lifetime. Perhaps you and I never really believed in it, or perhaps we did—but what is certain is that most of the powers-that-be *were* believers, or had no option but to be, whether in government, in industry, in banks, or in international institutions such as the IMF. I would suggest, however, in the wake of the events of 2008 that (protestations of the Chicago School notwithstanding), the *pure* free market faith is not coming back on a global level anytime soon—certainly not with the swagger it had in its hey-day in the 1980s and 1990s. The Occupy Movement of 2011 was one expression of the widespread unease felt in many societies about the economic reforms of the past thirty years. The central message of Occupy was not to be confused with Occupy's anarchic character, as it was something of far-reaching importance that has the potential (second only to the sheer failure of 2008) to upset the free market consensus. That message is this: neoliberal approaches to the market have generated from the very beginning, and all along the way, massive increases in economic inequality. While it is important to observe that the increase of inequality is not strictly part of the theory, and that most economic liberals appear genuinely to *believe* in the goal of decreasing inequality by creating opportunity (a version of "inclusivism"),[7] empirical observation of the effects of neoliberalism simply

---

[7] At one point, PM David Cameron pledged to spread "privilege" rather than to defend it in Britain:

do not bear out the claim that this works straightforwardly on the macro level. Or, to put the same thing another way, it may work in limited ways in particular times and places (e.g., in stabilizing prices in Moscow under Boris Yeltsin), or it may work in a nation like Britain for some tens or hundreds of thousands of entrepreneurs, but it does not work for millions of their fellow-citizens. The doctrine of the pure and perfect market, whether found dressed in the spats of the 1920s or the fancypants super-computer algorithms of investment bankers since financial deregulation, has been something of a failure.[8]

All of this, however, is mainly by way of a rehearsal of what has been argued by others, and there is no further need to labour the point. What I wish to do now is to turn to the question of theological analysis and response, and to pick up on certain of the themes with which I began. For if it is true that we live in an age of dogmatism, then the question arises, what happens when the dogmas prove to be unbelievable? What happens when the nexus of authority and trust of which I spoke earlier breaks down?

Failed "gods"

Part of the argument that I have been constructing is that ours is still in a rather strange sense an age of "faith"—but that we have dubious and hidden gods. I shall argue shortly that a particular problem for Christianity is that the Christian God has been assimilated to these dubious ideas, or that the Christian God is construed in such a way as to serve the same ends, but let us leave this aside for the moment. To make this claim about the ubiquitous character of contemporary religion will perhaps be controversial, and requires a certain clarification of what is meant by the term. To begin at the beginning, the Latin word *religio*, according to Lewis and Short at any rate, has in ordinary usage the basic sense of a system of worship or a public cult, though the word also has associations with the concept of sanctity, and can even be used for the idea of an obligation between citizens or friends, in the kind of bond which is commonly thought to be sacred. Modernity is occasionally accustomed to thinking of religion as something private rather than public—indeed, widespread use of the

http://www.telegraph.co.uk/news/politics/conservative/9598922/I-will-spread-privilege-in-aspirational-Britain-Cameron-tells-conference.html .

[8] A recent measure of such failure, and a classic Social Democratic response to it, can be seen in the Broadbent Institute's recent report, *Towards a More Equal Canada*, dated October 2012: http://www.broadbentinstitute.ca/.

word "religion" itself is something mostly modern, part of the age of enlightenment and individualism[9]—but in fact none of the senses of the Latin word is consistent with the notion of religion as something private.

Contrariwise, and even more in the modern period, the sociology of religion has insisted, to quote Emile Durkheim, that religion is inherently "something eminently social,"[10] and in that sense distinct from a person's faith, which in Durkheim's analysis is more a matter of individual taste and experience. Durkheim's importance for the sociology of religion easily ranks alongside that of Max Weber, and has, if anything, been even more influential in the field of religious studies, but he has been largely neglected by theologians themselves. Durkheim, rather more even than Weber, effectively eviscerates the whole theological enterprise when he opines flatly that society is God: "I do not see in the divinity any more than society transfigured and thought symbolically."[11] Yet, whereas this might seem to mark the end for religion, the truth is that for Durkheim it is not possible to conceive of religion's disappearance, since religion is constituent of the social. That is to say, what is generically called "the sacred" serves to organize and reinforce those social structures without which it is impossible to live in a community. So long as there is society, in short, there must be religion.

One of the interesting things about Durkheim's analysis is that it allows for the variety of religion empirically observed, and for varieties of expression of the core of religious life as something inherently social. Curiously, what Durkheim fails adequately to consider is that what is called religion in his analysis can operate in a society that is overtly "secular." This should scarcely have given him pause, in my view, given that his position is that, in effect, society is God. Durkheim's generation had, after all, inherited the philosophical inversion of the 19th century, whereby the finite world came to be vested with absolute meaning and the theological came to seen as derivative of it (so that God is our creature rather than the converse), and finally came to be regarded as merely epiphenomenal. The

[9] This is a now-classic argument, formulated by Wilfred Cantwell Smith, *The Meaning and End of Religion* (New York: Macmillan, 1963).

[1010] Emile Durkheim, *The Elementary Forms of the Religious Life*, trans. Joseph Ward Swain (London: George Allen & Unwin, 1915), p.10.

[11] É. Durkheim, *Représentations individuelles et représentations collectives* (1898), in: *Sociologie et Philosophie*, (Paris: Presses Universitaires de France, 1951), 36; as cited in Jesús Romero Moñivas, "Science And Religion in the Sociology of Émile Durkheim," *European Journal of Science and Theology* 3 (2007): 26.

classic 19th century humanist contention that "humanity is God," since it is the source of all that we value—so that it is to be literally served and adored—is clearly echoed in Durkheim's view, even if the latter has its roots in a more explicitly ethnographic analysis, and is to that extent a more scientifically-grounded claim.

Nevertheless, the coming down of heaven to earth in 19th century thought is not sufficiently reflected in Durkheim's sociology of religion, which consequently misses what I want to suggest is the really decisive thing. That is to say, the vesting of the earth with all the significance that had once been accorded heaven—including the generation of law, meaning, and life itself—means that one actually no longer needs to generate an overtly "religious" symbolic system by which to order society, since one already has one's god or one's absolute in the *this-world* of life, society and nature as such.[12]

It is Pierre Bourdieu (died 2002), arguably the greatest French sociologist since Durkheim (died 1917), who more than any other sees this point, and works it out in his theory. This, I think, is despite its being apparently more in tune with Weber because of Bourdieu's preoccupation with questions of power. Bourdieu's sociology has been aptly described as 'a "generalized" sociology of religion (with religion presenting in paradigmatic fashion properties common to all spheres of symbolic activity).'[13] To put the same thing another, hopefully less complicated way, the theoretical tools stemming from an analysis of religion are everywhere present in Bourdieu's treatment of society, so that, even though he writes very little about religion directly (considering it essentially an unviable proposition actually to *be* religious in the conventional sense in the West today), he is considered by virtue of the strategies employed in his analysis of secular society *per se* to be a major source for the contemporary sociology of religion. He was clearly right about large parts of the West. There are, as we know, no longer groups of religious specialists who stand at the centre of the social order (Bourdieu's "priests"), but nevertheless, there is certainly still abundant generation and imposition of "givens" that have the potential "to make visible and to make believable" the otherwise arbitrary claim to

---

[12] One suspects that this underlies, for instance, the "religious" quality of so much of the ecological movement, even among its ostensibly secular adherents.

[13] Erwan Dianteill, "Pierre Bourdieu and the sociology of religion: A central and peripheral concern," in David L. Swartz and Vera L. Zolberg, eds., *After Bourdieu: Influence, Critique, Elaboration* (New York: Kluwer Academic Publishers, 2005), p.66.

power of some over others.[14] Bourdieu speaks of this capacity in terms of "symbolic power," "symbolic capital," or even "symbolic violence," and what is of direct relevance to our theme—his contention is that just this underlies what he deems to be the free market "faith."[15]

I am not wanting to argue that either Durkheim or Bourdieu have got hold of the theological question rightly, nor do I wish to suggest that their (necessary) sociological reductionism ought to go unnoticed or uncritiqued in this or any other theology. I am not, as it happens, a social-scientific reductionist, but we do not have scope at present for this digression, and in any case, the point of this discussion is rather different. It is to alert us to two possibilities: first, that a culture may be *symbolically organized* in ways directly comparable to what is operative in religion, even though it may be avowedly "secular"; and second, that religion proper needs to be aware of the criticism that its fundamental function is to validate a particular social order that is, at bottom, arbitrarily constituted. Indeed, in all the great sociological theorists, this is really the singular and decisive function of religion, to generate some *mythos* that precedes and grounds the possibility of public *logos.*

What I want to suggest is not only that the *mythos* that has shaped the economic practices and the political discourse of neoliberal societies for nearly a generation has been constructed in subterranean ways by a set of assumptions that really operate as a kind of religion, though refusing to entertain open acknowledgment of that fact. It is also that many, at least, of the Christian churches have also done precisely what Durkheim suggests they must, which is to provide the symbolic validation of the dominant structures obtaining in the social order, which is to say in the present context, *the neoliberal economic order*, upon which the whole system rests. That is to say, the Christian religion in the modern West has served, and serves even today, to ground and justify precisely the neoliberal social agenda. The fact that a given church might reject such claims, citing innumerable left-leaning or "progressive" reports and policies produced over the years that fly in the face of the neoliberal polity, matters little on this analysis, since at its deepest level, it preaches and forms people into precisely the kind of free subjects and consumers who are the axle around which the whole economic machine turns. And since this is the case, then

---

[14] Pierre Bourdieu, "Sur le pouvoir symbolique," *Annales ESC*, 32 (1977):410, as cited by Dianteill, "Pierre Bourdieu and the sociology of religion," p. 79.
[15] Bourdieu, "The essence of neoliberalism."

the churches (the bulk of them in the West, at any rate) must in a manner of speaking be considered complicit in the making of the financial crisis.

One of the really telling characteristics of intellectual life in contemporary "churchland" is that few people really ask this question, despite the fact that a goodly number of our religious leaders have at least a cursory background in sociological theory, as do a considerable number among the active membership. Perhaps the chasm it opens up is too deep for them to cross; perhaps, to the contrary, they merely enjoy the (often considerable) symbolic capital they have accumulated as things stand. I would tend to suggest myself that the process of religious enculturation, or what may well be the same thing, the desire to be "relevant" to the world in which we live, blinds the church to the possibility that, instead of working for the word's transformation, it merely grounds, mirrors and reinforces its excesses. It is easy, of course, to apply the sociological critique to, let us say, the Catholic Church in Chile under Fascist rule in the mid-20th century, or to the Dutch Reformed in South Africa. What we are less prepared to see is that our own preoccupation with the question of the experience, flourishing, and freedom of the individual, whether as expressed in "decisions" made for Christ, or in the characteristically "liberal" non-prescriptive approach which insists that the act of authentic believing (anything at all, seemingly) is what matters, or for that matter in that non-directive nurturing and counselling that became so characteristic of the pastoral care movement in the late 20th century, equally explain and reinforce a social world in which de-socialized, atomized, abstractly free individuals are really both source and goal. Just these, however, sustain the system of private interests and tastes of modern individuals, the highest function and purpose of whom in life is to consume. Protestant denominationalism, as Lesslie Newbigen often argued, serves the same destructive ends: denominationalism, as he tended to put it, is consumerism in a religious mode. The denominations have, on the whole, fiercely resisted the intrusions of the ecumenical movement (which they tend to regard as a means of *affirming* themselves as they are rather than of actually ending their existence); ecumenism threatens denominationalism, however, because it threatens the notion that the church is an association of abstract individuals who share the same private opinions.

There would be a number of ways of illustrating the same dynamic. To take one of the most obvious that I have drawn attention to elsewhere, it ought to be a scandal to Christians that the same principle used in modern political polity to defend the legitimacy of religious belief, namely, freedom of speech and of conscience, is equally employed to defend the existence of pornography on supermarket and stationery shelves. Instead, a good many Christians actually thank God for such freedom of speech and conscience on a weekly basis in liturgical settings in the modern West. Liturgically and theologically, however, this is a barbarism, for it means that they also thank God for the ubiquity of pornography, which is made available to them under precisely the same principle. The courts have merely been consistent in applying the logic here. It is an insufficient defence to say that the churches do not "mean" to say this in their prayers, for the fact of the matter is that, by literally sacralising the principle of individual freedom in public worship (and indeed at every step along the way in churches which assert the supremacy in matters of religious faith of the individual), they validate the very thing that makes the freedom to say or to publish absolutely *anything* legally and philosophically necessary. Examples of this could be multiplied further; the disappearance of the concept of blasphemy, never mind in Western society, but also in Western Christian churches, could be mentioned, not least because there are societies in which this omission and commission is simply incomprehensible. But we must leave the matter aside and move on.

The claim is that the atomized individual of modernity, upon which depends also the concept of the economic risk-taker, producing in turn a cult of the winner, of the economic survivor who accumulates reserves of capital by virtue of his or her individual initiative, is symbiotically reflected in and underwritten by the religious individualism that dominates the lives of Western Christians and is represented in the core of contemporary Western Christian practice. It is no accident, from this point of view, that south of the Canadian border a few years ago, a disproportionate number of evangelical Christians stood among Mitt Romney's most fervent supporters in his run for office, there being no functional difference between the particular way in which the sacralization of individual freedom occurs either in evangelicalism or in Mormonism. American evangelicals were perhaps surprised to find themselves supporting a member of a "cult," as was said, but to employ our earlier argument, the *mythos* in each case validated precisely the same *logos*. The two, in short, amounted at this level to one and the same thing. From this point of view, I confess, I found developments in the last American Presidential election both theologically horrifying and fascinating: horrifying, because of the associations of Christian "commitments" with an obviously extreme neoliberalism—which is now imprinted on the minds of millions of onlookers in the general population; and fascinating, because the whole show reveals how deeply the political and the religious are in fact tightly bound together, despite the fiction of the firewall standing between American church and state.

My basic contention, however, is that these symbolic systems, these “gods,” have failed. They have failed in the churches that owned them, which are disintegrating before our eyes; they have failed in the political arena, which under their influence becomes ever more polarized and destructive; and they have failed in an exquisitely spectacular way in the financial crisis that began in 2008 and that, in many nations, still continues. These gods can no longer be trusted; indeed they *are* no longer trusted, or at least, not in quite the way that they were. We are brought to the position of needing to explain why we became so committed to them. And, we need to learn how to let them go.

On such terms, the financial crisis of 2008 and beyond ought to be a watershed for Christian theology in the West. Rather like an Augustine facing the challenge of untangling the meaning of the fall of Rome, we ourselves need to learn to say that God was never in the city of the world in quite the unambiguous way that the old “religion” assumed. Not only do we need to say this, but we need to acknowledge how deeply impacted all that was by a kind of idolatry. And this means nothing less than that in the church, a great many of us need to learn how to speak of God in the public square all over again.

A Theological Response

To speak of idolatry is, of course, to use rather strong language. The word evokes such images as that of the Golden Calf, and of the errant people of God who, it is said in holy scripture, sat down to eat and drink before it, and then “rose up to play” (Exodus 32:6; 1 Corinthians 10:7). Perhaps the cavorting in question today is less obvious, but in the present context, the rough equivalent of the Golden Calf would indeed be the Charging Bull of Wall Street, the bronze sculpture representing profit that stands at the edge of the Financial District in New York City. Idolatry does not necessarily require literal physical expression, or literal sacrifice and offering; for to fashion a god “in the form of anything that is in heaven above, or that is on the earth beneath, or that is in the water under the earth,” and to “bow down” to such gods (Exodus 20:4-5) can, as we have seen, happen in subtle, insidious and ingenious ways. It is possible (the sociologist might actually say that it is necessary) to fashion a god who is the servant of a socio-political system, whose principal function is to validate and sustain it, and in our age as in all ages, it takes considerable independence of mind and courage to speak the truth about this to the princes of the church. But we theologians have helpers in the social sciences. If nothing else, the sociology of religion ought to provide a warning to the church of the permanent possibility that all it says is a service to something on the earth beneath rather than to God, who is Lord and Judge of all.

It was out of the sorrows of the trenches of World War I, in reaction against the *Kulturprotestantismus* that publicly sought to justify the carnage, and then again amid the furnace of the European Fascism that sought to assimilate the Christian churches and to employ religion in its own project, that a subtle political theology developed in the 20th century that I suggest needs to be learned and appropriated again. Its central figure was Karl Barth, although ultimately the same tones can be heard in the work of leaders equally profound, if less prolific, such as Dietrich Bonhoeffer (who was, interestingly, an expert in sociology) or, in England, the Anglican Bishop George Bell. In a nutshell, that theology is this. Because God is God, and is not to be fashioned in the image of anything in the world, God is not to be aligned with any political or economic system. To be sure, the Christian can make common cause with varied political projects as provisional expressions of central Christian teachings. A politics that vilifies the refugee, the sick, the young, or the elderly, for instance, can only be resisted by the Christian, in alliance with those political parties and processes that would oppose such evils. But there is a delicate line to be negotiated and not crossed that stands here, between making common cause and identifying this or that political or economic stratagem as what it means to be a Christian or what it means to be the church. In fact, each of these theologians tends to insist that the Christian gospel prescribes no particular political polity. The church is capable of existing in any political context—and indeed even in recent history certain forms of the Christian church have thrived under the most oppressive regimes, such as in the Cultural Revolution in China. What the church must do above all else is keep its distance, since what is at stake in its life is the name of God and its witness to God. For God is *semper maior*, "always greater," or "always more." God, as God, does not fall into any of our usual categories, whether metaphysical, moral, political or economic (*Deus non est in genere*). This, I would suggest, is the basic thing that has been forgotten by so many of the churches of the modern West.

Barth makes a most interesting point here, maintaining that one of the great and perennial questions of Christian theology, which needs to be asked in the most searching way, is whether or not the church in any given historical epoch allows God to be domesticated to the prevailing structures of power. For when the church puts its shoulder to the wheel of the world, allowing the name of God to be used in ways that chime in with the central ambitions and power claims or any epoch, then, we can be sure, it has slipped into idolatry. For this reason, Barth rejected *Kulturprotestantismus* as a perilous danger, and claimed that what is essential for the Christian church in approaching questions of political and social importance is to disown any claim that a particular politics or economics is straightforwardly to be identified as God's will. This was why Barth himself, in the context of the middle decades of the 20th century, took the view that Nazism literally had to be preached against from the pulpit—and the later, difficult war against Nazism too—because it made overtly religious claims about God's will as expressed in the *Führerprinzip* and the rhetoric of blood and soil. Yet, for the very same reasons, he also resisted the claim of the West in the Cold War, precisely because of the thread of divine warrant that was asserted both in European and North American Christianity for the Western polity.

This is a delicate, nuanced position that might well be remembered as much in the face of the "My Little Pony"[16] approach to questions of economic justice that infests so many pulpits, as in response to the theology that sacralizes our own cultural individualism, and with it, the free market "faith." It is not simply that one or other of such approaches is bad for us, or even that it may be bad for the poor—or for that matter any other group in society (since perhaps the rich might also be targets of persecution under some system in our lifetimes). It is that too close an identification of God's way with this or that human way necessarily misrepresents God, because it makes God in the image of this or that thing "on the earth beneath," which for theology is among the most serious of all human errors.

Thus what emerges here at the end is the need to assert the freedom of theology, and indeed, the freedom of God in theology: a rediscovery of the idea of transcendence, and a recovery of the true wealth of "religious capital," is in order. Such a rediscovery is in order first and foremost for the church itself, since without these it will inevitably find that it has nothing genuinely new, or different, or really radical to say to the socio-political order, and it will instead be reduced inevitably to what merely mirrors and reinforces that world as it already is.

What does this imply, finally, for us in the church who ask the question with which we began, the question of God and the financial crisis? The

[16] The phrase is happily borrowed from Francis Spufford, *Unapologetic* (London: Faber and Faber, 2012), p. 12. Spufford uses it rather differently, however—to critique the simplistic politics and anti-religion of the John Lennon song, "Imagine."

answer is that because we and what we preach in so much of the church has been woven into the fabric from which the crisis was cut, there is need first and foremost for a kind of intellectual repentance. I would say myself that we need a new Augustine on the scene—or at any rate, a new *City of God* to guide—so entwined with the foundations of the free market "faith" is so much of our own Christian faith in modern times. This would entail that the task of theological renewal, which has become so imperative amid the moribund character of Western Christianity, might well need to begin with insights gleaned from "public theology," the conviction that theology is not well practiced in the religious ghetto, because its central message is bound up intimately with, and is profoundly affected by, great public questions. That the gods so clearly embraced in the subjectivism and atomistic individualism of neoliberalism and Western Christianity alike have failed is a signal, in short, that we have gotten things badly wrong, and that some new direction is needed.

CHAPTER TWO

OUT OF SORTS: ETHICAL REFLECTIONS ON THE FISCAL CRISIS AND THE GREAT RECESSION

FREDERICK BIRD[1]

Introduction

In the several years since 2007, North American and European countries have experienced, in differing degrees, a financial crisis and a prolonged economic recession. As a result, millions of people have suffered extensive losses. They have lost homes, savings, income, and jobs. In some areas, some countries, and for particular groups of people, especially the young, unemployment rates have been experienced at levels as high and higher than 20% of the labour force. Many others have suffered from aggravated levels of under-employment. Although they will find ways of getting by, most of those who have lost their homes and their jobs will not be able to recover from these losses anytime soon. The fiscal crisis and ongoing recession have aggravated personal strains, deprivations, and losses especially for those less well off. To be sure, many wealthy and affluent households suffered huge losses as well in their investments, savings, pensions, and expectations. Expecting to retire in a few years, many older workers have decided they cannot afford to retire soon, because of these losses. The strain on the millions who have lost their homes and jobs has been extensive.

What many, many people have found especially galling about this situation has been the inability of governments and businesses to find ways of improving the overall operation of their economies in any decisive ways. Thankfully, at the height of the fiscal crisis emergency, governments and

[1] Frederick Bird is Research Professor in Political Science at the University of Waterloo, and Distinguished Professor Emeritus, Concordia University.

central banks intervened in dramatic ways so that the crisis did not become much, much worse, in ways that seemed very likely at the time. Nonetheless, although they come from different countries and hold diverse political views, people generally are feeling aggravated by a wide range of issues and problems—from job loss to increasing size of student debts, from the steady rise health care expenses to inequities in the tax system—associated with this on-going economic recession. Two decades ago, after the Soviet Union collapsed, Western industrialized countries congratulated themselves on the vitality and resilience of their economic and political institutions. Clearly, we assured ourselves, these events demonstrated the strength and resourcefulness of our systems of free markets, private enterprise, and liberal democratic government institutions. Now we wonder why the political and economic institutions we were celebrating so recently have been unable to act more effectively with respect to prolonged periods of economic woe.

Although experiences vary, sometimes markedly from country to country, from region to region, and for some rather than other social groups—for example, think of the current prospects in Germany and Greece—people generally seem to be suffering not only directly and indirectly from the economic losses, but also from profound feelings of anger and disenchantment. How did we get into this mess? Why can't our leaders act more forcefully to address these problems effectively? Many people experience a sense of threat. They feel precarious, and they worry that things may well get worse for them. Will they be able to find opportunity for better employment? Will their saving be sufficient when they retire? In ways that we do not always clearly understand, we wonder whether larger climate changes, growing government debts, increased government spending on social insurance and public welfare, and/or our dependence on fossil fuels adversely affect us. For diverse reasons, this fiscal crisis and ongoing recession leave us feeling out of sorts. Given the wealth our economies have produced, the continued discoveries of our scientists, and the innovations of social and business entrepreneurs, we feel very deeply that things could and should be different. In general, we feel we have worked hard and lived responsibly. So we are inclined to wonder how these problems could have become so aggravated and have remained this way so long. Many of us feel quite upset. We still seem to be in the midst of a crisis, global both in scope and character. How can we make sense of this situation? What can and should we do?

In ways that are sometimes similar but generally dramatically different, both the Tea Party and Occupy movements have voiced anger with respect to this on-going crisis in terms that have gained widespread support. Both have expressed discontent felt by millions. Both point to fundamental problems that seriously do need to be addressed. Both reflect understandable feelings of frustration. The current patterns of government and business are not, they complain, working the way we think they could and should. Both movements argue, as I will argue, that the fiscal crisis and great recession have occurred because of a larger set of factors—what I will call social malpractices—which not only have functioned to shape the character of these events, but also have adversely affected public and private well-being.

The Tea Party movement emerged in the United States in the spring of 2009 and spread quickly, largely as a grass roots movement interested in changing the character of partisan politics. Those involved have broadly compared themselves with popular movements of dissent in the Middle East, China, and from American history. As part of its basic agenda, the movement has directly sought to shape political processes by supporting political candidates that aligned with its philosophy. The movement has opposed the extension of Medicare, efforts to expand regulatory controls over polluting emissions, and policies that would liberalize immigration policies. The Occupy movement emerged in the fall of 2011, staged its initial occupation in the financial district in New York City, and quickly spread to other cities and countries. By October 15th of that year there were sit-in or live-in demonstrations in more than 950 cities in more than 82 countries. Using public protests and acts of civil disobedience, the Occupy movement especially called attention to the power exercised by those with the most wealth. They sought to embody a new kind of egalitarian and participatory political process, sometimes referred to as "horizontalism," which provided occasions for people to assert control over their lives as communities of people apart from the established, hierarchical systems of administrations and politics.

Both initiatives represent popular grass root movements, whose organization and rapid expansion have been facilitated by the uses of social media. Both initiatives share a deep suspicion of large banks and leading financial institutions. Both movements see themselves as representing the average people over against the excessively influential special interests. However, for the most part these movements seem to hold diametrically opposite views, both with regard to what is especially wrong with the way political and economic institutions operate, and what should be done to improve the situation.

A number of people, associated both with the Tea Party and groups on the political Right, argue that the inability to emerge from the on-going recession reflects the ways governments have acted to waste public resources and interfere with and obstruct otherwise productive business practices. They complain about the ways government budgets continue to rise in part because of over-staffed government bureaucracies and irresponsible support for people on welfare, who, they insist, should be supporting themselves. They point to the way excessive regulations add needless expenses to businesses that make firms less able to perform profitably. Given the on-going recession, they complain about excessive taxes. They allow that recessions do happen from time to time, but they believe economies will largely correct themselves if governments do not excessively interfere. These criticisms of what they regard as "big government" are typically combined with complaints about a variety of groups that seem to pose threats to the commonweal, such as illegal immigrants, convicts, drug users, and diverse minority groups. Overall, these groups on the political Right fear that matters will likely get much worse unless action is taken to restrain governments. In particular, they point to the huge and growing government deficits as an imminent threat likely to lead to a much larger and more devastating economic crisis.[2]

In large part, these critics, at least in the United States, from groups like the Tea Party and the political Right seem to connect our inability to emerge from this on-going recession with the ways in which governments and the public have allowed themselves to deviate from traditional values. In spite of government spending, in very broad terms they note how schools are not performing as well as they should, how crime rates remain high, how family values seem threatened by new mores, and how people generally feel less happy. They point to the ways in which government spending has steadily increased, government regulations have become more costly and complicated, and tax policies have become more convoluted and complex. In the process, these critics have encouraged and fostered both increasing suspicions of governments and aroused fears that matters may well become worse. In ethical terms, these right-leaning critics have addressed the fiscal crisis and economic recession in large part by identifying both some people and practices, associated with governments, liberal elites, and those adopting questionable moral practices that seem especially blameworthy.

---

[2] Paul Ryan, *Path to Prosperity: A Blueprint for American Renewal* (House Budget Committee: March 20, 2012).

In contrast, a number of groups, associated with the Occupy movement and characteristic of the political Left, have argued that the current crisis has occurred because of the greedy, self-aggrandizing practices of those with the greatest wealth, the one percent, whose nominal incomes at least in the United States, grew by 277.5% between 1979 and 2007.[3] Many on the political Left have argued that it was people and organizations from these privileged groups of overpaid executives, investment bankers, and financial speculators, whose risky behaviour occasioned the financial crisis in the first place. Yet, it was these groups who have especially benefitted from government bailouts. Although the actions of these well-to-do people and organizations have wrought extensive harm, they have suffered comparatively little from the fiscal crisis and great recession. The political Left argues that the ways these powerful groups have managed to weather the crisis seem fundamentally unfair in relation to the millions who have suffered and continue to suffer in so many ways. Groups associated with the Occupy movement complain that those with great wealth and power have shaped business practices and government policies in their own interest. In the process they have been causing widespread ecological harm and undermining basic democratic process. The Occupy movement and critics on the political Left argue that these wealthy and powerful elites have conspired, and continue to conspire, to subvert political and economic institutions to their own advantage.

For those adopting the kinds of contrasting stances I have just described, these positions seem both empirically credible and emotionally satisfying. Although the positions taken by these movements often seem extreme—especially when proponents on one side or the other make quite radical proposals—in many ways these movements express pessimistic sentiments about current economic and political problems that are much more widely held. In an ironic way, these positions are mutually reinforcing. Because so many seem to embrace the alternatives they oppose, their own views seem more compelling and the alternatives seem more morally questionable. In many ways, those adopting Tea Party and Occupy-like views of the fiscal crisis and great recession seem to talk right past each other. Still, viewed as a whole in complementary ways, both movements raise important and serious concerns. Various politically unaccountable elites have increased their wealth and political influence in troubling ways. In many areas, government regulations have indeed become excessively complicated and offer new opportunities for circumvention. Interestingly,

---

[3] Data from the Congressional Budget Office, cited by Paul Krugman, *End This Depression Now* (New York: W. W. Norton, 2012), p. 76.

after being criticized for their complicity and the laxity with which they pursued their auditing tasks, accounting firms have ironically found new employment opportunities helping firms comply with new regulations established by governments both recently and nearly a decade ago. Tax laws have become excessively complex and still allow loopholes for those clever enough to find them. Far too many businesses are operating in ways that cavalierly ignore the ecological limits of their activities.

However, I am not making reference to the contrasting views associated with movements like the Tea Party and Occupy in order to propose a mediating middle ground that combines features from both camps. Rather, I am calling into question both kinds of responses—both of which are not without merit—because both tend to become excessively moralistic; both lack historical perspective; and both tend to be reactive. In his essay *On the Genealogy of Morals*, Nietzsche referred to the moral tone of complaints such as those voiced by groups like the Tea Party and Occupy as a product of resentment. He argued that ethics far too often are voiced primarily to express sentiments of loss and unhappiness rather than self-affirmations based on what people genuinely value. Far too often people articulate moral views to find compensation in imaginary revenge, sanctifying such feelings of revenge by referring to them as claims of justice.[4] From my perspective, both alternatives tend to become excessively moralistic. They are inclined to characterize those they oppose as deeply morally culpable while, at the same time, voicing statements that paint their own position as particularly morally virtuous. While these groups have raised truly important issues, they have also tended to express their views in morally self-righteous terms. Both groups have tended to respond to, while then going on to aggravate, feelings of suspicion, fear, and resentment.

While expressing a number of particularly important observations, neither group goes far enough in its critiques and analyses. This crisis has to do with more than the effects of a bubble in the housing market. It reflects more fundamental issues than those associated with the painfully slow movement back toward something like full employment. It has to do with more than our views of public debt. It reflects deeper issues than the ways banks created especially risky new financial instruments. In many ways, as I will demonstrate in due course, the fiscal crisis and great recession represent the tip of a much larger and more basic set of issues. If we are to re-

[4] Friedrich Nietzsche, *On the Genealogy of Morals*, trans. Walter Kaufmann and R. J. Hollingdale, in Nietzsche, *On the Genealogy of Morals and Ecce Homo*, ed. Walter Kaufmann (New York: Vintage Books, 1967), First Essay, Section 10.

spond to this crisis responsibly then we are called upon to gain perspective on this larger set of concerns. Both the Tea Party and Occupy movements forcefully express feelings that the ways current economic and political institutions operate have been fundamentally unjust. While they have forcefully expressed feelings of injustice about many of these matters in ways that seem not unreasonable, these movements have not been as able to articulately analyze the underlying ethical issues in ways that seem morally balanced, historically informed, and globally encompassing.

Viewing the Fiscal Crisis and Great Recession from a Truly Global Ethical Perspective

In the remainder of this paper I will draw upon a broad tradition of ethical discourse often referred to as Biblical Realism. Aside from an abiding concern for those who are least advantaged and a fundamental commitment to just economic and political practices, this tradition does not make claims for the priority of any particular economic principles or practices. What this tradition of discourse upholds is a truly global ethical perspective. This tradition, articulated in formative ways by figures like Augustine and Calvin, and more recently expressed in the writings of people like Reinhold Niebuhr, his brother H. Richard Niebuhr, Karl Barth, and Pope John XXIII, sets forth a view of humans as ultimately responsible before God for taking care of the earth and its inhabitants. Fundamentally, the earth is the Lord's, and humans are charged to exercise fiduciary responsibility to care for and govern the planet as God's agents. This tradition, correspondingly, expresses an intense sense of the way humans are accountable in the present for how we manage and care for the earth, and the difficulties which the earth and its inhabitants are facing. We are not only accountable to our contemporaries and our descendants; we are also accountable fundamentally before the sovereign who governs the cosmos. Humans are viewed both as being competent of assuming this responsibility—because among other capabilities we can reason, love, work, communicate, learn, and engage in cooperative enterprises—as well as being fallible creatures, because we are often inclined to act in ways that are destructive, self-deceptive, and excessively self-centred.

This tradition of ethical discourse is especially characterized both by its commitment to realism and by its underlying affirmation of hope. It is realistic in two senses. First, it presumes that we must begin our ethical analyses by fully recognizing the world as it is and has become in all of its complexity, and in relation to all of its difficulties. We are cautioned against the inclination, associated with expressions of false prophecy, to view the world as corresponding to our categories of thought and to our dreams. The world is God's world and we are called to take care of it as it is, and as it has become. Secondly, the tradition reminds us of the human tendency to subvert the common good to advance private goods, and to foolishly regard ourselves as being as virtuous as our ideals. The realism of this ethical tradition is often associated with sober acknowledgements of the limits of what can be accomplished. However, at the same time, this tradition of ethical discourse remains basically hopeful. It remains hopeful but not optimistic. This hope does not grow out of a belief in progress or even from a recognition of the constructive role of science. Rather, trusting in God's providence, this tradition assumes by God's grace that difficulties can sometimes be overcome and that possibilities sometimes arise out of disasters.

This tradition of Biblical realism has had a strong commitment to foster justice among humans in light of a transcendent view of justice as the way God governs the cosmos. This is not a simple matter as any review of works like Job, Isaiah 53, Paul's letter to the Romans, and Augustine's account of the barbarian attacks on Rome in *the City of God* make quite evident. Human standards of justice are important and often wise, but only relatively so. In the face of crises, these standards cannot always be mechanically invoked. New lessons may need to be learned, new perspectives may need to be entertained. Still, views of justice, associated with traditions of Biblical prophecy, natural law moral traditions, as well as more recent philosophy, should be consulted. Informed by traditions of Biblical Realism, ethicists are likely to view crises as occasions for re-thinking current issues from a broader perspective, for exercising judgment thoughtfully in light of how to the best of our ability humans can discern the outlines of God's judgment in midst of these crises.

One of the best expressions of this sense of judgment and justice informed by the traditions of Biblical realism was Abraham Lincoln's Second Inaugural address. As the Civil War was ending, in this speech President Lincoln briefly but articulately challenged Americans to understand that that crisis was one that could not just be blamed on particular others, but rather grew out of institutions and ways of life that had to be abandoned because they were fundamentally unjust. Out of the extensive suffering and widespread discord and animosity that this war occasioned, a new way forward could be charted. Lincoln articulated his understanding of the Civil War crisis using Biblical language. He confessed that he had striven to understand the purposes of the Almighty, whose judgments he believed to be wise, with regard to this war. Without casting blame narrowly on any groups or parties, he ended this address by calling all to act with "malice towards none; with charity for all; [and] with firmness in the right as God gives us to see the right...." Interestingly, Lincoln invoked the themes of realism, accountability, and hope. In particular, he called for his contemporaries to view this crisis as an expression of God's providence and judgment, not because it was now important to condemn those especially blameworthy, but because it was now time to exercise judgment so that all could move forward and allow the past to become past.

There are several characteristic features of Biblical realism as a tradition of ethical discourse that I would I would like comment on. To begin with, this is an inclusive and holistic perspective. As we act, we must take into account past, present, and future generations, living beings as well as the earth itself. From a Biblical perspective, these are all God's creatures. Humans are special only in their responsibility to take care of—to collaborate with God in governing—this earth and its creatures. Hence, above all we are charged to seek and promote the common good. We are accountable for how well we manage the challenges and threats we face. We are responsible before God, not just our before our friends and families, our creeds and rules, but before the being that oversees the whole of creation. Minimally, because we called to be responsible, we are called to be responsive to on-going contingencies, as possibilities and as dangers. At the same time, we are inherently fallible, prone to seek our own advantages at a cost to others, and inclined to overrate our ideas as higher wisdom especially when these ideas seem to serve our interests. As the apostle Paul confessed, the good we ought to be doing, we often do not do. Hence, the crises we experience are characteristically occasioned by human actions, often actions that we have come to regard as morally acceptable. When crises do occur, they often most deeply scourge those who have been least responsible and are least able to cope. Hence, it is important to act with compassion towards the poor and others especially vulnerable. Overall, the Biblical perspective remains hopeful. God is gracious. New beginnings are possible.

In what ways might the tradition of Biblical realism help us think about and respond to the current economic crisis? I will first answer this question in broad terms, and then proceed in light of this frame of reference to make a number of pointed substantive arguments. Broadly, in times of crises, such as the present moment, we are first called to act with compassion toward those most adversely affected. Moreover, we are furthered called to search for ways to reframe what is going on, not from our own parochial points of view, but from a truly global and historical perspective that takes into account the good for all, present and future. In practice, we are reminded that crises like the present one, similar to the crises Judea experienced at the time of Jeremiah, and that the United States experienced at the time of Lincoln, grow out of long held social practices that may well need to be re-examined so that we can constructively move forward. We are cautioned to recognize that many people will not easily relinquish social practices from which they in part benefit, even when the harmful consequences of these practices for themselves and others seem quite evident. We are especially challenged to widen the scope of our thinking—to think broadly and expansively as global citizens. In decisive ways we are directly addressed and authorized to take charge, recognizing our accountability and responsibility, to make a difference. While acknowledging our accountability and obligation to respond thoughtfully with open minds, we are reminded of our own fallibility. Correspondingly, we are counselled to see in what way the immediate causes of this crisis may have grown out of generally accepted, but largely unexamined, social practices that now seem questionable when viewed in light of the present crisis.

As reformers sought to overcome the Great Depression in the thirties, they also attempted to address underlying factors that gave rise to that economic crisis. In particular, they came to recognize that while the modern processes of industrialization helped to create great wealth for many, many people, these same processes were associated with increased vulnerabilities and risk especially with respect to employment income and banking practices. They correspondingly developed a wide range of institutions, from deposit insurance to unemployment insurance, from old age pensions to banking regulations, from minimum wage laws to provision for bankruptcy, which have fostered expanded wealth creation in the context of manageable risks.

The recent financial crisis and on-going great recession is a similar crisis. As Paul Krugman argues, probably much could be fairly easily undertaken to address the worst features of this situation.[5] At the same time, however, in many ways this on-going crisis reflects several serious unaddressed problems to which in different ways both the Tea Party movement and the Occupy movement have called attention. However, to act responsibly now, it is not enough to complain about perceived wrongs. It is not enough to point judgmentally at the greed and self-serving practices

[5]Krugman, *End This Depression Now.*

of particular others. It is inappropriate to view this situation as some kind of morality play in which we castigate the evils of those we oppose. Together with those affected in this and other countries, sympathetic to those who have suffered while seeking opportunities to converse with those with whom we disagree, we must do more than feel out of sorts. We can and must explore avenues for responding to widely experienced feelings of injustice, experienced in such contrasting terms, by finding the means to reform basic economic institutions in ways that address in common the symptoms viewed so differently by protesters on the political Right and political Left.

In the discussion that follows, I shall also draw upon and enlarge upon notions of fairness in exchanges associated with traditions of commutative justice. Commutative justice seeks to identify norms that mark fair and unfair interactions between those engaged in exchanges, whether these be between buyers and sellers in commercial markets, employers and employees in labour markets, investors and enterprises in financial markets, or investigators and subjects in research settings. The tradition has especially emphasized two normative principles: namely, one, those engaged in these exchanges should do so freely by their own choice and, two, they should be fully informed with respect to what is likely to take place in these exchanges and what the outcomes are likely to be. In practice, these principles have been elaborated to recognize various constraints that make choices less than ideal and to call attention to the ways access to relevant information may be asymmetrical and less than transparent. Clearly, many sellers of mortgages violated these principles when they sold low income house buyers low interest loans that included subsequent much higher interest payments that were not fully disclosed. I think we should add two additional principles to these basic notions of fairness in exchanges. These principles more fully spell out the basic taken-for-granted assumption of what is involved in fair exchanges. Thus, three, the benefits which people gain from fair exchanges ought in proximate terms to be proportionate to efforts they make, including foregone opportunities they have had to relinquish in order to participate in these exchanges, the contributions they make (or are expected to make), and the risks they face in the process. Accordingly, we justify higher salaries for those who exercise more highly valued skills, like corporate executives; those who manage greater risks, like pilots; and those who make more significant efforts gauged in relation to time spent, skills exerted, and attention required, like many professionals. This notion of proportionality is widely accepted, although imprecisely defined. It is typically invoked to complain when benefits gained seem disproportionate in relation to efforts, contributions, and risks which people have made. Finally, four those involved in any exchange ought to respect and not undermine the conditions and/or institutions that make it possible for them to engage in these exchanges. People characteristically invoke this principle when they argue that businesses should pay taxes to support governments which provide the security, public order, as well as social and physical infrastructures that make it possible for businesses to operate. In practice, much more may be involved as we more fully examine the institutions and conditions associated with diverse markets and exchanges. For example, many people would now argue that businesses have to respect and not undermine the ecological services provided by the natural environment. Businesses have far too long taken these services for granted.

The first two principles of commutative justice have often been invoked in a very narrow way by the political Right.[6] However, even these principles more fully examined have been utilized by the political Left, especially to point to the way asymmetrical access to information distorts so many market exchanges.[7] However, I think a strong argument can be made for adding the third and fourth principles not as extraneous norms, but as standards implied in the very notion of a fair exchange.[8]

In quite different terms the Tea Party and Occupy movements have called attention to perceived wrongs related to experiences of economic inequalities, the ways economic markets have been operating, and the characteristic systems used by governments to collect taxes. Both movements have had much to say about how current practices in unjust ways have aggravated social and economic problems by deviating in fundamental ways from core values. I have made reference to principles of commu-

---

[6] E.g., Robert Nozick, *Anarchy, State, and Utopia* (New York: Basic Books, Inc., 1974).

[7] See various works by Joseph Stiglitz, including especially *The Price of Inequality* (New York: W. W. Norton and Company, Inc., 2012). One might argue that Karl Marx's elaborate analysis of labor markets in volume one of Capital represents a thorough-going effort to demonstrate the ways the choice exercised by laborers were constrained both by their own relative immobility and by the enormous power exercised by employers. From this perspective, any analysis of exchanges that does not also examine the relative power exercised by the parties involved is likely to be superficial.

[8] I have more fully developed this model of commutative justice in an essay, "Justice in International Businesses," in Frederick Bird and Manuel Velasquez, eds., *Just Business Practices in a Diverse and Developing World* (New York and Basingstoke, UK: Palgrave-Macmillan, 2006), pp. 37-69.

tative justice in order to provide a common reference for evaluating these claims of injustice. Like the traditional story of the blindfolded men trying to determine the shape of an elephant by their close observation of part of the larger reality, these protesters have called attention to certain aspects of the larger set of problems. Their observations should not be ignored. However, they should be included in a much more encompassing analysis aimed at reforming basic economic institutions for the common good.

Reducing Excessive Economic Inequality

Both the Tea Party and the Occupy movement have called attention both to their particular views of aggravated economic inequality and to social, economic, and political consequences of economic inequality. The Tea Party has complained about the ways big government and high finance have exerted disproportionate power to make matters worse for average, hard-working citizens. The movement has also complained about a number of social ills—from higher delinquency rates to higher rates of drug abuse, from higher rates of teenage pregnancy to lower levels of social trust—that seem to have become aggravated in recent years. While they typically blame these problems on a declining attachment to core values, there is strong evidence that these social ills have become more aggravated to the degree that economic inequality has become greater. In contrast, the Occupy movement has called attention to ways the one percent of household with the highest incomes have since 1980 dramatically increased their share of wealth, while the wealth of middle and lower income households have stagnated or declined.

Over the past thirty plus years, inequality between household incomes has indeed become much greater, not only in a number of industrialized countries, like the United States and Britain, but also between industrialized and developing countries. In a book on global inequality, Milanovic documents the steady increase since 1980 in the difference in the *per capita* income levels of the richest and poorest countries, as well as the equivalent disparities between the wealthiest and poorest citizens in industrialized countries. This growing inequality traps many of the poorest regions in continuing poverty. After all, at present, in spite of the remarkable degrees of economic expansion since the Second World War and in spite of the recent and dramatic economic growth in China, India, and Brazil, one in three humans still live in impoverished households, defined somewhat arbitrarily as having household incomes of less than $2.25 per person per day. After analyzing the global growth in inequality, Milanovic points with concern to an overall corresponding global decline in the size and influences of the middle classes. He raises this concern because the rise in the size of the middle classes has been associated with the growth of civil society and the development of viable democracies. Alternatively, increasing global inequality seems to be associated with the rise of political extremism.[9]

Between 1930 and 1980, economic inequality between households declined steadily in industrialized countries. The increased equality resulted especially from greater investment in public education at all levels, the marked expansion of old age social insurance, the enactment of minimum wage laws, and the growth of both public health insurance as well as publicly subsidized employer funded private health insurance. The incomes and especially the wealth of the richest households still greatly exceeded that of the lowest households, but the gap had declined. Since 1980, economic inequality has greatly expanded, especially in countries like the United States, Britain, and Australia. It has remained high in countries like Portugal and Brazil. In the United States, the top one percent of households earned more in one week than the bottom 20% earned in a whole year.[10]

This growth in aggravated economic inequality has been associated with a number of disturbing consequences, such as increased political polarization and greatly diminished sense of community between those living at the economic extremes. There was much more bi-partisan political collaboration during the decades when inequality was declining. Furthermore, economic growth itself seemed to be correlated with reduced levels of economic inequality.[11]

In a book entitled, *The Spirit Level*, Richard Wilkinson and Kate Pickett analyze the growing inequality over the past thirty years within a number of industrialized states, including especially the United Kingdom and the United States. After reviewing information from 20 industrialized countries, they observe the way societies with higher levels of inequality also experience higher levels of a number of social problems, including drug abuse, homicide rates, teenage pregnancy, lower aspiration levels for

---

[9]Branko Milanovic, *Worlds Apart: Measuring International and Global Inequality* (Princeton: Princeton University Press, 2005), chapters 6, 7, 10 and 12. Cf. Paul Krugman, *End This Depression Now*, pp. 88-89, and Zanny Minton Beddoes, "For Richer, For Poorer: Special report on the World economy" *The Economist* (October 13, 2012).

[10] Stiglitz, *The Price of Inequality*, p. 4.

[11] Stiglitz, *The Price of Inequality*, chapters 3 and 4.

15- year-olds, higher rates of mental illness, and low levels of trust. Moreover, in studies comparing rates for these social problems and inequality levels over time, in the 50 U S states as well as in the UK and in America as a whole, as inequalities levels became more aggravated, the rates for these social problems have increased. To be sure, these problems have worsened in these countries as a result of other factors as well, including racial prejudice and social conflicts. Nonetheless, increasingly aggravated inequalities do seem to have had a measurable adverse impact on a wide range of social problems. Interestingly, groups on the political Right, like the Tea Party, while ignoring the way growing inequality affects the least advantaged, have voiced concern about the growth of these kinds of social problems, which they attribute to the declining attachment to basic values. Wilkinson and Pickett argue that these social problems have worsened in large part because increased social inequality exacerbate feelings of relative deprivation and loosen sentiments of social interconnection. Ironically, if the political Right were really seriously concerned about the growth in crime rates, delinquency, loss of trust, and teenage pregnancy, then it would make sense for them to join with the political Left in seeking ways to reduce levels of economic inequality.[12]

The marked increase in economic inequality in countries like the United States and the United Kingdom has been caused by four factors, each of which are sources of concern in their own right, and each of which has either contributed to the current economic crisis or made it more difficult to emerge from this crisis.

First of all, the growth in economic inequality has in part been caused by the tremendous increase in "winner-take-all" economic rewards.[13] The most successful entertainers, sports figures, lawyers, executives, and consultants increasingly gain disproportionately huge compensation packages while most of the others pursuing careers in these professions earn only modest incomes. Compensation levels for executives have grown much faster than the value of the firms they manage. The ratios of their earnings to that of average workers have become even more disproportionate.[14] The

---

[12] Richard Wilkinson and Kate Pickett, *The Spirit Level: Why Greater Equality Makes Societies Stronger* (New York: Bloomsbury Press, 2009).

[13] Robert H. Frank and Philip J. Cook, *The Winner-Take-All Society* (New York and London, Penguin Books, 1995).

[14] Many economists defend the size of executive pay, arguing that higher pay levels do seem to correspond to higher share values. A representative view can be found in Schumpeter, "American chief executives are not overpaid," *The Economist* (September 8, 2012), p. 67.

steep rise in the pay levels of the top performers, professionals, and executives has aggravated inequalities and occasioned resentment by those who have not benefited as well.

It is worth calling attention to the fact that increasingly executives are paid by receiving shares in the firms they manage. Thus, in principle because the value of these shares should reflect how well their businesses are doing, executives will be financially advantaged or disadvantaged by the corresponding success or failures of their firms. However, this practice involves a moral hazard because executives in general, who as a group often sit on the boards of related firms, have an overall vested interest in increasing the share value of firms. It then comes with little surprise that in the two decades prior to the fiscal crisis, share value of firms increased exceedingly much more than the overall productive value of these businesses.

Various justifications have been offered for supporting this dramatic increase in size of compensation for top professionals, entertainers, and executives. If people willingly are prepared to pay more for their entertainment or goods and services they purchase—because of these compensation packages, then, it is sometimes argued, it would be an infringement of their liberty to interfere with that choice. However, in response, one can easily argue that consumers exercise no real choice over how these enterprises choose to reward these highly paid individuals. Again, it is often said by proponents that these high compensation packages are simply reflective of the character of these very competitive markets for especially talented people who can perform in these highly valued roles. Compensation levels are further justified on the basis of the decisive role these individuals play in fostering the well-being of their enterprises. However, in answer to both of these arguments, we can observe that these businesses have not produced proportionately more benefits than competitors in other countries paying much less. Overall, chief executives in Japan have performed correspondingly as well as their counterparts in the United States even though their levels of compensation are only 16 times greater than those of their average employees rather than 200 times as is the case in the United States.[15]

Secondly, in industrialized countries like Britain and the United States, increased levels of aggravated inequality have also been caused by continued patterns of corporate welfare. Over the years, governments have intervened in support of businesses in ways that especially benefit those who

[15] Stiglitz, *The Price of Inequality*, p. 21.

are well-to-do. These include extensive land grants to those building railway systems, huge public subsidies in agriculture, which especially advantage large farming operations, recent bailouts of a number of huge financial institutions viewed as being too large to fail, as well as procurement policies that *de facto* benefit firms in the defence industries. Other examples of corporate welfare include major reductions in royalties required of oil companies drilling offshore and mining companies mining on public lands, subsidies for the use of ethanol as well as prolonged copyright protection for new discoveries by pharmaceutical companies.[16] We can point to a number of additional examples whereby governments have offered extensive financial support for particular firms and industries. What is important to observe is that the amount of public finds used in one way or another to offer assistance to businesses has been staggering.

Both the vocal political Right and the vocal political Left have called attention to problems of winner-take-all patterns of compensation and corporate welfare. The Right, however, has been wary of proposed solutions to the problem of excessive pay levels because of their fear that government interventions in these matters, like other forms of government regulations, will result in interferences that may well make matters worse. Many on the political Right may secretly admire those who have succeeded so well. In any case, while complaining about the inequalities experienced by middle and working class households, their potential critique of winner-take-all economic contests remains comparatively mute. However, they join with the political Left in complaining about corporate welfare. Here, again the range of topics about which these groups protest remain spotty. While characteristically criticizing the bailouts of the banks, the Right tends to ignore other instances of corporate welfare such as the extensive corporate welfare embodied in farming and ethanol subsidies, inflated prices for defence contracts, and the way pharmaceutical companies raised prices to take advantage of changes in government-funded drug programs.[17]

The problems associated with winner-take-all economic contests and unjustifiable expressions of corporate welfare can and should be addressed. Both practices aggravate patterns of household inequality in ways that violate traditional notions of fair play. Both practices encouraged excessive risk-taking by financial institutions and the wealthy in ways that

[16] James Surowski, "Corporate Welfare Queens," *The New Yorker* (October 8, 2012), p. 42.
[17] Stiglitz, *The Price of Inequality*, p. 97.

were connected with financial crisis. Because many people hope they might be lucky enough to win, like people who regularly buy lottery tickets even though they typically spend more than they get back in their occasional winnings, they invest a lot of their lives working to compete in winner-take-all economic contests and settling for quite meagre economic rewards. No doubt many of those who found themselves far from the winner circles in these economic contests were enticed by lenders who persuaded them they could still get the family homes they desired by borrowing and paying back as the value of their houses increased as housing prices had been increasing for a number of years. The extensive spread of winner-take-all economic contests and corporate welfare represent social malpractices. Both practices can and should be limited and judiciously reformed.

Thirdly, over the past thirty years, economic inequalities have been aggravated as well by a steadily growing practice of hiring ever larger numbers of employees on a part-time and/or part-year basis. In many industrialized states, an increasing larger proportion of the labour force is being offered conditional rather than full-time work. Retail firms hire people to work just during the hours when they have the most customers. Many business offer larger percentages of their workers limited term contracts even when they typically renew their contracts at the end of these periods. These practices make sense to the firms involved because they often do not then have to contribute toward fringe benefits of part-time and part-year workers, or their contributions are greatly reduced. Firms reduce their labour costs by hiring employees for fewer hours. Furthermore, part time and seasonal workers are typically less likely to become members of trade unions, and therefore less likely to bargain for higher wages.[18] For whatever reasons, the proportion of workers hired through conditional labour markets has greatly increased since 1980. Because these employees work markedly fewer hours per year and typically also receive low wages, they take home less income. Correspondingly, many of the households these workers support live with household incomes at or below the poverty line. While often not being unemployed, these workers are under-employed. While the current levels of unemployment have raised much public concern, the levels of under-employment are much higher. The proportions of young men who are unemployed or underemployed have become alarmingly high, especially in the countries surrounding the Mediterranean Sea in North Africa, the Middle East, and southern Europe, as well as in southern Africa.

---

[18] Naomi Klein, *No Logo* (New York: Picador, 1999), chapter 10.

The steady growth of the conditional labour force is a worrying phenomenon, especially since those who seem to be most affected are young people just entering the labour force. The social cost of this practice is enormous. Just when it seems to be most advantageous for young people to be working to begin careers and families, increasingly large numbers are being offered part-time and part-year work that does not in any meaningful way seem related to the development of viable careers. Correspondingly, many of these young people seem to be more interested in their private lives or political protests than the public good. Thus, the practices associated with conditional labour markets not only add to the factors productive of aggravated patterns of economic inequality but also occasion serious social problems of their own.

Fourthly and finally, aggravated inequalities in household incomes have also been exacerbated by changes in tax laws, which merit more extensive discussion. I will be discussing the question of fair taxation later in this essay.

For millions of people, clearly, it will not be enough to find ways of ending the Great Recession, unless actions are also taken to address the malpractices and institutional arrangements that have both aggravated patterns of inequality and led to a number of serious social problems, in turn made worse by increased inequality. In their own ways, both the Tea Party and Occupy movements have called attention to aspects of this larger set of problems. But the interlocking issues, associated with increasingly aggravated inequality encompass more than the problem to which these movements direct attention. Fundamentally increased inequality and the social problems that it aggravates—like declining trust, increased delinquency, lower school achievement scores and decreased social mobility—result neither from excessive government intervention nor the greed of elites. Rather, they are fostered and reinforced by a set of institutional arrangements like pay systems that excessively reward highest earners, unfair taxing systems, excessive corporate welfare, and the growth of conditional labour markets.

Facilitating Open and Effective Economic Markets

Both the Tea Party and the Occupy movements seem convinced that the contemporary economic malaise has arisen because of current patterns of market practices. In by-passing monologues each movement assumes that the overall economy has been under-performing because it has been too closely shaped by policies supported by those on the opposite end of the political spectrum. The political Right argues that weak economic performance has occurred because of the way governments have excessively intervened with regulations that have occasioned market rigidities and stymied economic growth. While the political Right seems to believe that current economic problems could be solved by strengthening markets, the political Left is inclined to believe that current problems have emerged precisely because of excessive reliance on markets. Correspondingly, the political Left points to the ways efforts by British and American governments since 1980 to reduce regulations have not in any demonstrable ways fostered increased economic growth. Rather than fostering increased productivity, efforts at de-regulation have simply facilitated rent-seeking behaviour by those with the most economic influence. Moreover, the Left worry about the insidious ways the logic of markets seems to have invaded all aspects of social life. For example, Michael Sandel and others have called attention to the disturbing ways we seem to think about ever larger areas of life in terms of economic markets. We pay children to do their homework; we solicit blood donors by offering them pay; and so forth. Voluntary associations and religious groups often adopt business plans in order to render their operations more successful. We seem to think of more and more aspects of our lives in terms of the cash nexus.[19]

However, while the political Right and Left have called attention to some issues that merit genuine attention, their positions seem reactive, focused more on symptoms rather than underlying problems. With regard to market practices, these groups seem at times excessively wedded to their own rhetoric. With respect to economic markets, the fundamental problem is neither an over-reliance on markets—although that can become an issue—nor excessive government interference in markets—although that too can become a problem as we saw with respect to the growth of corporate welfare. Rather, the fundamental problem is the way open markets characteristic of industrialized market economies have in a number of diverse ways been subverted over the past several decades. As Acemoglu and Robinson have argued in their recent book *Why Nations Fail*, these markets in industrialized societies operate effectively to foster wealth creation rather than wealth extraction to the extent that governments help to create a range of public institutions to establish and to protect these mar-

---

[19] Michael J. Sandel, *What Money Can't Buy: The Moral Limits of Markets* (New York: Farrar, Straus, and Giroux, 2012).

kets. Markets are subverted when these market-establishing institutions are undermined.[20]

The recent fiscal crisis and current recession challenge us to re-examine to what extent economic markets have been in practice operating in keeping with widely shared free market assumptions. Concerns have been raised about a number of practices that seem to subvert accepted market norms. For example, alarms have been raised about predatory lending to low income households, initially charging them below market interest rates that were subsequently steeply raised to prices many of these households could not afford. Questions have been asked about the practice of cleverly disguising the risks of financial packages, designed especially to mask this risk. Many have protested the ingenious ways many international businesses avoid taxes by depositing earnings in off-shore bank accounts.[21] Rather than acting as exchanges promoting wealth creation, many observers worry about the extent to which at least some markets are becoming exchanges to facilitate the wealth extracting interests of those well-placed to pursue these ends.[22]

To get a sense of how widespread these problems are, consider the following examples in which governments have ignored basic market norms in order to favour particular enterprises at great expense to the public. For example, after first reducing regulations with respect to the thrift industry in the United States, the government then spent billions of tax payers' dollars to bail out savings and loans associations that had become bankrupt because of risky practices.[23] Similarly, the federal government offered huge loans to keep Chrysler and General Motors in business when they faced bankruptcy during the recent fiscal crisis. At an enormous expense to the public and in contradiction to basic free market norms, governments in Europe, Canada, and the United State for decades have offered huge subsidies and tax breaks to the agricultural sector. These subsidies, sometimes supported as well by corresponding tariffs, directly obstruct the opportunities of millions of farmers in developing countries who might otherwise market more of their produce and finished agricultural goods in industrialized societies. Initially undertaken temporarily to foster econom-

---

[20] Daren Acemoglu and James Robinson, *Why Nations Fail: The Origins of Power, Prosperity, and Poverty* (New York: Crown Publishers, 2012).

[21] Matthew Valencia, "Storm Survivors: Special Report: Offshore Finance," *The Economist* (February 16, 2013).

[22] Stiglitz, *The Price of Inequality*, chapter 2.

[23] Martin Mayer, *The Greatest-Ever Bank Robbery: The Collapse of the Savings and Loan Industry* (New York: Charles Scribners' Sons, 1990).

ic growth in the housing industry after World War Two, the federal government in the United States continues to offer significant tax credits for mortgage payments. More recently, governments have intervened with extensive loans and grants to protect a number of financial enterprises from folding. In all of these examples, governments have interfered in normal market processes in order to promote what seemed like worthy public purposes, at least to some enterprises. They have done so not only often at cost to consumers and tax payers, but also at costs to present and potential competitors. In the process, they have contravened accepted norms regarding market exchanges.

In a number of ways businesses have also acted on their own to subvert markets. For example, some larger businesses subvert ordinary market processes by the practice of predatory pricing. At a loss, they deliberately sell a number of items at below what it cost to produce these goods or services in order to attract customers away from competitors, who will then be forced to abandon their businesses.

A number of international businesses distort their marketing transactions through practices of abusive transfer pricing and deliberate mis-pricing. Transfer pricing refers to accounting practices by which firms determine the cost of items traded between different national branches of the same international companies. By these practices, firms in one country will decide how they will price goods and services that are delivered to them from other branches of the company headquartered in other countries. According to basic principles of transfer pricing, items should be priced as if they were determined by impartial market forces at arms' length. In practice, firms exercise considerable discretion. Insofar as possible, firms will price items so that it appears that the largest earnings are in countries with the lowest tax rates. Thus, for example, in 2011 Microsoft declared it had made 15.5 billion dollars, 55% of its gross profits in Puerto Rico, Ireland, and Singapore, countries all of which have very low corporate tax rates.[24] While technically legal, the abuse of transfer pricing means that many countries lose huge amounts of potential revenues. Moreover, in the process, transfer prices are seldom really set in keeping with an objective assessment of market forces. Mis-pricing refers to the widespread practice of setting different prices for internationally traded items in the country of origin and in the countries where they are finally sold. This practice allows firms to price items produced in various devel-

[24] "Tax Avoidance: The rights and wrongs of moving profits off shore to cut taxes," *The Economist* (September 29, 2012), p. 78

oping countries quite low, therefore generating little or no taxable profits from their operation, and selling them to intermediaries nominally located in offshore tax havens where they are re-priced before they are then sold at much higher prices to eventual customers. Huge profits are then made by these intermediaries while the governments and workers in the developing countries gain little in taxes and wages from the items produced. Both of these practices aggravate international inequalities. Both practices have been encouraged as examples of smart business practices. Both, nonetheless, represent clear efforts to avoid or subvert ordinary trade markets.[25]

Markets have been further subverted by various expressions of corruption, including the abuse of offices, whether as public servants or organizational officials, for private gain; the use of private influence to gain public contracts; and the manipulation of information to secure market advantages. These kinds of problems have grown in the recent past, even while the public denunciation of corruption continues. It sometimes seems that excessive outrage has been directed against comparatively minor abuses, such as the misuse of executive prerogatives or customary payment of facilitation fees. At the same time, much larger and more consequential abuses, connected with securing major government contracts or the manipulation of relevant information regarding the risks connected with new financial instruments, have received comparatively less attention.[26]

Financial markets have been subverted both by excessive de-regulation and by the failure to update regulations to keep pace with the creation of new and ever more complex financial instruments.[27] The Financial Crash of 1929 and the Great Depression of the thirties were in part occasioned by excessively risky financial transactions. In an effort to moderate and manage these risks, the US federal government established deposit insurance for bank accounts, and with the Glass-Steagall Act of 1933 separated the practices of commercial and investment banking. With these institutional arrangements in place, the banking industry flourished, and the economy steadily grew during the next half century. However, in the past thirty years these institutional arrangements have been deliberately weakened. Banks learned from the Savings and Loan crisis of 1987 that the government would protect them after their excessively risky practices cost home

---

[25] Raymond W. Baker, *Capitalism's Achilles Heel: Dirty Money and How to Renew the Free-Market System*(Hoboken, New Jersey: John Wiley & Sons, Inc., 2005), pp. 23-49, 163-173.

[26] Stiglitz, *The Price of Inequality*, chapter 3.

[27] Krugman, *End This Depression Now*, chapter 4.

owners and the public billions of dollars. In 1999, the government repealed the Glass-Steagall Act, thereby allowing commercial banks to engage in the same kinds of risky practices that had occasioned the Great Crash.

The current recession with its accompanying high rates of unemployment and under-employment also call for us to explore ways in which contemporary labour markets have functioned much less well at helping workers find employment than they have functioned to help employers find employees. This situation represents a major market dysfunction. If they are functioning effectively, labour markets are supposed to connect jobs with workers and workers with jobs. As a recent *Economist* essay noted, at present globally there are more than 300 million young people who would like to work but who are neither regularly employed full-time nor in training or education. To be sure, some of these people remain unemployed because they do not possess the skills needed for possible jobs, and some remain unemployed because they lack information about real job prospects or cannot easily apply to the firms where the jobs exist.[28] However, fundamentally, labour markets are not functioning well because there has been for a number of years a growing global lack of demand for labour. As at the time of the Great Depression, this situation calls for governments to explore initiatives, through industrial policies, tax incentives, and/or the use public subsidies to expand employment opportunities to further targeted public purposes.

As we reflect on the current crisis, it is important to make two different points. One, wherever free markets occur, they have been established not only because of expanding commerce and industry, but also because appropriate institutional arrangements have been developed by governments. In their recent wide-ranging study of the wealth and poverty of nations, Acemoglu and Robinson point to the decisive role in the development of free markets played by corresponding development of political institutions, including the rule of law, legal definitions of contract and property, rules standardizing trade and credit transactions, as well as rules and agents used to identify and to protect those involved from fraud.[29] When public institutions like these are absent or weak, powerful interests tend to utilize markets exploitatively in order to extract wealth from existing sources for their own ends. In a book entitled *The Moral Ecology of Mar-*

---

[28] "Generation Jobless: Youth Unemployment," *The Economist* (April 27, 2013), pp. 58-60.

[29] Acemoglu and Robinson, *Why Nations Fail*.

kets, Finn demonstrates how all markets presuppose the existence of a set of publicly established institutions, including those that provide for public security and those that manage the increased economic risks associated with market economies. These institutions facilitate the development and maintenance of markets. At present, it is noteworthy that in all industrialized societies governments have established a range of publicly funded institutions—including old age pensions, unemployment insurance, workers' compensation programs, deposit insurance for banks, as well as bankruptcy laws—all of which operate to help these societies manage the risks associated with modern labour, commercial, and financial markets.[30]

A second fundamental point regarding markets has to do with the fact that not all markets are the same. In terms of the character of the risks occasioned by market transactions, the kinds of alternative opportunities foregone, and the shape and duration of expected corresponding commitments, there are huge differences in the exchanges associated with labour, credit, investment, retail, and wholesale markets. Vast bodies of law and guidelines for accounting practices have been developed to spell out and protect these differences. To treat all of these market exchanges as if they operated in keeping with the same set of normative assumptions not only over-simplifies matters. It also is likely to produce unjust outcomes.

In response to the current crisis, several initiatives seem to be especially important. We need to discover ways to reduce the extent that markets are distorted and subverted by business people, governments, and accountants. In keeping with classical notions of commutative justice, we need to reduce areas where particular parties to market transactions are adversely affected by asymmetries in relevant information. We need to work to insure greater transparency with respect to all aspects of market interactions. More forthrightly, we need to acknowledge the extensive role that governments play in establishing the institutions that help to construct and facilitate open and competitive markets. We also need to respect the characteristic ways in which different kinds of markets vary. It is indeed appropriate to call attention to the valuable ways over time open markets with respect to trade, labour, and credit have functioned to create wealth and raise standards of living. However, in light of the fiscal crisis and the great recession, it is also necessary now to call attention to the multiples ways we have allowed markets to be subverted by rent seeking practices. Disturbingly, many of the organizations and people who engage in these

[30]Daniel K. Finn, *The Moral Ecology of Markets: Assessing Claims about Markets and Justice* (Cambridge University Press, 2006).

market-distorting practices invoke the rhetoric of free markets in order to obstruct the responsible efforts by governments to address these very problems.

As both the political Right and the Political Left have argued, the recent financial crisis and great recession have been occasioned and aggravated by current market practices. Particular commercial and financial markets have been subverted. Labour markets have become dysfunctional at least for hundreds of millions living with un- and under-employment. These problems can indeed be addressed by acting in keeping with core values both, one, by strengthening and reforming the public rules and institutions that facilitate open and competitive markets and, two, by using public resources to increase demand in labour markets.

Fostering Fair and Effective Tax Policies

Both the Tea Party and Occupy movements argue that current tax practices are unjust in fundamental ways. The political Right contends that taxes are higher than they need to be and that excessive amounts of tax revenues are used wastefully by governments both for useless government programs and to support people who have allowed themselves to become dependent on welfare assistance. These beliefs in part reflect the actual fact that the real income of most middle income and working class household in the United States, Britain, and a number of other industrialized countries have not risen in the past thirty years even though the economies of these countries as a whole have grown modestly, although not as much as they grew between 1950 and 1980. Many have been inclined to look for tax relief—and to oppose tax increases—because they fear any further threats to their modest household wealth, including the worry that tax increases might impede economic growth. Correspondingly, they have welcomed tax cuts, even when these primarily benefit wealthiest households, because of the promise that these cuts might help the economy expand in ways that would benefit them. The political Right has so successfully raised fears about tax increases that almost no political party seems prepared to entertain proposals for general tax increases even as government deficits increase, the quality of many public services declines, and public infrastructures deteriorate. They worry that efforts to reform tax systems may serve as the occasion for raising taxes.

In contrast, the Occupy movement has attacked the ways current tax practices seem to favour the rich. They point to numerous ways in which wealthy households and large corporations have been able dramatically to reduce their taxes by making use of special tax credits and deductions, for example, for mortgage interest payments and for particular kinds of investments. They note how the wealthiest households especially benefit from recent tax cuts. They call attention to the fact that many of the wealthiest households pay taxes at lower rates than most working class households.

Many of these arguments of the political Left have merit. Many of the arguments of the political Right are also understandable. Both express deeply-held suspicions that current practices of taxation are unfair in many different ways. Certainly, current taxing practices in a number of industrialized countries, like the United States, Britain, Portugal, and Spain, as well as in many developing countries like Brazil and Mexico, reinforce and/or aggravate inequalities in household income. Correspondingly, both the political Right and political Left argue further that present taxing practices are not only unfair to large proportions of the population, but also excessively complicated and unreasonably costly.

Current tax systems have indeed become complicated and costly and, in addition, they have functioned to encourage some practices that led directly and indirectly to the recent financial crisis and great recession. For example, to cite a quite varied sample of examples largely from the United States, the current pattern of corporate taxes encouraged many firms increasingly to raise funds by borrowing rather than attracting investors because interest payments can be deduced as business expenses while profits are taxed; tax policies thereby fostered excessive borrowing. Tax deductions for mortgage interest payments encouraged many families to purchases houses they could not presently afford in hopes that continuously rising house values and correspondingly reduced taxes would benefit them in the long run. To cite another example, tax cuts during the early years of the current century, at a time the United States was fighting two major foreign wars, markedly increased public deficits, without having any impact on economic growth, thereby putting the government in a position where it was much less able to respond to the financial crisis when it arrived. Additionally, the current tax system encourages a number of questionable practices by people to reduce their taxes. As an indirect evidence of these practices, we can note that as people chose not to declare certain forms of income and resorted to varied strategies of tax avoidance and tax evasion, there was in 2005 a gap of $1.3 trillion dollars between the total income people actually earned based on information from sources and the amount of income declared in tax forms as the basis for calculating taxes owed.[31]

Current tax systems in industrial countries assume the complex forms they do today because they have been developed, modified, amended, expanded, reduced, tinkered with, and adjusted in response to the diverse agendas of many different interests. They have been variously designed and/or cobbled together to raise public revenues, foster investments, fund public insurance schemes, encourage savings and/or spending, overcome particular perceived abuses, and benefit targeted constituencies. For example, several tax policies in the United States function to deliver what amounts to huge public welfare benefits—i.e. government transfers—to particular constituencies who then regard these benefits simply as tax breaks.[32] Tax systems are so complex that they are not easily reformed. Every initiative on one part of the system seems to have its unanticipated consequences for other parts. It is no wonder then that many of those aware of particular injustices perpetuated by the tax system despair of attempting any kind of broad reform. Often driven by feelings of resentment and despair, movements like the Tea Party and Occupy champion either tax cuts in general or tax hikes for the very rich because both initiatives will, they hope, reduce, if only marginally, tax burdens for citizens generally.

Neither of these strategies is likely to address the underlying problem associated with perceived injustices associated with current tax practices. In order to address these real underlying problems, three changes need to take place. First, people need to develop a new appreciation of the ways the benefits they have received and expect to receive as citizens grow out of the taxes they are called upon to pay as citizens. What we need with respect to tax policies is a new and renewed sense of citizenship. Secondly, basic reforms must be undertaken so that citizens feel that systems of taxation are legitimate, reasonable, and fair. In many ways the Scandinavian countries provide useful examples of how to proceed. Their economies

---

[31] Bruce Bartlett, *The Benefit and the Burden: Tax Reform—Why We Need It and What It Will Take* (New York: Simon and Schuster, 2012), p. 157.

[32] I have in mind the following programs: a) the tax credit home owners receive for mortgage payment, which cost the government approximately $100 billion per year; the fact that employees do not have to pay taxes on medical benefits employers provide then through employer funded private health schemes and employers can deduct the cost as business expenses, which cost the government approximately $184 billion per year; and c) the Earned Income Tax Credit which allows workers with low wages tax credits. Cf. Bartlett, *The Benefit and the Burden*, pp. 92-93.

are thriving. The citizens of these countries enjoy wide public benefits and regard their tax systems as fair.[33] Thirdly, in order to meet current claims upon our governments, many of which are statutory requirements associated with social insurance, public revenues in a number of countries, like the United States, will have to increase. We shall consider each of these points in what follows.

1. Taxation and Democratic Citizenship

Any efforts to deal responsibly with perceived problems with tax systems must begin with a renewed assessment and appreciation of the way public welfare systems have grown and evolved over time as major industrial democracies have industrialized. As these broad systems of public welfare have grown, the taxes collected by governments have also grown. Systems of public welfare have grown in these countries in response to the historical processes associated both with industrialization and with democratization. Accordingly, it is fitting to regard modern public welfare systems as integral to both processes. Modern public welfare systems include a wide range of government funded programs and services including public schools, old age and unemployment insurance, tax credits for employer-provided health services and the interest payments on mortgages, publicly enforced standards guaranteeing minimum wages, occupational safety, and patent protection, as well as publicly supported research. A very tiny part of modern systems of public welfare are involved with what many of those alarmed by abuses of welfare think of as welfare, namely public assistance programs for dependent children, single mothers, handicapped persons, and the indigent.

Modern public welfare programs and services have been established in large part to manage the risks occasioned by modern labour, commercial, and financial markets. Hence, the development and expansion of social insurance programs for retired, unemployed, and injured workers; deposit insurance for money people place in banks; minimum wage laws and tax credit to guarantee minimally adequate incomes for low income workers; and bankruptcy laws to protect businesses against vicissitudes of market fluctuations. Because of the size and complexity of modern markets and businesses, and because we are therefore affected by the behaviour of many whom we do not know, modern systems of public welfare include as well provisions to guarantee safe and healthy working conditions as well

---

[33] Adrian Woolridge, "Northern Lights: Special report on the Nordic Countries," *The Economist* (February 2, 2013).

as safe and healthy consumer products. Because modern industrial business require workforces with appropriate skills, modern welfare systems have expanded publicly-supported systems of education and training at the secondary, college, and university levels. Because certain markets that produce publicly valued goods and services remain weak, modern public welfare systems have been expanded to provide and guarantee subsidies, price supports, tax credits, and purchases with respect to agriculture, housing, and defence. As industrialization has proceeded and markets have expanded, modern systems of welfare have grown proportionately. Modern industrial capitalist societies in the process have thereby become homes for large, complex, many-faceted modern public welfare systems.

At the same time, the growth of modern welfare systems represent as well a response to the desires of citizens in increasingly democratized societies. The relationship between democracy and the growth of public systems of welfare was recognized more than 170 years ago by de Tocqueville at the end of the second volume of *Democracy in America*. He observed that in democracies, as citizens gained increasing capacity to express their wants for goods and services such as education, public roads, safety and security, public parks, as well as public guarantees of basic rights, they will ask governments to act to address these concerns. In response governments will grow in size as they act to meet these desires.[34] Interestingly, the provisions established to guarantee basic human rights are costly. Most people recognize that the social rights to education, old age pensions, and basic protection in response to natural disasters involve public costs. However, the rights to free speech, freedom of contract, and protection of property are costly as well.[35] Everywhere as countries have become more democratic, and as citizens have correspondingly demanded greater public guarantees of their basic human rights, certain features characteristic of modern public welfare systems have grown as well. It is worth observing that many of the least developed countries face severe limits in guaranteeing the full range of human rights for their citizens precisely because their own lack of economic development leaves their governments with only modest tax revenues that might be used to provide the corresponding guarantees and services.

---

[34] Alexis de Tocqueville, *Democracy in America* (New York: Vintage Books, 1945), Vol. II, Part IV, chapter 6.

[35] Charles Holmes and Cass Sunstein, *The Cost of Rights: Why Liberty Depends on Taxes* (New York: W.W. Norton, 1997).

What is especially unique and interesting with respect to the United States is how much of their own modern system of public welfare remains hidden right in front of them. Overall, the extent of spending associated with the modern system of public welfare in the United States compares favourably with most other industrialized countries. As a percentage of GDP, US welfare spending is slightly less than that of France or Sweden but higher than the average for all industrialized countries.[36] Over time, the US systems were especially noteworthy for their commitment to public education and the generosity of social insurance for the aged. They were also noteworthy for the diverse and complicated ways they delivered public welfare services and the extent they used tax expenditures—that is, tax credits—to deliver some of the most costly benefits, like tax credits for mortgage interest payments, no taxes for employer-provided health insurance, and tax credits for low income workers. Together these latter welfare programs cost more than $300 billion per year. What is also noteworthy about the American systems of public welfare is the extent to which they provide the most generous services for the middle, working class, and the wealthiest classes.[37]

Just as the citizens of most industrialized democracies recognize the multiple ways they benefit from modern public welfare systems, Americans are challenged to overcome the widespread moral amnesia that allows them not to acknowledge as publicly-funded welfare programs the many services, entitlements, prerogatives, and opportunities from which they benefit. Any serious efforts to address the injustices associated with current tax practices in industrialized countries generally, and in the United States in particular, must begin by first recognizing the diverse ways modern welfare systems have helped to create the institutions they have benefited from and have come take for granted. Just as they receive these services as an integral aspect of their citizenship, so they are correspondingly expected to support these services as citizens through the taxes they pay.

[36] Irwin Garfinkel, Lee Rainwater, and Timothy Smeeding, *Wealth and Welfare States: Is America a Laggard or Leader* (New York: Oxford University Press, 2010); Molly C. Michelmore, *Tax and Spend: The Welfare State, Tax Politics, and the Limits of American Liberalism* (Philadelphia: The University of Pennsylvania Press, 2012).

[37] The average middle and working class households receive benefits from these welfare services worth more both in absolute terms and relative to their overall income levels than do households in the lowest classes.

2. Tax Reform as an Urgent Priority

Therefore, two, concerted efforts must be undertaken to restructure and reform the policies and institutions in terms of which taxes are collected. There are no panacea formulae, like the proposed flat tax, for bringing about changes that will be politically feasible, effective, and fair. However, it is useful to identify several basic principles that seem effective and fair and are likely to attract wide support. I will briefly discuss three: namely, the principle of proportionality: taxes should be paid in proportion to the ability of people and organizations to make these payments; the democratic principle: all citizens ought to be expected to contribute to the extent they are able; and what might described as the principle of fair business taxes, which will be discussed further on in this essay.

Thus, in the first place, most observers would agree that people ought to pay taxes in proportion to their ability to pay. The overall system should be progressive. For lower income households, much of this progressivity can be achieved by raising the level of personal exemptions both for tax payers and their dependents. During the past three decades a number of tax cuts have been introduced in the United States and Britain that have especially benefited the wealthy in ways that have rendered the overall system of taxes significantly less progressive. These tax cuts, especially those introduced by the Bush administration since the turn of the century have thereby aggravated the overall patterns of inequality and have had little or no impact, as promised, on economic growth. Any promising tax reform should seek to attempt to make the overall pattern of taxes generally progressive, in ways like the systems instituted by the Scandinavian countries.

In the second place, to the extent that all citizens benefit from modern public welfare systems as well as other government services, then it seems fitting to ask all citizens to contribute to the degree they can, even if quite modestly. What seems especially unfair about the current practices are the multiple ways many households pay little or no taxes because of tax deductions, tax credits, exemptions, and the way certain kinds of wealth-creating sources are not counted as income. In part the attacks by the political Right on welfare abuse stems from a misperception that many recipients of public assistance receive huge benefits while paying no taxes. In reality the situation is far more complex. Most impoverished households pay sales taxes and pay rents that are used to pay property taxes. At the same time many working class households gain tax credits—and therefore indirect welfare benefits—to compensate for the payroll taxes deducted by their employers. Because they are able to take advantage of various tax deductions and tax credits as well as particular legal definitions of what counts as income, many wealthy households pay little or no income taxes. The basic principles of fairness and equity seem to be compromised in many different ways by these diverse tax policies and practices. It would seem fair that all citizens should be expected to pay taxes as citizens—albeit in many different ways—whether they are rich, middle class, or poor to the extent that they can. It would also seem reasonable and fair duly to recognize that as citizens they may pay their taxes in quite different ways.

One of the appeals of the value-added tax (VAT) as it has been instituted in European countries is the fact that it is a tax that all citizens pay as they consume. Since value-added taxes have been instituted so widely in the industrialized countries of Europe, it makes sense for industrialized countries without them to consider the merits and problems associated with this form of taxation. The VAT is collected from businesses at every stage of the production process. However, at each stage in the process, businesses get credit for price additions they have to pay suppliers for taxes already collected. In the end the price for goods and services are increased by the amount of taxes paid. The overall system for collecting taxes is administratively simple. VAT has fewer problems associated with compliance. Indirectly consumers pay for value added taxes in proportion to the value of the purchases they make. Accordingly, wealthy households pay much higher taxes because they make more purchases overall, and purchases of more expensive items. VATs possess a number of virtues. They are administratively effective and simple. Since everyone pays them, they reinforce the connections between citizenship, taxes, and the corresponding benefits of modern public welfare systems. They do not function to discourage investments and savings.

Nonetheless, where they have not been introduced, VATs have been strongly criticized by both the political Left and the political Right for opposite reasons. The Left has opposed VATs because, as a tax on consumption, they are in part regressive. If a straightforward VAT were introduced in America, low income households would end up paying modestly more for the items they consume. These households would be paying moderately more in taxes than they do now. The political Right has opposed VATs because this form of taxation is largely hidden and not viewed as a tax and could, therefore, be used fairly easily to increase the overall level of taxation. Nonetheless, a VAT could be introduced in ways that addressed both of these concerns. The regressive character of VATs could be mitigated in several quite decisive ways: food items could be made exempt from VATs. So could other items that represent disproportionately large parts of the budgets of low income households, such as rents below a certain level and the cost for utilities and public transportation. At the same time, taxes could still be levied on incomes above several hundred thousand dollars. In the meantime, many of the intricacies of the current taxing practices could be eliminated. In response to the fears of the political Right, we can observe that adoption of VATs by other industrial states has not led to excessively higher taxes. At present the overall levels of taxes as a percentage of GDP remain comparable. Again, the Scandinavian countries provide interesting examples, where legislators in response to public concerns have moderately reduced tax revenues over the past several decades.

I am not here proposing the VAT as the central platform for any serious tax reform. However, I do think those considering tax reform should seriously consider how this system of taxing has worked in European countries over the past four or five decades. In interesting ways, this system addresses a number of current concerns. It provides a way of addressing the problem of noncompliance. It is administratively simple. On the whole it addresses the two principles we have thus far discussed: namely, it remains generally progressive in character, when thoughtfully introduced, and it operates in keeping with the basic democratic principle of universal participation.[38]

In the third place, any serious tax reform must address a series of complicated issues with respect to taxes of business enterprises. Although the political Left often calls for increased taxes of businesses, in practice the cost for paying these taxes are often passed along in terms of higher costs for consumers, lower wages for employees, and increased dividends for shareholders, because in this case tax rates on capital gains are much less than taxes on profits. More disturbingly, many businesses have over time become very proficient in tax avoidance practices. They locate their major offices of their companies in countries with very low tax rates, thereby paying much lower corporate taxes. They make effective use of account-

[38] We might add as an additional principle that the tax system should be used sparingly as a means of delivering social welfare benefits. For example, it would seem fair and reasonable to address *directly* a number of social problems, such as low wages among the working poor, rather than managing them *indirectly* through the tax code. Thus, it would seem simpler, more effective, and more fitting to address this problem by raising minimum wage levels and, in order to keep small business competitive, provide these employers with corresponding tax credits for transitional periods of time.

ing practices and transfer pricing arrangements to reduce their apparent profits and thereby the taxes they are required to pay. Thus, in practice taxes on businesses often do not end up taxing the excess wealth which proponents of these taxes hope will be taxed. Are there more effective ways to tax this excess wealth that do not act as disincentives for desired investment in further business enterprises? Might an effective wealth tax on income and capital gains, whether earned domestically or abroad function to address this problem better? There are no simple solutions to these inter-related issues and abuses. Any lasting and significant tax reforms must look at all of these issues related to taxes of business enterprises.

Complaints about current taxing practices are widespread. The Financial Crisis, the Great Recession, and the public responses to these troubles have occasioned both more impassioned complaints and diverse calls for varied incompatible reforms. Any serious efforts to address these concerns must adopt a large view, acknowledge the extensive role modern public welfare services play in industrial democracies, listen much more attentively to concerns raised by those they oppose, consult the experiences of other industrialized countries, and look for common grounds.

3. Increase Tax Revenues

Three, any effort seriously to address the injustices associated with current tax practice will probably call for those concerned to explore reasonable ways to increase revenues available for governments. The political Right vehemently opposes this idea and with minor exceptions the political Left seems to concur, adding only that they think additional revenues might come from higher taxes of corporations and the wealthiest households. Higher taxes are necessary for a number of very significant reasons. Thus, as traditional conservatives would argue, they are required in order to find ways of limiting and reducing huge public deficits. While these debts may not now be alarming,[39] they may in time become so because so much of this debt is connected with the growing cost of statutory government programs, such as old age pensions, public health insurance, and interest payments on existing debts.[40] Tax increases are required as well in order to address the steady deterioration in physical and social infrastructures. There are widespread complaints about the declining quality of transportation systems, public schools, and mental health services. There have been corresponding complaints about the declining quality of urban

[39] Paul Krugman, *End This Depression Now*, chapter 8.

[40] Bartlett, *The Benefit and the Burden*, chapter 20.

life. Most importantly, tax increases are called for in order to enhance the demand for labour so that millions of un- and underemployed people can find regular employment opportunities. Finally and decisively, tax increases are necessary because none of these objectives can even approximately be realized by the prevailing initiatives taken to reduce government spending.

Since the 1980s, the political Right has argued that the problems associated with increased government expenditures could be effectively addressed through carefully instituted tax cuts. They assumed that fitting tax cuts would stimulate economic growth, as it seemed to have done so briefly when the Democratic Administration in the United States introduced tax cuts in 1964. However, within a few years, that administration had to introduce new tax increases in part to pay for the costs of the Vietnam War. However, the underlying assumption, shared by liberals and conservatives, was that governments would find ways of funding increased expenditures because the economy would grow and as a result tax revenues would be increased without having to institute any tax increases. Beginning in the early 1980s, tax laws were changed in Britain and America to reduce income taxes of the wealthy, capital gains taxes, inheritance taxes, and corporate taxes. New reductions have been added in subsequent years in hopes that these reductions would help to foster economic growth, because —it was argued—those now paying lower taxes would use their added wealth to consume more and to make added investments. In fact, these reductions seem to have had almost no impact on economic growth. The overall economies of the industrialized countries, especially Britain and the United States, grew at a higher *per capita* rate during the generation prior to 1980 when taxes were higher than in the subsequent generation. Interestingly, in terms of the impact of taxes on economic growth, in the United States the economy expanded during the middle 1990s as taxes increased but growth slowed as taxes were cut after 2003.

To be sure, when viewed from the perspective of their own household budgets, even modest tax increases still represent costs even if they are used to support public services that these households value and take for granted, whether these be infrastructure developments, social insurance, tax credits for mortgage payments, or health care services. Viewed from the perspective of the economy as a whole, increased taxes have typically functioned within limits to support the services people count on and to augment demand and expand employment. In practice, given the current structure of taxes, which seem complicated and costly, many resent even modest tax increases when others seem to be paying much less than seems fair. However, this myopic perspective on taxes, viewed apart from the wide range of public services funded by these taxes, neither serves the interests of those who protest nor the public good.

It is easy to despair about the possibilities for genuine tax reform. However, concerns about the dysfunctions, complications, and inequalities associated with current practices have become widespread in a number of industrialized countries. Therefore, it seems worthwhile to attempt to explore ways of reforming the overall systems of taxes that go beyond attempts to address particular abuses. In the above paragraphs I have attempted to spell out some basic principles that might serve as basic assumptions or debating points. Clearly, any discussion of reform must begin, as I have argued in this essay, with a revaluation of the meaning of citizenship in modern industrialized societies, in relation both to basic benefits people receive as citizens as well as their corresponding responsibilities.

Conclusion

As a result of the Financial Crisis and Great Recession, millions of people in the United States, Canada, Europe, and around the world have suffered from long periods of unemployment and under-employment, lost their homes, and seen sizeable shares of their savings vanish. The losses in economic terms amount to several trillion dollars. The losses in personal and social terms have probably been even greater. Although overall economic conditions have improved, nonetheless the long term prospects for many millions of people do not seem very promising in spite of huge expenditures by governments. Many people feel out of sorts. Telling themselves and those who sympathized with them quite different stories, the Tea Party and Occupy movements reflect the larger, shared more pervasive sense that basic economic and political institutions have not been working well. Both movements assumed that these institutions perpetuated unjustified and unnecessary injustices, occasioned the crisis and recession, and failed to develop effective responses to these problems in large part because they had lost touch with traditional core values. Both movements gave voice to similar feelings of resentment.

I have argued that it is important to attend to the concerns raised by these movements, not necessarily because their analyses or proposals were especially insightful or particularly promising, but because of the several ways these movements have alerted us to a number of serious underlying issues that must be addressed. In this essay, echoing concerns regarding particular issues raised quite differently by these movements, I have discussed three large concerns.[41] These are as follows: one, the growth in aggravated household inequality; two, the several distinct ways economic markets have been subverted or become dysfunctional; and, three, the ways tax practices have become increasingly complicated and unfair. In order to address these concerns responsibly, it is necessary to undertake a number of reforms related to factors that have given rise to aggravated inequality, subverted markets, and various problems associated with current tax practices. Thus, for example, in order to reduce the growing inequalities related to household income, we must reduce the degree to which labour markets have become distorted by winner-take-all economic contests. We must undertake these reforms in part because these kinds of economic contests become socially dysfunctional as they aggravate feelings of resentment and discontent, and attenuate feelings of social connectedness. In part winner-take-all economic contests affront our basic notions of fair play according to which economic rewards people enjoy ought to be in some ways proportionate to the efforts they make, the risks they face, and the value of their corresponding contributions. Growing inequalities in household incomes also reflect the extent to which economic exchanges have also been affected by the growth both of corporate welfare and conditional labour markets. These phenomena need to be addressed both because they are socially dysfunctional and because they interfere with our basic assumptions about fair play.

In this essay I have discussed a number of what might be described as social malpractices. In each case I have examined the ways these malpractices in part functioned to occasion the financial crisis and great recession and were in turn aggravated by them. I have noted the ways both the Tea Party and the Occupy movements have in different terms called attention to these practices. I have indicated why these malpractices need to be addressed both because of the social costs associated with them and because each seems to violate basic notions of fair play. Invoking notions associated with traditions of commutative justice, I have also attempted to analyze

[41]This list of concerns is not meant to be exhaustive. We might add several other underlying issues, of which the financial crisis and the Great Recession have been symptoms, such as the widespread disenchantment with political processes, looming ecological crisis and associated increased costs for energy, and continuing poverty in the developing world. While the most severe forms of poverty (*per capita* income of less than $21.25/day) seem to be declining, the extent of less severe poverty (*per capita* income of less than $2.25/day) does not seem to be declining in total numbers affected.

these malpractices in terms that are in part responsive to observations made by both the political Right and the political Left.

As we explore ways of addressing these issues responsibly, we face particularly troubling circumstances. As an indirect result of the increase in aggravated inequalities, occasioned by the increase in winner-take-all economic contests, tax cuts favouring the rich, the growth in conditional labour markets, and increase of corporate welfare, the sense of commonality among citizens of these countries has been markedly attenuated. The increase in the incidents by which businesses and individuals use and thereby subvert open markets to extract wealth from others rather than create wealth through reciprocating exchanges further aggravates these inequalities and undermines public trust. As a result of these developments, it has become much more difficult to explore the bases for finding common grounds. However, in this essay, while taking seriously concerns raised by both the political Left and the political Right, I have attempted to find broader more encompassing ways framing these underlying issues in hopes of identifying genuine bases for reforms.

As Lincoln stated in his Second Inaugural, the crisis we have been experiencing results from practices with which we have all been involved. It is not enough to blame particular others for their greed, their lack of effort, or their corruption. We need to need to seek a way forward that addresses the kind of underlying issues discussed in this essay with as much wisdom as we can hope to achieve, with compassion for those most adversely affected, with an enlarged commitment to the common good, and with a renewed sense of justice.

CHAPTER THREE

FADING "RELIGIOUS CAPITAL": A CAUSE OF THE FINANCIAL CRISIS? THINKING OUTSIDE THE MAINSTREAM

ROBERT H. NELSON[1]

Not surprisingly, given the very large costs that the financial crisis of 2007 to 2009 and the following Great Recession imposed on American society, there have by now been many scholarly and other studies of its causes (see the partial bibliography at the end of this essay). There is now wide agreement that a host of factors played significant roles. Princeton University economist and former vice-chairman of the Federal Reserve, Alan Blinder, wrote in 2013 that, "Americans built a house of cards, piece by piece, starting in the late 1990s and continuing right up until disaster struck in 2007." The build-up to the financial crisis was "based on asset-price bubbles, exaggerated by irresponsible leverage, encouraged by crazy compensation schemes and excessive complexity, and abetted by embarrassingly bad underwriting standards, dismal performance by the statistical rating agencies, and lax financial regulation."[2]

If there is one party that was the most responsible, as Blinder suggests, the leading candidate is the top executives of the credit rating agencies such as Moody's and Standard & Poor's.[3] Others throughout the financial system relied specifically on these agencies to provide accurate assessments of the levels of risks associated with mortgage-backed securities and other key financial instruments, the very purpose of their existence, based

---

[1] The economist Robert H. Nelson is Professor of Environmental Policy in the School of Public Policy at the University of Maryland. He has a longstanding interest the relation between economics and religion.

[2] Alan S. Blinder, *After the Music Stopped: The Financial Crisis, the Response, and the Work Ahead* (New York: The Penguin Press, 2013), p. 84.

[3] Ibid., p. 79-81.

in part on a federal mandate that many securities have ratings. In this especially critical role in the financial system, they systematically abdicated their responsibilities and failed miserably.

The next most responsible party was probably the top executives of the large mortgage lending institutions such as Ameriquest, Washington Mutual, and especially Countrywide. They were unusually well positioned to see and understand the poor quality of the large numbers of subprime mortgages they were writing, the rapidly growing risks of defaults, and the potentially very large losses for both the borrowers and the investors in mortgage securities. Yet, even though it appears in retrospect that many top executives of these firms were aware of the developing problems, they showed a blatant disregard for others in a headlong rush to maximize their own individual and firm incomes.[4]

There were, however, a number of other significant contributors to the financial crisis. A significant share of blame should be assigned to Fannie Mae and Freddie Mac which lowered mortgage lending standards and lobbied aggressively against proposed legislative or regulatory limitations on their own ability to take large financial risks, even as they were implicitly backed by federal taxpayer guarantees.[5] Some scholars have argued that the Federal Reserve helped to stimulate the housing bubble by keeping interest rates too low and for too long in the early 2000s.[6] Under the leadership of Chairman Allan Greenspan there is little question that the Fed failed badly in its assigned task of regulating mortgage risk taking, as his successor in 2006 as Fed chairman Ben Bernanke (who also was slow himself to act in this regard) would later acknowledge.[7] From the 1990s onwards, leaders of both political parties in the Congress and the executive branch aggressively pushed for major expansions of mortgage lending into lower income and minority areas of big cities, by the mid 2000s saddling many people in these areas with debts that they could not pay.

---

[4] *The Financial Crisis Inquiry Report: Final Report of the National Commission on the Causes of the Financial and Economic Crisis in the United States* (New York: Public Affair, 2011), pp. 104-105.

[5] Gretchen Morgenstern and Joshua Rosner, *Reckless Endangerment: How Outsized Ambition, Greed and Corruption Led to Economic Armageddon* (New York: Times Books, 2011).

[6] See discussion of this issue in the dissenting statement of Commissioners Keith Hennessey, Douglas Holtz-Eakin, and Bill Thomas, *The Financial Crisis Inquiry Report*, pp. 420-422.

[7] Ben S. Bernanke, *The Federal Resource and the Financial Crisis* (Princeton, NJ: Princeton University Press, 2014), p. 121.

Wall Street investment banks such as Merrill Lynch and Lehman Brothers were altogether negligent in failing to perform due diligence in monitoring the actual high risks associated with the housing market securities they were both holding on their own books and selling to trusting investors around the world—reflecting in part the new shorter term incentives that resulted from shifts in investment banking in the 1980s and 1990s from partnerships to corporate ownership.[8] The list could go on to include additional lesser contributors to the financial crisis among government regulatory agencies in Washington and private actors on Wall Street. Financial journalists and academic students of financial markets as well cannot be absolved of any blame.[9]

Given the many contributors, analysts of the financial crisis have typically concluded that there was no one cause, no one core explanation—Blinder lists seven key "villains." This is true in the sense that no one institution or single category of actors was principally responsible all by itself. If others had behaved responsibly, any one party of transgressors would have had less impact, their financial misbehaviour contained by the corrective actions of the others. But as events unfolded, there was a wide failure on almost all financial market fronts.

Why, however, would failure in the Washington regulatory apparatus and in the actions of Wall Street have been so systematic? Martin Wolf, the distinguished economic columnist for many years for the *Financial Times*, has advanced three explanations. First, there was a general intellectual failure to which professional economists were principal contributors, the idea that free-market principles were generally applicable throughout the entire economy, even including the special circumstances of the financial markets. As Wolf writes about the financial crisis, "behind all this was the assumption that self interest would, via Adam Smith's invisible hand, ensure a stable, dynamic, and efficient financial system," thus fostering an attitude of complacency among both Washington regulators and Wall Street participants, even as evidence of mounting financial market problems accumulated in the 2000s.[10]

---

[8] Alan Greenspan, *The Map and the Territory: Risk, Human Nature, and the Future of Forecasting* (New York: Penguin, 2013), pp. 51-52.

[9] Adair Turner, *Economics after the Crisis: Objectives and Means* (Cambridge, MA: MIT Press, 2013).

[10] Martin Wolf, *The Shifts and the Shocks: What We've Learned—and Have Still to Learn—from the Financial Crisis* (New York: Penguin Press, 2014), p. 136.

Indeed, reflecting a professional preoccupation with heroic abstraction and market theory, most economic and other analysts were unaware of the details of recent developments in the financial sector. Their confident free-market assumptions were in reality more a statement of faith—a tenet, one might say, of one particular form of "economic religion" that was ascendant at the end of the twentieth century—than the product of any rigorous scientific analysis by economists of the detailed economic circumstances and workings of contemporary markets such as in the financial sector.[11]

A second key underlying factor, as Wolf argues, was global in character, the large imbalances being created by international capital flows in the 2000s. In the United States, these were resulting in large foreign account deficits while other countries such as China were financing these deficits by massive purchases of U.S. government bonds. As Wolf explains, a "global savings glut and associated imbalances" led to the following: "debt exploded relative to incomes; assets became increasingly leveraged; and the financial sector grew hugely. In the process, the financial sector itself became more unbalanced, with more leverage, more reliance on short-term wholesale funding, and more complexity, irresponsibility, and dishonesty."[12] A third general contributing factor advanced by Wolf is the long period of macroeconomic stability prior to the financial crisis, thus dulling critical awareness of actual risk potentials among regulators and financial market participants.[13]

In this essay, I will suggest an additional fundamental element underlying the financial crisis, a breakdown in "religious capital" that was concretely manifested in the weakening ethical standards of Washington and Wall Street. As is chronicled over hundreds of pages in exhaustive detail, the final December 2010 *Financial Crisis Inquiry Report* found that there had been "a systematic breakdown in accountability and ethics" throughout the financial system in the 2000s.[14] As also found in other studies of the financial crisis, a change had occurred in the culture of the financial sector that worked to undermine the principles of honesty and trustworthy behaviour necessary to the successful functioning of most markets—and especially the financial markets where the financial instruments are often less transparent and have become increasingly complex to the point of being impenetrable for many people. Ethical breakdowns of such a sys-

[11] Robert H. Nelson, *Economics as Religion: From Samuelson to Chicago and Beyond* (University Park, PA: Pennsylvania State University Press, 2001).
[12] Wolf, *The Shifts and the Shocks*, pp. 173, 172.
[13] Ibid., p. 132.
[14] *Financial Crisis Inquiry Report*, p. xxii.

temic character have historically often had a religious basis, as I will argue—interpreting religion broadly—was again the case for the financial crisis.

Thinking Outside the Mainstream

This will, admittedly, lead into unfamiliar territory for most social scientists and financial analysts. In seeking to understand the financial crisis, they have looked to traditional legal and economic explanations such as the workings of financial regulations, the set of private incentives faced by the various participants in financial markets, and the impacts of specific organizational forms. Among economists, there has in general been a reluctance to develop cultural explanations—and this has been particularly true when the key shaping force of a culture might be religious.

For a typical economist, he or she might well feel at a loss even to try to characterize the shifting religious territory of Wall Street and the factors seen in religious change there. A novelist or an essayist such as Michael Lewis might be able to say valuable things about such matters but "harder" analysis, according to the conventional expert wisdom, would be necessary for shaping future government financial market policies. If the real problem was the culture of Washington regulatory agencies and of Wall Street, social science has little confidence in its ability to provide a roadmap to needed cultural change. Embarrassingly, theologians—broadly understood—rather than economists, might be the most relevant group.

Yet, I am not the only economist to conclude that religion was central to the financial crisis, and that a religious understanding may therefore be required in order to preventing recurrences in the future. Reflecting a growing scholarly interest in the role of religion in government and business affairs, the *Journal of Religion and Business Ethics* published its first issue in 2009—this yet another consequence of the many efforts to understand the financial crisis. In a 2010 issue, economists Kim Hawtrey and Rutherford Johnson argue that the new "moral infrastructure" of the financial markets in the 2000s created a vicious circle that led to a "viral moral atrophy" that undermined the workings of these markets themselves. At least since the time of Adam Smith, it has been widely understood that "moral-philosophical pillars and socialized sentiments underpin the economic judgments that help lead to a cohesive society under a market regime."[15] But the necessary "socialized sentiments" collapsed in the financial markets in the 1990s and 2000s in the run up to the financial crisis.

Understanding the causes of the moral deterioration that fed the financial crisis will thus be "about more than law, and goes deeper than ethics" as a philosophical inquiry alone. Rather, Hawtrey and Johnson argue, theology must come into play because the deepest cause of the financial crisis "involves belief....When a community is unsure of its religious faith, then the moral path can easily become a slippery slope" that can undermine the socially beneficial workings, for example, of free markets.[16] As one might say, a well functioning economy depends not only on physical inputs such as land, labour, and capital, but also on an adequate level of "social capital" that is often derived in significant part from religion.[17]

Another outgrowth of the financial crisis was the 2009 Encyclical of Pope Benedict XVI, *Caritas in Veritate*. As James Stormes writes, the Pope "understands sin precisely in our rejection of...interdependence and overemphasis on individualism."[18] Benedict condemned the fact that "many people today would claim they owe nothing to anyone, except to themselves." In the Encyclical, the Pope considered that "in the list of areas where the pernicious effects of sin are evident, the economy has been included for some time now." It was possible for "authentic human social relations [to] be conducted within economic activity," but contemporary economic structures often worked against this outcome. Indeed, as Benedict wrote, "the conviction that man is self sufficient...and that the economy must be autonomous [from the wider society]...had led many to abuse the economic process in a thoroughly destructive way," as illustrated most recently by the social and economic devastations of the financial crisis.[19]

In the United States, the religion of Wall Street was once Protestant Christianity, which—despite some significant breaches in the 1920s and other years—set the overall value foundations for fair dealings among

---

[15] Kim Hawtrey and Rutherford Johnson, "On the Atrophy of Moral Reasoning in the Global Financial Crisis," *Journal of Religion and Business Ethics*, 1:2 (2010), pp. 21, 16.

[16] Ibid., p. 23.

[17] Robert Putnam, *Making Democracy Work: Civic Traditions in Modern Italy* (Princeton, NJ: Princeton University Press, 1994).

[18] James R. Stormes, S.J., "Pope Benedict XVI's 'Caritas in Veritate'": A Challenge to Business Ethics," *Journal of Religion and Business Ethics*, 1:2 (2010), p. 4.

[19] Pope Benedict XVI, *Caritas in Veritate*, quoted in ibid., p. 4.

mostly Protestant financial market participants until the middle of the twentieth century. Over the later course of the century, however, the influence of mainstream Protestant Christianity in American public and private life declined sharply. Religion, as many increasingly believed, should not only be separated from the state but from business as well. The leadership of American business also became much more diverse, including more Catholics, Jews, Asians, agnostics and atheists, and others to reflect the growing religious diversity of the United States itself.

If a common religion would still be necessary to provide the "religious capital" of the financial markets, in such a newly diverse environment this bonding faith would have to be a more widely acceptable "secular religion." Writing in 1992, Yale humanities professor Harold Bloom explained that "the American Religion is post-Christian, despite its protestations, and even…[it] has begun to abandon [residual] Protestant modes of thought and feeling. If we are Americans, then to some degree we share in the American Religion, however unknowingly or unwillingly."[20] Former Treasury Secretary Timothy Geithner would write in his memoirs that Federal Reserve chairman Alan Greenspan "did have an almost theological belief that markets were rational and efficient."[21]

For much of the second half of the twentieth century, a widely shared secular religion in American life was in fact the religion of economic progress, or what I have called "economic religion."[22] Economic progress, as a powerful modern faith in Europe and the United States, offers the prospect of saving the world by economic actions alone. As this essay will relate, however, by the 1980s and 1990s, the secular religious faith in the transcendent powers of economic progress was rapidly fading—with major implications, as I will argue, for many American institutions such as Wall Street.

Instead, in those years traditional forms of religious fundamentalism were newly resurgent around the world. Moreover, not all turns away from economic religion took traditional religious courses; American environmentalism amounted to a new secular fundamentalism opposed in many

---

[20] Harold Bloom, *The American Religion* (New York: Chu Hartley Publishers, 2006 [1992]), p. 11.
[21] Timothy F. Geithner, *Stress Test: Reflections on Financial Crises* (New York: Crown, 2014), p. 85.
[22] Nelson, *Economics as Religion.*

ways to economic religion.[23] None of the increasingly influential forms of religious fundamentalism, however, gained a wide following among the players in the financial markets. Lacking a religious substitute and given a waning economic faith, there was a religious vacuum developing on Wall Street. It thus lost its moral moorings, culminating in the 2000s in multiple forms of individual and organizational misbehaviour that helped to set the stage for the financial crisis.

This is not to suggest that the traditional objects of economic analysis such as the workings of supply and demand, the structure of individual incentives, opportunity costs, and so forth were not present in the workings of financial markets of the decade of the 2000s. But when the entire financial system began to go awry, there was not enough religious capital—traditionally or secularly based—to guide and provide a vocabulary for high-level corrective leadership. There were few, if any, prominent Wall Street or Washington heroes.

As matters developed, the public and private workings of the financial markets were like an open rangeland or other commons in which—lacking any effective societal regulatory or normative restraints—rampant opportunism was given wide scope across the entire financial sector. As 2009 Nobel economics prize winner (her receipt of the award was another outgrowth of the financial crisis) Elinor Ostrom emphasized, there are three institutional ways to resolve a commons problem: private property rights, collective public regulation, and informal normative controls.[24] None worked in the lead-up to the financial crisis.

Social Science as Religion

In order to explore more closely such central religious developments on Wall Street, it will be helpful to provide some wider religious context. From the mid nineteenth century, the emerging social sciences sought to model their efforts after the physical sciences that had been so astonishingly successful in providing a technical basis of knowledge for a human mastery of nature for human benefit. As a result, the average person in the

---

[23] Robert H. Nelson, *The New Holy Wars: Economic Religion versus Environmental Religion in Contemporary America* (University Park, PA: Pennsylvania State University Press, 2010); also Robert H. Nelson, "Calvinism Without God: American Environmentalism as Implicit Calvinism," *Implicit Religion*, 17:3 (2014).

[24] Elinor Ostrom, *Governing the Commons: The Evolution of Institutions for Collective Action* (New York: Cambridge University Press, 1990).

developed world today lives better materially than a member of a royal family did in the seventeenth century—a virtual miracle on earth, as it seems to me at least.[25]

By contrast, despite an enormous expenditure of time and effort since the nineteenth century, the social sciences as a whole—at least by the standards of the physical sciences—have been a large disappointment. Despite a few decades in the mid twentieth century in which Freudian psychology was the rage in the United States, and some other western nations, the inability of psychology to develop a scientifically valid understanding of the workings of the human psyche is today manifest. Bloom thus writes that "the Freudian Fundamentalists (of the Ego Psychology sect) are as literal minded as the Southern Baptist Fundamentalists, and both groups believe that their sacred texts, the Standard Edition of Freud and the Holy Bible, somehow interpret themselves and are inerrant."[26]

It is equally apparent that the workings of American government and politics today defy the efforts of political "scientists" to establish reliable technical explanations and predictions (although opinion polls have greatly improved the quality of monitoring of public thinking). Even much more ambitiously, the founders of sociology in the nineteenth century such as Auguste Comte once proclaimed that there would soon be a comprehensive scientific (a "positive") understanding of the full workings of every aspect of society.[27] As it developed, however, the field of sociology never remotely succeeded in approaching this original aspiration.

As a surprising number of observers have concluded, the modern developments in the fields of psychology, political science, and sociology may be today better understood in religious than in scientific terms.[28] The social sciences, as it increasingly seems, are part of a modern spread of new forms of religion that are commonly described as "secular religion"

---

[25] Deirdre N. McCloskey, *Bourgeois Dignity: Why Economics Can't Explain the Modern World* (Chicago: University of Chicago Press, 2010), pp. 4-6.
[26] Bloom, *The American Religion*, p. 7.
[27] Robert H. Nelson, *Reaching for Heaven on Earth: The Theological Meaning of Economics* (Lanham, MD: Rowman & Littlefield, 1991), pp. 114-122.
[28] Paul C. Vitz, *Psychology as Religion: The Cult of Self-Worship, second edition* (Grand Rapids, MI: Eerdmans, 1994); William M. Epstein, *Psychotherapy as Religion: The Civil Divine in America* (Reno, NV: University of Nevada Press, 2006); Emilio Gentile, *Politics as Religion*, trans. by George Staunton (Princeton, NJ: Princeton University Press, 2006).

(or some call them "implicit religion").[29] They have been part of a wider modern process in which the traditional functional role—and to a surprising degree also the core traditional messages—of Judaism, Christianity, and other historic religions have been recast to a new language that says little explicitly about God, but is no less religious for this fact.[30]

Among the social sciences, whatever the manifest failings of recent years, the field that has been seen as making the strongest claims to a scientific status has been economics. It is true that many economic phenomena do lend themselves to quantitative representations, making it possible to develop formal mathematical models of economic behaviour and outcomes and to apply rigorous statistical tests. But economics is not an exception to the religious character of the social sciences.

Economics as Religion

I have examined the religious content of economics—and its role as a leading potential source of "religious capital" (an especially important form of "social capital") in American life—as a main theme of three books of mine, *Reaching for Heaven on Earth: The Theological Meaning of Economics* (1991); *Economics as Religion: From Samuelson to Chicago and Beyond* (2001); and *The New Holy Wars: Economic Religion versus Environmental Religion in Contemporary America* (2010).

Admittedly, when I attended economics graduate school in the late 1960s, none of my professors then saw a religious content to economics. That does not mean, however, that theology was altogether absent from economics. My PhD thesis advisor, and the most influential member of the Princeton economics department in those days, was William Baumol. When Baumol was asked a while ago to explain why he had entered the economics profession, his response was that "I believe deeply with [George Bernard] Shaw, that there are few crimes more heinous than poverty. Shaw as usual, exaggerated when he told us that money is the root of all evil, but he did not exaggerate by much."[31] Evil in the world, in short,

---

[29] Edward Bailey, "Implicit Religion," in Peter B. Clarke, ed. *The Oxford Handbook of the Sociology of Religion* (New York: Oxford University Press, 2009); and Edward Bailey, "Implicit Religion," *Religion* 40:4 (2010).

[30] Robert H. Nelson, "The Secularization Myth Revisited: Secularism as Christianity in Disguise," *Journal of Markets and Morality* (forthcoming Fall 2015).

[31] William J. Baumol, "On My Attitudes: Sociopolitical and Methodological," in Michael Szenberg, ed., *Eminent Economists: Their Life Philosophies* (New York: Cambridge University Press, 1992), p. 51.

for a professional economist such as Baumol arose from dire economic circumstances.

In the Bible, however, the sin of the Garden of Eden is the "root of all evil." In Baumol's new alternative theology, characteristic not only of many economists but also of numerous other progressives, socialists, and other social theorists over the course of the twentieth century, there is a new secular explanation for the presence of sin in the world. Severe economic deprivation, the dire poverty in which human beings have lived for most of human history, is the actual cause that has driven most people to lie, cheat, steal, and commit other "socially offensive" acts.

If poverty is the true explanation for sin in the world, moreover, the astonishing economic successes of the modern age have created a radical new human possibility. If severe poverty—indeed, all major economic deprivation—can eventually be eliminated, it may be possible to save the world through human actions alone. The Biblical God—more and more difficult for many people in the modern age to believe in—will no longer be necessary. Indeed, traditional religion may become a diversion from taking the necessary economic steps. In short, according to economic religion, in the long run economic progress will eliminate the old conflicts and divisions among human beings grounded in resource and other material scarcities, in the end thereby leading to a new heaven on earth.[32]

Arguably the greatest economist of the twentieth century, John Maynard Keynes, thus once wrote that rapid economic growth would "lead us out of the tunnel of economic necessity into daylight." In the new world of the future, perhaps only 100 years away, as Keynes wrote in 1930, we shall finally be "free, at last, to discard" the uninhibited pursuit of self-interest, the obsessive accumulation of capital, and other "distasteful and unjust" institutions of our present-day economic system.[33] These unpleasant features of our lives today should be seen as merely a temporary expedient that are now appropriately justified as necessary short run sacrifices on the long run path of a human earthly salvation.

At the annual meetings of the American Economic Association, the Richard T. Ely lecture is one of the most prestigious platforms in economics. Ely is remembered as the leading early American economist who in

[32] Robert H. Nelson, "The Secular Religions of Progress," *The New Atlantis* (Summer 2013).

[33] John Maynard Keynes, "Economic Possibilities for Our Grandchildren," (1930) in Keynes, *Essays in Persuasion* (New York: W.W. Norton, 1963), pp. 369, 371-72.

1885 was a key founder of the Association. Although he regarded himself as a devout Christian, the Kingdom of Heaven for him—characteristic of the social gospel movement of the time in which he was a prominent figure—was to be achieved in this world, not in the hereafter. As Ely would write, "Christianity is primarily concerned with this world, and it is the mission of Christianity to bring to pass here a kingdom of righteousness." As a "religious subject," the teachings of economics should provide the critical base of technical knowledge for "a never-ceasing attack on every wrong institution, until the earth becomes a new earth, and all its cities, cities of God."[34] For many people in the secular American progressive movement that would soon follow, the Christian setting was no longer necessary. They adapted such thinking to create what is today commonly described as the American secular progressive "gospel of efficiency."[35]

Efficiency was of such transcendent importance because the attainment of higher and higher levels of economic productivity (i.e., efficiency) would continue the economic progress that would lead to the ultimate perfection of society. At first, the leading experts in efficiency were seen by secular progressive thinkers as the engineers and administrative scientists of society. With time, however, the key experts came to be seen by the second half of the twentieth century as the members of the economics profession.[36] As such, they had the essential knowledge of the workings of the economic system to show the way to a long run elimination of material deprivation—and thus by the premises of economic religion to the salvation of the world.

The members of the economics profession (to be assisted by other social and administrative scientists) would then appropriately become the new priesthood of the progressive American gospel. As advocates for efficiency—the new good over against evil—economists would be the guardians of American public morality in matters of policy and administration, largely replacing in the twentieth century the core historical role once played by the Protestant ministry in the public affairs of state.

---

[34] Richard T. Ely, *Social Aspects of Christianity and Other Essays* (New York: Thomas Y. Crowell, 1889), pp. 15, 53, 73.

[35] See, for example, Samuel P. Hays, *Conservation and the Gospel of Efficiency: The Progressive Conservation Movement, 1890-1920* (Cambridge, MA: Harvard University Press, 1959).

[36] Robert H. Nelson, "The Economics Profession and the Making of Public Policy," *Journal of Economic Literature* 25:1 (March 1987).

In economic religion, Wall Street must have an especially critical role because it is responsible for allocating the uses of capital across the American economy. The commercial and investment banks and other institutions of Wall Street become leading "temples" of American economic progress. They are to be among the chief overseers of national economic efficiency and growth. All this must be accomplished within a framework of democratic political institutions. This blend of economic and political beliefs provided the core tenets of what the American sociologist Robert Bellah famously labelled in 1967 the American "civil religion."[37] At the time Bellah wrote, Wall Street had many such true believers.

A Waning of Progressive Economic Faith

Faith in economic progress was not only central to the religion of Wall Street, but also of most of the faculty and students of the top universities, and other members of the governing classes of American society. As with other religious causes, America's civil religion—with economics at the centre—fostered a culture in which individual gain alone should be tempered by various greater collective purposes and obligations. The people working in financial markets might be amply compensated individually for their efforts, but they should never lose sight altogether of the larger national social and economic purposes they were expected to serve as well. This was especially important because the principles of free market economics did not apply as well in the financial sector where a few institutions had long held great power and where trading in information was a principal commodity that often lacked clear property rights and other normal market characteristics.

The heyday of such a progressive moral compass on Wall Street and elsewhere in America was from the end of World War II into the 1980s. But even in this period, the belief in the saving powers of economic progress was living on borrowed time. The deaths of nine million soldiers on the battlefields of World War I, and six million civilians, seemingly to no real purpose, had already fundamentally challenged the progressive economic utopianism of the late nineteenth and early twentieth centuries. The events of the 1930s and 1940s, including the rise of Hitler and Stalin, made it abundantly clear that there was much more to sinful human actions than the material circumstances in which human beings lived.

---

[37] Robert N. Bellah, "Civil Religion in America." *Daedalus: Journal of the American Academy of Arts and Sciences* 96:1 (Winter 1967).

The holocaust was the most powerful symbolic event of the twentieth century. What it revealed with such terrible clarity was that there existed a potential for unspeakable horrors in even an economically advanced nation such as Germany. The creation of the atom bomb in 1945 meant that human beings were now in possession of the physical power—if not carefully managed—of their own annihilation as the ultimate consequence of human scientific and economic mastery of natural processes. The pursuit of economic progress might have yielded unparalleled material gains in the modern age, but could no longer offer a sure promise of a path to heaven on earth. Indeed, there was no guarantee that there might not even be a future hell on earth in store.

It is difficult, however, for most people to change their fundamental thinking—their religion—once they have reached mature adulthood. So a belief in the transcendent powers of economic progress was still broadly accepted in American thought and society for three or four further decades after the end of World War II. By the 1960s, however, a new generation was reaching adulthood that had grown up in the full knowledge of the awful historic events of the first half of the twentieth century. As Yale professor Sydney Ahlstrom put it in his magisterial *A Religious History of the American People*, the turmoil in American society of the 1960s amounted to a "violent and sudden…moral and theological transformation" of the nation, beginning the death throes of economic religion.[38]

By the 1980s the baby boomers were reaching their 30s and 40s and becoming newly important in American life. What would be the new source of "religious capital" for them in the years to come? Unfortunately, none took hold widely in financial circles (or among many other power brokers within the American elite). If a strong, shared belief in a religion is required to limit individual opportunism, the checks were becoming weaker and weaker. As these trends continued in the 2000s, they were manifested in a declining ethical commitment that would be observed in financial markets and in Washington regulatory circles. In the wake of the financial crisis, more and more Americans have come to see their government, Wall Street, and other large leading American institutions as "dysfunctional."[39]

---

[38] Sydney E. Ahlstrom, *A Religious History of the American People* (New Haven, CT: Yale University Press, 2004 – first ed. 1972), p. 1091.

[39] Francis Fukuyama, "America in Decay: The Sources of Political Dysfunction," *Foreign Affairs* 93:5 (September/October 2014).

Environmentalism: A Sign of the Times

First becoming an important influence in American life in the 1960s, the rise of environmentalism was among the most important signs of the times. The old economic progressives had seen nature as a "natural resource" to be used for human benefit, as a source of key inputs to serve the core goals of economic growth, progress, and efficiency. Environmentalists now contended, however, that nature had an "intrinsic" value independent of any human benefits. The old economics was falsely "anthropocentric," they said. In failing to respect its intrinsic value, human beings in their callous treatment of the natural environment were themselves behaving in an unethical—in Christian language, a "sinful"—fashion. For some plant and animal species, it had even meant their complete extinction from the earth. Proclaiming the rise of new values in American society, the Wilderness Act was enacted in 1964, establishing a national system of environmental "cathedrals" to be defined by the fact that human impacts were absent from these areas as far as was practically feasible—and thus permanent signs of the sinful character of fallen human beings were minimally present.[40]

A leading environmental philosopher even went so far as to write an article published in 1991 in a well-respected scholarly journal, *Environmental Ethics*, addressing the question of "Why Environmentalists Hate Mainstream Economists."[41] For the leading theorists of the environmental movement since the 1960s, their writings have been filled with themes of human economic progress as a double-edged sword, human mastery of nature that has led to human abuse of nature, human beings becoming too powerful for their own good, and even more so for the rest of the natural world, the whole of "creation" now therefore endangered, human beings trying to play God in the world (the ultimate sin of the Garden of Eden), the necessity for human beings to reform their ways, and the catastrophic results for human beings and the rest of nature if they do not. Although such thinking in the United States showed a distinctly Calvinist flavour, it has been spreading more widely around the world in the twenty first century.[42]

---

[40] Robert H. Nelson, "Environmental Religion: A Theological Critique," *Case Western Reserve Law Review* 55:51 (Fall 2004).

[41] Bryan G. Norton, "Thoreau's Insect Analogies: Or, Why Environmentalists Hate Mainstream Economists," 13 *Environmental Ethics* (Fall 1991), p. 250.

[42] Nelson, *The New Holy Wars*.

While Roman Catholics historically played a lesser role in the shaping of the worldwide environmental movement, Pope Francis, for example, in his 2015 Encyclical *Laudato Si*, newly developed such environmental messages in the language and theology of the Roman Catholic Church. He was also critical there of secular economics with its implicit religion of progress, seeing it as a false idol, a harmful belief that tragically promotes 'a tendency to believe that every increase in power means "an increase of 'progress' itself", …as if reality, goodness and truth automatically flow from technological and economic power as such.' For the Pope, economic religion is thus a modern heresy. It is significantly attributable to the powerful influence of economic religion on modern thought that "the earth's resources are…being plundered because of short-sighted approaches to the economy, commerce, and production." It is thus essential that we "leave behind the modern myth of unlimited material progress," as Francis declared.[43]

It was not only environmentalists (and Vatican theologians) who found basic reasons to question the redeeming quality of modern progress. By the end of the twentieth century, even small groups of terrorists—perhaps even lone individuals in the future—held the power to do great harm to a whole society. Both environmentalism and the war on terror involve an attempt to protect the world from potentially harmful products of modern technological and economic "progress." The war on drugs has similar origins and appeals to related public fears and anxieties. If environmentalism is concerned with chemicals in the external environment, the war on drugs is concerned with the internal environment of the human brain and body. Cocaine, heroin, LSD, amphetamines, and other mind-altering substances are all, to varying extents, products of modern scientific discovery.

Together, environmentalism, the war on terror, and the war on drugs have had a great cumulative impact on American public life. Although they are sustained by much different political coalitions, and their advocates are often critical of and opposed to one another, these outward differences mask a fundamental underlying similarity. In the face of the deep public fears that have been aroused in these areas, and the extraordinary pace of technological change, these three leading moral crusades of our time seek to offer the hope of restoring—however improbably—the past certainties of a true "natural" order in the world. If the progressive economic goal was to further advance human powers over and mastery of

[43] *Encyclical Letter Laudato Si of the Holy Father Francis, On Care for Our Common Home*, June 2015, Paragraph Nos. 105, 32, 78.

nature, the ascendant moral causes of more recent times have had a much different fundamental concern.

The Crisis of Keynesianism

Unlike the environmental challenge that arose outside the economics profession, there was another source of progressive economic disillusionment that originated within economics. A key part of progressive economic religion was the conviction that the economic system operates according to objective laws that are discoverable by economists and can be manipulated for human benefit—as physical laws had been discovered by physicists for such purposes. The triumph of Keynesianism in the economics profession after World War II meant a new wide public acceptance of this element of economic faith.

As perhaps the leading economist of the twentieth century, Keynes himself in 1936 presented his ideas in scientific terms in *The General Theory* (the title was seemingly intended to draw parallels with Einstein's discovery of the "general theory" of relativity). More than most economists, Keynes recognized the existence and importance of emotional and other "non-rational" qualities in the market behaviour of investors and consumers. But in the hands of MIT economist Paul Samuelson and others of his followers, Keynesian macroeconomics was intended to be the application of a technical understanding of the dynamic laws of a modern economic system. It would put into practice the "scientific management" of the American "market mechanism" based on the discoveries of economic science, ensuring a future of rapid economic growth, high employment, and low inflation.

In the last decades of the twentieth century, however, the confident claims of Keynesian economics were subject to strong empirical and theoretical challenges. The economic outcomes of the 1970s were characterized by "stagflation" which should not have happened according to a Keynesian analysis—and thus Keynesian economists also found it difficult to offer any credible policy solutions. Rather, the most lasting economic impact of Keynesianism, as can now be seen in retrospect, may well have been moral and philosophical. Keynesianism broke the ethically based bonds of fiscal discipline that had existed prior to the Great Depression in the 1930s that had required governments to balance their budgets as a moral imperative. This could be traced in part to the powerful Puritan and Calvinist strain in American religious history.

Thus, owing much to the Keynesian undermining of an earlier form of national "religious capital," American government management of the economy since then has been characterized by a pattern in which one generation could hope to sustain its own generous levels of consumption by passing on a significant part of the burden to a successor generation. This is a mode of operation that, like other Ponzi related phenomena, cannot go on indefinitely. But it can still last a long time. Indeed, when the internet and information technology bubble in the stock market collapsed in 2000, many Americans were threatened with the prospect of actually curbing the high levels of consumption that they (baby boomers in many cases) had come to take as a birthright. The Federal Reserve, however, once again came to their rescue by pushing interest rates to near zero (as it did once again in the aftermath of the financial crisis), thereby helping to shift the stimulus of an asset bubble to a new part of the economy, the housing market.

The great theologian St. Augustine once famously wrote (I paraphrase *City of God*, IV.4) that an individual pirate is a criminal, but when piracy occurs on a large enough scale we instead call it a government. It is harsh to say, but in the long run the verdict of history might be that Bernard Madoff was a pirate of our times, while the federal government has been stealing legally from future Americans. Both Madoff and the Federal Reserve offered remarkably stable high returns—in the latter case sometimes labelled on Wall Street as the "Greenspan put"—over much the same period from the late 1980s until the year 2008, when both of these Ponzi-like schemes finally crashed and burned spectacularly.

Economists in the Confessional

Given the importance to economic religion of public confidence in the actual scientific foundations of professional economics, it is disconcerting for true economic believers that the Keynesian story is not an isolated example. Indeed, since the emergence of the American economics profession in the progressive era (typically dated as 1890 to 1920), economic experts have often been caught by surprise. Large unexpected developments such as in the most extreme case the Great Depression of the 1930s have been a recurrent phenomenon. New or revised theories such as Keynesianism would then have to be improvised but later they would frequently have to be significantly altered or rejected altogether. Professional economics has found it impossible to sustain a steady advance of scientific progress in the manner of the physical sciences. Some have even questioned whether there is any advance at all, but rather mostly a process of old wine being regularly repackaged in new bottles—more like the processes of evolutionary change in religion than of science.

Having devoted many years to achieving professional success, the average working economist has a strong professional commitment to defending the scientific status of economics. Some of the more prominent members of the economics profession, however, can afford to be more skeptical. The internal doubts among a number of leading economists at the end of the twentieth century were explored in a 1991 special issue of *The Economic Journal* (the journal of the Royal Economic Society of England, one of the most prestigious in the world of economics). As a commemoration of its first hundred years of existence, the journal published a series of 22 articles on "The Next 100 Years" including some of the better known economists of the second half of the twentieth century. The articles provided an occasion for introspective reflection on the record of the economics profession over the previous 100 years, and the prospects for the future.

A few of the articles were optimistic about the future of economics, even as they had significant criticisms to make of the past. The majority of the articles suggested, however, that economics had become too narrow and that a widening of professional horizons and methods and a firmer empirical grounding for the discipline would be much to be desired. Dartmouth economist Andrew Oswald set the tone in his contribution to the centennial forum of *The Economic Journal*, describing a sense of malaise that he perceived in 1991 concerning the directions of the profession.

Oswald poses the question whether economics is going in the right direction. Some people did not think so. Former Harvard economist Wassily Leontief had argued that the discipline was deteriorating into a second-rate branch of applied mathematics in which, unscientifically, researchers eschew empirical investigations. According to Oswald, University of Chicago economist James Heckman says that the subject is "widely perceived to be discredited because it has so little empirical content and cares so little about developing it." Stanford economist John Pencavel concludes that economists do not want applied work to be done, because it is likely to reveal the irrelevance of their hypotheses and undermine their ability to derive sweeping implications from theoretical models.[44]

In surveying these views, Oswald states that he is at least sympathetic to, if not in complete agreement with, the critics of the profession. Profes-

[44] Andrew Oswald, "Progress and Macroeconomic Data," *The Economic Journal*, 101 (1991): 75.

sional economics is in a "downward spiral" that reflects the influence of a "post-war generation of mathematicians [who now] hold power" in the ranks of the profession. Among this group, "formal analytical ability," as opposed to empirical and other more useful knowledge, "is the criterion for advancement." In seeking desperately to uphold their scientific status, economists had been led to observe the outward form of science at the expense of genuine economic knowledge. Although few economists recognized the parallels, economics was taking on the character of a "new scholasticism," now spinning elaborate webs of reasoning directed to affirming the wondrous powers of a new modern divinity of economic progress.

Oswald considers that up and coming economists find it difficult to move beyond the scientific pretense because, "believing themselves to be an elite, the ruling class [in economics] aim to create future generations in their own image." Their manner of exercising control over the activities of the economics profession is "by accepting for publication only certain kinds of articles, by recommending for promotion young mathematical economists, and by changing graduate courses to stress technical skills at which they excel."[45] As the philosopher of science Francis Bacon complained long ago, the scholastic manner of argument "brings forth indeed cobwebs of learning, admirable for the fineness of thread and work, but of no substance or profit."[46]

Another leading economist, William Baumol found that a "peril" facing economics is that "few specialized students are allowed to proceed without devoting a very considerable portion of their time to the acquisition of mathematical tools, and they often come away feeling that any piece of writing they produce will automatically be rejected as unworthy if it is not liberally sprinkled with an array of algebraic symbols." If they engage in "the pursuit of alternative approaches"—such as the study of "religious capital" in the Max Weber tradition—their work will "not [be] respected" by the leadership of the economics profession. In looking toward the next century, Baumol stated that "it should by now be obvious that I am hoping that the future will bring some decrease in the display of technique for its own sake, with models constructed so as to increase what they tell us about the workings of the economy rather than just displaying

[45] Ibid.

[46] John Herman Randall, *The Making of the Modern Mind* (50th Anniversary Edition; New York: Columbia University Press, 1976), p. 214.

the properties of some analytical procedure."[47] Indeed, although Baumol might not have agreed, the very commitment to formal "models" might itself be a key element of economic scientism.

University of Chicago economist Milton Friedman (winner of the Nobel prize in 1976) is often ranked as second only to John Maynard Keynes (and some have put Friedman first) in terms of influence on the economic thought and policies of the twentieth century. Friedman is generally supportive of the turn during the twentieth century of the economics profession towards greater use of mathematical and statistical methods. However, much like Baumol, he finds in 1991 that things have now gone too far. Indeed, Friedman declares that the "reliance on mathematics and econometrics" has reached "the point of vanishing returns." As Friedman comments, "again and again, I have read articles written primarily in mathematics, in which the central conclusions and reasoning could readily have been restated in English" and thus been available for review and discussion among a much wider readership (and often a better informed readership in practical economic matters) extending beyond the members of the economics profession themselves.[48]

The growing emphasis on rigorous scientific methods in economics dated to the 1930s, as Friedman concluded in 1991, but had unfortunately not led to corresponding increases in economic understanding, perhaps because these methods were not appropriate to the full complexity and the interdisciplinary character of many economic questions. "[T]o summarize," Friedman writes, seen in historical perspective, "there has been little change in the major issues occupying the attention of economists: they are very much the same as those that Adam Smith dealt with more than two centuries ago. Moreover, there has not been a major sea change in our understanding of these issues." In physics and chemistry the writings of 200 years ago are ancient history. But it is still possible for a current economist, Friedman reports, to "read the *Wealth of Nations* and David Hume's essays *Of Money* and *Of Interest* with pleasure and intellectual profit."[49] Indeed, some might suggest that they contained more economic wisdom than the writings of contemporary economists.

---

[47] William Baumol, "Toward a Newer Economics: The Future Lies Ahead!" *The Economic Journal,* 101 (1991): 2, 6.
[48] Milton Friedman, "Old Wine in New Bottles," *The Economic Journal,* 101 (1991): p. 36.
[49] Ibid., p. 37.

Again, in re-examining old volumes of *The Economic Journal,* Friedman is struck by how "the substance of professional economic discussion has remained remarkably unchanged over the past century" since the first journal volume was published in 1891. If the substance was not much different, to be sure, "the language" had changed "drastically."[50] Displays of technical virtuosity had become more important for many economists than the development of genuine economic enlightenment.

Remarkably enough, coming from such a prominent figure in the economics profession, Friedman also is pessimistic in seeing little gain in the quality of economic understanding from the nineteenth to the twentieth centuries; it is poor in both periods. He quotes a statement of an economist, W.J. Ashley, in 1907 that "when one looks back on a century of economic teaching and writing, the chief lesson should, I feel, be one of caution and modesty, and especially when we approach the burning issues of our own day. We economists…have been so often in the wrong!" Friedman declares that this conclusion from 1907 "can serve as mine in 1990."[51] If he were alive today, Friedman might offer the financial crisis as a further example.

A leading French economist of the second half of the twentieth century, Edmund Malinvaud, offered yet another pessimistic assessment. In assessing developments in economics since World War II, Malinvaud declared that these years "were obviously marked first by a wave of optimism, then by the painful realization that most of the initial beliefs were the product of delusion. This applies whether one considers the broad development issues [in poorer countries] or the more modest current problems of industrial countries." In the 1950s, large numbers of development economists believed that their work would soon "lead to international economic order; it will gear development in the Third World; it will show the way to good socio-economic performance in alternative systems to capitalism." As the events of the second half of the twentieth century unfolded, however, "the beliefs appear to have been mainly unwarranted, following from wishful thinking and from bold or loose extrapolations of what economics really knew."[52]

In reviewing more recent intellectual history in economics as well, Malinvaud finds "the same sequence of confidence and disappointment occurred with respect to the role of economic management in market econo-

[50] Ibid., p 33.
[51] Ibid., p. 39.
[52] E. Malinvaud, "The Next Fifty Years," *The Economic Journal,* 101 (1991): 65.

mies, whether it concerned allocation of resources, distribution of welfare or macroeconomic stabilisation." Part of the problem has been the common failure of economists to understand that "public management is never a purely economic matter and cannot be immune from political interference, if only because the notion of an objective to be achieved can seldom be precisely defined beforehand." Another problem is that "side effects that had been taken as negligible turned out to be determinant." On the whole, there has been a demonstrated "inability to solve the real problems" that has acted to undermine the earlier high hopes of the economics profession.[53] Malinvaud's concerns in 1991 would prove prescient in the aftermath of the financial crisis.

A Shortage of "Religious Capital" on Wall Street?

Faith in economic religion thus was being eroded on two fronts at the end of the twentieth century. First, the old religious certainty that in the long run material progress would lead to a new heaven on earth was much less believable in light of the actual history of the twentieth century. Second, as the priesthood of economic religion, the economics profession had been unable to sustain in practice its original expert claims to be able to discover the scientific knowledge to lead the way of continuing rapid economic progress. Astonishing economic progress has occurred over the past 200 years, but the importance of economists to this outcome has been coming under increasing doubt.[54]

The waning American religious faith in economic progress—in the various denominations of "economic religion"—is not a matter of mere intellectual (and theological) interest. Every society requires some broader purpose and associated ethical glue to hold itself together—deriving from what I have been calling the "religious capital" of a society. If the sources of religious capital are threatened, the bonds that hold the society together will be threatened as well. Absent large elements of trust and a spirit of shared sacrifice, as it is said, "the centre will not hold." Lacking a common set of value commitments, the members of society will increasingly adopt an ethic of every person for themselves.

---

[53] Ibid.

[54] McCloskey, *Bourgeois Dignity: Why Economics Can't Explain the Modern World*; also *Deirdre N. McCloskey, The Bourgeois Virtues: Ethics for an Age of Commerce* (Chicago: University of Chicago Press, 2006).

On Wall Street the wider ethical issues were exacerbated in the investment banking world by the changing ownership structures there.[55] Investment banks such as Morgan Stanley or Goldman Sachs were created as partnerships. For various reasons, including the need for greater working capital, in the 1980s and 1990s all the major investment banks became public corporations with stockholders and a board of directors to oversee the firm. As a result, the top management was no longer personally responsible as partners for the financial obligations of the firm, becoming employees instead. They were compensated through high salaries and conditional payments such as stock options.

There were serious "agency problems," however, in that the great majority of the stockholders did not have the information to evaluate internal management practices accurately. Martin Wolf observes that in such circumstances "insiders can easily exploit in their own interest" corporate decision-making. When cultural restraints on self-serving management behaviour break down, as they did on Wall Street in the 2000s, large public "corporations are…vulnerable to looting by management."[56] Top financial firm management had incentives to emphasize short term results that drove up stock prices (and their compensation), and incentives to enter into risky investments that might offer exceptionally high payoffs—with only a small chance of a dire outcome within the time period in which they would be held accountable as current managers.

Although economists resist such explanations, this is where culture comes in. In the circumstances of Wall Street, where "outputs" are more difficult to measure than in, say, railroad transportation, it requires greater internal restraints to prevent top corporate managers from maximizing their own advantage at the expense of others. As Wolf says, for it to work properly "a complex financial system" on which the whole national economic system is dependent is necessarily based on a "fragile network of trust"—the existence of faith in the people and the system.[57]

Historically, many leading American corporations in the twentieth century did have cultures that emphasized a strong internal sense of collective obligation to the customers, to the firm, and extending to the society as a whole. In the end, such collective checks, which were forms of "moral/religious" capital, failed on a widespread basis in the financial markets

---

[55] Geithner, Stress Test, p. 106

[56] Martin Wolf, "Reforming Western Capitalism," in Janet Byrne, *The Occupy Handbook* (Boston: Back Bay Books, 2012), p. 344.

[57] Ibid., p. 341.

from the 1980s and especially after 2000. In the worst cases, whole public corporations became free-for-alls of individual self-aggrandizement—corporate cultures in which it had become acceptable for individual top managers to seek their own money, status, and power without significant external restraint. If challenged, they might, moreover, justify such behaviour as a particular manifestation of the free-market creed of self-interest, for some allegedly the foundational ethic of the whole market economic system. As a high level federal financial regulator at the time, Sheila Bair recalls attending a 2007 Wall Street conference and her surprise on being told that the members of the finance industry "have a right to make fat profits by any means."[58]

Wall Street Without Religion

In such an environment, the proximate causes of the financial crisis are now clear enough. Wall Street and other parts of the financial markets had created a set of working relationships that, lacking broader cultural restraints, were set to fail at various steps of the process. Those who originated mortgages to homes often wrote them indiscriminately, failing to ensure that the mortgagee could pay and was otherwise well served (making large individual commissions for the mortgage originators in the process). Wolf, among many others, strongly condemns such "predatory practices seen so egregiously in subprime [mortgage] lending in the United States."[59] Often with Fannie Mae and Freddie Mac as an intermediary, Wall Street firms (again very profitably) then assembled and bundled the mortgages, creating new high interest securities (collateralized debt obligations, or CDOs) that were sold to investors who did not have the means to do the necessary investigations of the actual risks involved.

The main burden of risk assessment was passed to the credit rating agencies who themselves had come to lack the motivation and the analytical skills to provide accurate risk assessments. But this would not be widely recognized until after the financial crisis. Hoping to take advantage of leverage and boost profits still further, investment banks and traditional commercial banks alike kept large holdings of the new high interest mortgage backed securities on their own books, thus exposing themselves to large risks (of events they hoped were unlikely to occur, certainly within a short time horizon).

---

[58] Bair, *Bull by the Horns*, p. 356.
[59] Ibid., p. 342.

The potential overseers of this Wall Street system among the federal regulators; among the members of the economics profession (some in business schools); and finally in the media; never made the necessary effort to understand fully its evolving complex workings and dangers. Among the few who did understand, most of them did not shout it out to the world (likely in itself to be a low-payoff strategy in the short run), remaining passive bystanders. Such potential overseers all had their own individual incentives that they followed, and their own professional cultures were not strong enough to create collective obligations to the wider society to transcend the narrower incentives.

What is common to all of the above participants in financial markets? In an ideal world, they would have all felt a sense of responsibility for their actions to the successful workings of financial markets, to the nation, and even to the whole world. They would have felt a sense of internal personal obligation to uphold professional standards and to serve the needs of their business customers. They would have been motivated to give close scrutiny to the full contemporary workings of the whole financial system. Significant numbers of them would have warned the wider world of the developing large dangers of financial market failure that might be triggered by unforeseen events. One would hope that they would have demanded corrective actions, occurring at the mortgage origination level, within their own Wall Street firms, in the rating agencies, in the regulatory arena, and among those who had professional responsibilities for studying financial markets.

There were some people who did, in fact, issue such warnings. But they were few in number and small in influence. Most of the individual members of the financial system remained focused on their own actions and the individual rewards (money, prestige, power, etc.) that might accrue to them personally. Paul Volker writes, however, that in the actual complex circumstances of Wall Street, there is a need for a healthy balance "between the need to compete, to prosper, to grow, and the need to treat clients fairly, to maintain high fiduciary standards, and to respect the broad public interest reflected in regulation and supervision."[60]

In his memoirs, Henry Kaufman—for many years the director of research for Salomon Brothers and a prominent Wall Street figure in the 1970s and 1980s—explains that market discipline will not work in circumstances such as found on Wall Street where American businesses are

---

[60] Paul Volker, Foreword to Henry Kaufman, *On Money and Markets: A Wall Street Memoir* (New York: McGraw-Hill, 2000), p. vi.

too important and "too big to fail." As he observes, the largest Wall Street corporations are "less like ordinary business enterprises and more like public utilities." In some other nations, such organizations have simply been nationalized outright, for better or for worse. In the United States, it would almost certainly be for worse, given its 200-year-old constitution and the frequently dysfunctional character of its national political system (imagine hiring staff for such nationally critical organizations as are found on Wall Street under standard American civil service rules and regulations and tight salary limitations).

But a corollary is that nominally "private" Wall Street firms—which are actually distinctively American *de facto* forms of "public utilities"—must operate according to internal norms transcending the mere maximization of corporate profits. As Kaufman writes, given their "awesome role and responsibilities in the larger society," and the difficulty of imposing outside public control over their internal activities, and if they are to continue to be regarded as socially legitimate by the wider American public, the "leading financial institutions must adhere to an unusually high code of business conduct. They must take into account not only their narrow private interests, but also their considerable public responsibilities."[61] From the 1970s onwards, however, Wall Street leadership increasingly failed to recognize or respect such wider social norms. Over the same period, not coincidentally, the historic central role of economic religion within the shared "civil religion" of the United States was coming under growing challenge.

In 2009, the CEO of Goldman Sachs, Lloyd Blankfein, famously told a reporter that he and other bankers at his firm were "doing God's work."[62] Although Blankfein was widely derided for saying this, there was an element of truth in it—in the objective he stated at least, if not its actual realization in many real world instances. For many people in the twentieth century, the pursuit of economic progress had become the path to heaven on earth. A well functioning financial system is essential to the maximally efficient use of the resources of society, and thus to the pursuit of economic progress. Many people on Wall Street had once been true believers, and were willing to commit themselves to this purpose. As they saw it, they could do well and do good at the same time. But religious belief in the

---

[61] Kaufman, *On Money and Markets*, p. 228.

[62] Blankfein quoted in Andrew Ross Sorkin, *Too Big to Fail: The Inside Story of how Wall Street and Washington Fought to Save the Financial System—and Themselves* (New York: Penguin Books, 2011), p. 550.

redemptive powers of progress gradually faded on Wall Street, as it did throughout other areas of American life, as new generations slowly assumed the reins of power from the 1970s onwards.

In short, there was not enough religious capital to hold the financial system together. The once prominent place of traditional Protestant religion in government and business affairs had been fading since the late nineteenth century. Forms of secular religion—especially the true belief in economic progress as the salvation of the world—substituted another form of shared religious faith, but they also began to fade on the American scene in the last part of the twentieth century. Without mutual trust, honesty, and a sense of a collective wider purpose, spiralling downward events would lead to the financial crisis from 2007 to 2009.

A Case Illustration: Moody's

There were many parties who contributed to the events leading up to the financial crisis. But three firms, as noted earlier, bore a particularly large burden of responsibility for the Great Recession and all that has followed. They are Moody's, Standard and Poor's, and Fitch Ratings, the three main credit rating agencies. They were well positioned and had the ability all by themselves to bring a halt to the financial market dysfunctions that reached a boiling point in 2007 and 2008. The securities marketed by Wall Street firms, including the collateralized debt obligations of the 2000s, normally have to be rated by at least one (and often two) of the rating agencies for the degree of payment risk that they pose. As a result of Securities and Exchange Commission policy dating to 1975, it was legally necessary to have a rating to sell many securities, so the rating agencies, despite their nominally private status, actually had a quasi-governmental role. Seldom have the actions of so few in American "business" had such large negative consequences for the nation as a whole.

At the height of the Wall Street follies, the rating agencies gave high ratings (the highest AAA ratings supposedly assuring that there would be very low or even close to a non-existent risk) to many mortgage backed securities. These ratings proved to be fundamentally flawed, as unfortunate investors in the securities (all around the world) would subsequently learn. If their ratings had been accurate, many securities that ultimately defaulted would either have been unmarketable or would have required much higher interest rates. With accurate ratings of risk, it seems likely that the financial market history of 2007 and 2008 would have turned out to be much different from the actual result.

One of the better books chronicling the events of the financial crisis is by Bethany McLean (who had personal experience working on Wall Street and was a business writer for 13 years for *Fortune* magazine) and Joe Nocera (a business writer and top editor at the *New York Times*). In *All the Devils are Here: The Hidden History of the Financial Crisis*, they have a chapter on how Moody's was transformed from a responsible business to a good case illustration of all that went wrong on Wall Street in the next decade.[63] A key event, as suggested above for the investment banking sector, was that Moody's became a public corporation for the first time in 2000, significantly altering the incentive structures for top management.

But at the same time the incentive problem was exaggerated by another large change in the culture of the firm, much for the worse. (The incentive factors interacted with the cultural factors so that they were not, strictly speaking, separable). As McClean and Nocera explain, the historic culture of Moody's involved taking the firm's critical role in the credit markets seriously as a matter of the fulfilment of a strong professional duty as well as a firm obligation to perform a service critical for the whole nation. But this did not survive the 1990s.

In the 1970s, Moody's and other rating agencies first began charging the issuers of securities for doing the ratings, thus tying their own business fate to the satisfying of their new paymasters. It was an obvious conflict of interest, but concern to take strong action to address such matters potentially of importance to the whole nation was already waning among the top business and political leadership of the United States, and nothing was done to correct the situation. For a time, however, the Moody's implicit religion of social service and culture acted as a sufficient corrective of its own. As McClean and Nocera write:

> In retrospect, the surprise is not that the rating agencies would eventually be corrupted by their business model, but that it took so long to happen. For many years, whatever [the many] mistakes they made were the result of misguided analysis, not out-and-out cravenness. This was especially true of Moody's, which had a reputation among bond issuers as a "hard ass."…The Moody's culture, introverted and nerdy, was more akin to academia than Wall Street. Analysts would answer their phones after many rings, if at all. Moody's analysts were standoffish toward the issuers who paid their salaries—a little like journalists during the heyday of newspapers, when they could thumb their nose at advertisers. Credit analysts at Moody's didn't worry about the revenue that might be lost if they refused

[63] Bethany McClean and Joe Nocera, *All the Devils are Here: The Hidden History of the Financial Crisis* (New York: Penguin, 2010).

> to give an issuer [of a security] the rating it sought. That was someone else's problem. In the early 1990s, Moody's actually refused to rate a then popular structured product, on the grounds that a [favourable] rating might lead investors to expect more than they were likely to get.[64]

This last story was recounted in a 1994 article in *Treasury and Risk Management* magazine entitled, "Why Everyone Hates Moody's." After polling ninety-nine corporate treasurers, the magazine concluded that "ingrained in Moody's corporate culture is a conviction that too close a relationship with [Wall Street security] issuers is damaging to the rating process" and thus unacceptable for a person working for Moody's.[65] The reliability of the rating process was critical to the efficient allocation of capital in the American economy and thus to the cause of American economic progress, giving the Moody's priesthood a true religious purpose.

McLean and Nocera relate that a key Moody's employee, Mark Adelson, was a "careful, cautious, somewhat skeptical analyst" in the 1990s. Adelson recognized many of the developing problems that would lead eventually to the financial crisis of 2007 and 2009. As they put it, "he was always less willing to accept uncritically many of the arguments made for [the] mortgage backed securities" that would soon fail on a large scale. Rather, he argued within Moody's that "the fact that an asset class like housing had performed well in the past said nothing about how the same asset class was going to perform in the future"—as was a necessary assumption to justify the virtually risk free ratings of many supposedly "higher quality" mortgage backed securities.[66]

Adelson was a throwback to the traditional Moody's culture that regarded itself as committed to "the truth" of disclosing actual securities risks. As it says in the Bible, "the truth shall make you free"—free of sin and bondage.[67] By 2000, however, he was out of step. As McClean and Nocera report, "in 2001, he quit," unwilling to compromise his personal integrity to get along with the new management team that was taking over at Moody's—a team with ethical attitudes much different from the historic Moody's culture, if typical of a cut-throat culture of individual success that was rapidly spreading across much of Wall Street at the time.[68]

[64] Ibid., p.114.
[65] Ibid.
[66] Ibid., pp. 115-116.
[67] John 8:32.
[68] McClean and Nocera, *All the Devils are Here*, p. 116.

A critical moment occurred in 2001 when the public corporation Enron went bankrupt, virtually wiping out its stockholders. Moody's and the other credit rating agencies had failed abysmally, maintaining the high rating of Enron's debt until four days before it collapsed. This was a strong indication that Moody's lacked the technical capability to analyze at least the Enron forms of corporate risks. But it was also a cultural failure on Wall Street. McClean and Nocera report that at a Congressional hearing "the S&P [Standard and Poor's] analyst who had covered Enron confessed that he had not even read some of the company's financial filings." But the ultimate result was that "not a single analyst at either Moody's or S&P lost his job as a result of missing the Enron fraud.... Enron taught them how small the consequences [in the rating agencies] of a bad reputation [now] were."[69] The importance of being objectively correct for its own sake was seemingly an old fashioned idea that had been slowly going out of favour at least since the 1970s. Admittedly, now lacking some stronger form of religious capital on Wall Street to maintain collective standards, why should anyone really care?

More than a few people may have recognized that things were spinning out of control at the rating agencies and Wall Street more broadly. But regarded from an individual point of view, what was the incentive to try to do anything about it? After 2000, quite a few new arrivals on Wall Street—many still in their 20s with their sense of ethics largely formed by the university world and popular culture of the late twentieth century—would soon be making enough to retire for life with a mere few years of work experience. Lacking some moral compass, what was the point of being concerned about individual "reputation" in such circumstances? The financial collapse of 2007 and 2008 caused losses of hundreds of billions of dollars for investors in overrated (by companies such as Moody's) mortgage backed securities, but the Wall Street firms that had touted the securities had already sold most of them to investors and were out of the picture by then (unless they had foolishly retained the securities themselves, which some did in surprising numbers).

It was not simply a matter of "greed" among the Wall Street firms, although that may have been a significant contributing factor. It was also that "no one took responsibility" for the wider economic results, as long as they did reasonably well themselves. Every society needs at least a few saints who are willing to make personal sacrifices. Rather than such people who might try to call a halt publicly to the increasingly flawed proceedings

[69] Ibid., pp. 119, 120.

in the mortgage origination and securities markets, McLean and Nocera write of the actual analysts found at Moody's:

> The Moody's analysts in structured finance (such as mortgage backed securities) were working twelve to fifteen hours a day. They made a fraction of the pay of even a junior investment banker on Wall Street. There were far more deals in the pipeline than they could possibly handle. They were overwhelmed. "We were growing so fast, we couldn't keep staff, and we were grossly under-resourced," recalls a former Moody's structured finance executive. Moody's top brass, he says, thought the mania would end, and as a result they wouldn't add staff. At both Moody's and S&P, former employees say there was a move away from hiring people with backgrounds in credit and toward hiring recent business school graduates or foreigners with green cards to keep costs down.[70]

Economists are sceptical of economic interpretations that depend on the behaviour of particular individuals. Explanations should be more systemic and grounded in wider economic circumstances. In the case of Moody's, however, the leading agent of change was a particular person—and events at Moody's (with the other two ratings firms) would have national and even international reverberations. Much of the damage at Moody's was done by a new hire to the firm in 1991 with a law degree, Brian Clarkson. By 2000, Clarkson had ascended to top management levels, including direct responsibilities for the ratings being developed by the asset-backed finance division. McClean and Nocera report that:

> Clarkson went off like a bomb inside Moody's. He developed a reputation for being nasty to those who wouldn't fight back and for never forgetting a slight. "At my level, any watercooler discussion of his management style included the words 'fear and intimidation'".... [He rose at Moody's partly because] the company's top executives "recognized in Brian the character of someone who could do uncomfortable things with ease, and they exploited his character to advance their [new] agenda." That agenda was using structured finance to boost revenues, market share, and—above all—Moody's stock price [and thus management compensation under the new public corporate status adopted in 2000].[71]

Moody's issued top AAA ratings (essentially risk free supposedly) for many mortgage backed securities, but under the companies ratings procedures, "nowhere in the process was anyone required to conduct real-world due diligence about the underlying mortgages," and so account for the

---

[70] Ibid., p. 123.
[71] Ibid., p. 115.

actual risks that some might default. Another problem was that the ratings were developed based on "a series of assumptions," including that any declines in housing prices "would not be severe" and that declines in one housing market would occur independently of declines in other housing markets in other regions (thus allowing the pooling of mortgages from many regions to reduce overall risks). The three ratings agencies competed to issue favourable ratings, and the investment banking community used its leverage to increase the pressure. McClean and Nocera report of one Moody's analyst who sought to give more accurate ratings: "Goldman Sachs once requested that he not be assigned to its deals."[72]

In retrospect, some have characterized much of what went on as a version of a "Ponzi scheme." Law professor David Westbrook comments that "investment bubbles have the structure of Ponzi schemes"—a point made originally by the economist Hyman Minsky.[73] While he does not use this label, Richard Posner writes of the financial crisis that it further revealed "the tendency of corporate management to cling to a bubble and hope for the best."[74] Current debt and payment obligations will be met by incurring new obligations. Indeed, as long as confidence holds up, this method can work well. As asset backed securities became more popular, and the credit ratings agencies assured minimal risk, their total sales on Wall Street soared from $69 billion in 2000 to around $500 billion in 2006. So there was always plenty of new money coming in to pay off old obligations. McClean and Nocera observe that "the rating agencies were at the very heart of the madness. The entire edifice would have collapsed without their participation."[75] Overseeing all this at Moody's, as noted above, was Brian Clarkson. McClean and Nocera conclude their chapter about Moody's by commenting acidly that "in August 2007, Brian Clarkson was named president of Moody's. His compensation that year was $3.2 million"[76] Whatever his religion was, it had never taught him the lesson of the Golden Rule.

---

[72] Ibid., pp. 118, 116.

[73] David A. Westbrook, *Out of Crisis: Rethinking Our Financial Markets* (Boulder, CO: Paradigm Publishers, 2010), p. 26.

[74] Posner, *A Failure of Capitalism*, p. 93.

[75] McLean and Nocera, *All the Devils are Here*, p. 123.

[76] Ibid., p. 124.

Gobbledygook, Silos, and Social Silences

Besides McClean and Nocera, some other of the most informative accounts of the developments leading up to and causing the financial crisis have also been by financial journalists (some of whom could draw upon previous work experience on Wall Street). One of the most helpful is by Gillian Tett, author of *Fool's Gold: The Inside Story of J. P. Morgan and How Wall Street Greed Corrupted Its Bold Dream and Created a Financial Catastrophe.*[77] She wrote there of how in 2008, "what was driving the price of super-senior risk was not so much 'hard' economic data, which could be plugged into models, but investor fear, which economists had long ignored in their modelling. In this new world, the 'quants' [quantitative analysts on Wall Street who tended to be true believing rationalists] were at sea. It was a terrifying, disorienting landscape, and the banking community was about to suffer a gut-wrenching case of vertigo." Tett covered these events, and then wrote authoritatively about them, as a top financial reporter for the London-based *Financial Times* (in 2009 she won an award as British Business Journalist of the Year for her coverage of the financial crisis in the *Financial Times*).

Three years after *Fool's Gold* appeared, Tett in 2012 summarized her observations on the causes of the financial crisis.[78] At the core, she found three basic "problems in modern finance: the cultural dangers of gobbledygook, silos, and social sciences." As she writes, there is little evidence of "any coordinated, *deliberate* plot by [Wall Street] bankers to conceal their activities or downplay the risks before 2007. Instead, many of the [most damaging] activities were hidden in plain sight." It was admittedly true that many Wall Streeters "preferred to keep their deals away from the limelight—and the noses of regulators—because that allowed them to boost their [profit] margins (and stop rivals from stealing their ideas)." But the necessary information to understand the situation was actually available, in admittedly obscure places such as "rating agency reports, bank filings and other data." Indeed, it would have been "possible for outsiders to spot that the system was spinning out of control and had become prone to excess." Doing this, however, would not be easy; it would require a person

[77] Gillian Tett, *Fool's Gold: The Inside Story of J. P. Morgan and How Wall Street Greed Corrupted its Bold Dream and Created a Financial Disaster* (New York: Simon and Schuster, 2009).

[78] Gillian Tett, "Hidden in Plain Sight: The Problem of Silos and Silences in Finance," in Janet Byrne, ed., *The Occupy Handbook* (Boston: Back Bay Books, 2012).

to "confront the gobbledygook" that was being produced on such a large scale, perhaps intentionally to hide things while still remaining legal, or to limit access to valuable information to select professional insiders, but also because of the very nature of large scale administrative and regulatory processes in America's legalistic culture.[79]

For Tett, an urgent question today is why there were no whistle-blowers on Wall Street; why did "so few people actually ask hard questions at all," including almost all the media? Owing to the lack of deeper scrutiny, the result was that "Western Society allow[ed] finance to spin out of control" —with disastrous worldwide consequences. As a partial answer to this question, Tett finds that the large organizations involved with financial matters on Wall Street had strong tendencies towards the compartmentalization of knowledge—to break into distinct "silos" that did not communicate with one another. As she writes, "inside the giant bureaucracies of the modern banks, it seemed that different departments existing almost like warring tribes: although the separate desks, or divisions, of banks were theoretically supposed to collaborate, in practice they competed furiously for scarce resources, knowing that whatever desk earned the greatest profits would wield the most power."[80] Thus, in Tett's view, profits were not necessarily the end in themselves for bank employees, but were often a means toward a higher end of "power"—and one might add, the related end of status and prestige. Tett does not take seriously the possibility that bank employees might have been religiously motivated by a commitment to include the greater public good as a further important goal—a reflection in itself of the spreading religious cynicism of the times.

Even within the same business firm, she writes, "desks tended to hug information. The right hand of the bank rarely knew what the left was doing in any detail—nor was the risk management department necessarily better informed." The very highest executives with cross-cutting responsibilities for the entire business simply could not keep track of and coordinate all this; in many cases they did not even understand, or even know about, what their own individual divisions were doing. The financial regulatory apparatus of the government was similarly fragmented and with similar results in terms of anyone being able to understand and evaluate the full picture. As Tett thus comments, federal regulation of Wall Street was "marked by tribal rivalries that mirrored (and intensified) those pri-

[79] Ibid., pp. 45, 46.
[80] Ibid., pp. 46, 46-47.

vate sector splits."[81] It seems that there was virtually no one to assume responsibility for looking over the actual cumulative workings of the U.S. financial system. Tett writes that "there were some journalists and some economists who could vaguely sense how the overall patterns were playing out. But trying to get a clear vision of how finance was developing as an entire system was hard. A sense of tunnel vision permeated the system—hampering bankers as much as anyone else."[82]

A key role of religion is to look at the larger picture; even ordinary church members attend Sunday services as their one moment to think about God and the world. Theology is in this classical sense the "queen of the sciences," in seeking an understanding of "the meaning of everything." The financial sector in the 2000s, however, was lacking in religious capital and in the motivating influence of belief to ask the biggest questions. Tett herself does not really try to answer the obvious question: why did no one perceive the dangers of gobbledygook and silos and then make a deep commitment to do something about them? If she had undertaken such an inquiry, it might have taken her into issues of the overall fading of religious capital on Wall Street and the seeming weakening sense of collective obligations—to the firm, to the finance industry, to the nation—among those who worked there.

Tett was, however, originally trained professionally as an anthropologist, and she does not ignore such wider issues of culture altogether. As the second of her basic factors in bringing about the financial crisis, she sees a particular problem in what she calls "social silences," drawing on the work of the French sociologist and anthropologist Pierre Bourdieu. This is a matter of addressing the question of priority setting within an intellectual elite and "what is not discussed" in a given society. Tett observes that in most societies "there is simply a tacit, half conscious recognition that it is better to simply avoid discussing an issue, or that there are cultural disincentives to peering into it—because it is considered either taboo or 'boring.'"[83] The latter certainly characterized "back in 2005 and 2006 the topics of credit derivatives and collateralized debt obligations [which] were considered to be incredibly boring, if not downright arcane."[84]

[81] Ibid., p. 47.
[82] Ibid., pp. 47-48.
[83] Ibid., p. 48.
[84] Ibid. pp 48, 49.

When Tett and a few other journalists did occasionally write about such matters before 2007, she thus found that "it was often tough to get these stories on the front page," no matter how fundamentally important they might actually be.[85] This partly reflected the existing lack of public interest, which meant that few people would actually read the stories. And adding another cultural factor, many top newspaper editors had become increasingly attuned to the commercial prospects of their publications and less committed to a sense of public obligation to inform the whole society about complicated policy issues. Thus, lacking journalistic intermediaries, and "faced with financial gobbledygook," Tett writes, "the general populace found it easier to leave the whole field of finance in the hands of technical experts, particularly since those technical experts were insisting before 2007, that modern finance [as practiced on Wall Street] was a wonderfully beneficial thing"—a refrain much repeated up to 2007 not only by the technical experts, but also by high level (and technically knowledgeable) Washington leaders such as Alan Greenspan, Robert Rubin, and Larry Summers (not political conservatives as some people might have suspected but all appointed—or in Greenspan's case reappointed—by the Clinton administration).[86]

Another lesson that many people learned from the financial crisis was that they had placed too much trust in "the experts" and their ability or willingness to meet their professed public obligations.[87] To some extent the professional failings were due to simple errors of professional judgment and method, but this was not the only factor. Levels of religious capital were not only fading in the American financial sector, but also among the American professional elites who were supposed to be responsible for the nation's future.

Tett's critique of the importance of areas of "social silence" applied here as well. For many Americans, the manner of formation and the content of ethical standards in business has been an uncomfortable subject—maybe better not explicitly discussed—because they find it difficult to reconcile the actual world of business practice that they experience personally with the sometimes conflicting religious and other obligations as they have heard preached by church leaders. If American businesses were to take seriously the religious message of Pope Francis in his 2015 Encyc-

---

[85] Ibid., p. 49.

[86] Ibid.

[87] David Colander, et. al, "The Financial Crisis and the Systemic Failure of the Economics Profession, *Critical Review* (July 2009).

lical *Laudato Si*, for example, it would require a radical overhaul in the culture of American business. Until the later part of the twentieth century, and even then reluctantly, the expert professionals of American social science also observed a deep "social silence" when it came to study of the role of religion in the workings of markets and society. As a result, their analyses would inevitably be missing a critical element and their policy recommendations would thus be correspondingly limited in scope.

As one might summarize all this, across a number of important areas of American life, there was a failure of "leadership." Much of this can simply be attributed to analytical mistakes or to other intellectual misjudgements among a large number of people. Foolishness and recklessness sometimes played a part. But in the end, there seems to have been a shortage of people who were motivated to penetrate the "gobbledygook," who perceived an urgent need on their part to break out of their own comfortable "silos," and who were willing to challenge the "social silences" by which societies frequently avoid discussions of uncomfortable (and in some societies literally dangerous) subjects.

By 2007, a dawning awareness of such matters was being expressed by a few members of the American leadership class. Gerald Corrigan, the former president of the New York Federal Reserve Bank, wrote to Treasury Secretary Henry Paulson that the banking industry "needs a renewed commitment to collective discipline in the spirit of elevated financial statesmanship that recognizes that there are circumstances in which individual institutions must be prepared to put aside specific interests in the name of the common interest."[88] But it was hard to know how to revive a spirit of collective sacrifice in a banking community where, as Tett writes, "Corrigan lamented that there appeared to be few such bankers left."[89]

A Failure of Economic "Science"

If a crisis of faith in economic religion was a key factor in forming the culture of the financial sector leading up to the crisis of 2007 to 2009, what are the prospects for reviving the old economic religion as a way of serving the critical need for a form of religious capital on Wall Street? It must be said that the prospects do not appear good. Indeed, they have probably worsened. If anything, the past confidence in the core idea of economic religion—that material developments such as economists study

[88] Corrigan quoted in Tett, *Fool's Gold*, p. 229.
[89] Tett, *Fool's Gold*, p. 229.

are the shaping factors in history—has been further eroded by events since the financial crisis in the Middle East, Russia and elsewhere.

The financial crisis itself, moreover, added to the doubts of those who had already questioned the scientific credibility of the economics profession. For the economics profession, the financial crisis of 2007 and the "Great Recession" that followed—from which the United States has still not entirely escaped as of 2015—have been humbling experiences. Very few members of the profession recognized in advance the potential hazards that existed in the linkages between mortgage lending in the U.S. housing market, financial practices on Wall Street, and overall American macroeconomic outcomes.

After the Great Recession began in late 2008, some leading economists offered predictions of rapid economic improvement that proved excessively optimistic. As the Great Recession continued longer than expected, leaders of the economics profession offered widely conflicting economic solutions, leaving the public bewildered. Robert Samuelson, a prominent economic columnist for the *Washington Post*, wrote of "an intellectual breakdown. There is a loss of faith in economic ideas—and government policies based on them—driven by most economists' failure to anticipate the financial crisis and many subsequent events."[90] Indeed, the lack of confidence in economists' ability to manage the economy might have become a causal factor itself, diminishing overall public confidence in the stability of the economic future, and thus potentially altering current consumption and investment decisions.

The history of the financial crisis was particularly embarrassing because in the period from 1990 to 2008, a number of prominent economists advertised a newfound professional ability to guide the American economy on a stable path. In his presidential address to the American Economic Association in 2003, the University of Chicago macroeconomist Robert Lucas (winner of the Nobel prize in economics in 1995) declared that "macroeconomics…has succeeded. Its central problem of depression prevention has been solved, for all practical purposes, and has in fact been solved for many decades." In a similar vein in 2004, Ben Bernanke, then a member of the Board of Governors of the Federal Reserve, observed in a speech to the Eastern Economic Association that "one of the most striking features of the economic landscape over the past twenty years or so has

[90] Robert Samuelson, "Behind the Economic Pessimism," *The Washington Post*, July 29, 2012.

been a substantial decline in macroeconomic volatility," a development labelled by Bernanke and other economists as "The Great Moderation."[91]

In seeking to understand the seemingly greater macroeconomic stability of the past 20 years, Bernanke attributed it in part to "structural change," among which he included as important helpful developments "the increased depth and sophistication of financial markets, deregulation in many industries, ...and increased openness to trade and international capital flows." A second key factor for Bernanke was "improved performance of macroeconomic policies" on the part of the American government. As Bernanke explained, "few disagree that monetary policy has played a large part in stabilizing inflation, and so the fact that output volatility has declined in parallel with inflation volatility, both in the United States and abroad, suggests that monetary policy may have helped moderate the variability of [national economic] output as well."

Bernanke acknowledged a third important possibility, "good luck." By this he mainly meant, however, that the period of macroeconomic stability since the 1980s had been free of wars and other large destabilizing events such as the OPEC oil price shocks of the 1970s. There was no suggestion that luck in another sense might have been an important factor. Perhaps, government economists might simply have promoted policies that fortuitously ended up working in the particular economic circumstances that happened to arise in the 1980s and 1990s. Bernanke had nothing to say in his summary 2004 macroeconomic assessment about any large growing risks posed by a growing bubble in the housing sector. He did not raise the possibility that Federal Reserve policies that stimulated the housing market from 2001 to 2004 might have bought some short term macroeconomic stability, but at the expense of greater long term instability—a view that is now accepted among some leading professional economists. The American economy, as it now seems, was virtually flying blind in terms of professional understanding of the actual deeper forces at work, fortunately with good results for more than 20 years until disaster struck in 2007 and 2008.

In the next several years following Bernanke's speech, economic analyses of the causes of the "Great Moderation" proliferated. In one particularly ill-timed article, just as Wall Street was collapsing and the economy was about to turn sharply downward, Steven Davis and James Kahn sought in a Fall 2008 issue of the *Journal of Economic Perspectives* (a

[91] Remarks by Governor Ben S. Bernanke, at the meetings of the Eastern Economic Association, Washington, DC., February 24, 2004.

leading economics journal published by the American Economic Association) to explain the reasons for the significantly greater macroeconomic stability of the times. Davis and Kahn noted, as had other economist commentators on the great moderation, "the abrupt drop in volatility of U.S. real GDP growth in the early 1980s," continuing to the present (and presumably into the indefinite future, as their article seemed to suggest).[92] One of the several significant explanatory factors described by Davis and Kahn ironically was the stabilizing benefits due to the rapid spread of "financial innovation" over the same two-decade period as the Great Moderation had occurred. (To be fair to the authors, this article was probably in final stages of publication by the spring of 2008, reflecting the slow processes of academic publishing).

Although some economists had advocated for the good luck explanation, Davis and Kahn wrote that this would amount to a confession of economic failure: it would simply indicate "the need for better models to explain the volatility reductions or for convincing evidence that measurable and plausibly exogenous, economic disturbances…can explain [past] observed declines in the volatility of economic activity."[93] Their implicit assumption, widespread in the economics profession, was that scientific investigations can develop complete explanations of economic events in the real world, resembling explanations provided in the physical sciences. Many ordinary people might exhibit such attitudes, but no physicist would ever think to professionally attribute a set of events in the natural world to "luck"—and the ultimate goal of many professional economists remains even to this day a "a physics of society."

In reviewing the writings and actions of the members of the economics profession in the period leading up to the financial crisis, the law and economics scholar (and Appeals Court judge) Richard Posner writes that they were "asleep at the switch." Many "leading macroeconomists, and prominent finance theorists as well, were simply silent as the storm gathered and broke." It was probably mainly that their economic models simply offered no adequate framework for understanding the events that they were observing. Moreover, few economists had studied the precise institutional workings of the financial markets in any great detail; the market practices and culture there were mostly a mystery to them. Posner suggests that, at

---

[92] Steven J. Davis and James A. Kahn, "Interpreting the Great Moderation: Changes in the Economic Volatility of Economic Activity at the Macro and Micro Levels," *Journal of Economic Perspectives* 22: 4 (Fall 2008), p. 157.
[93] Ibid., pp. 155, 156-157.

least in the case of the finance professors, there might have been an element of ethical failure as well. They faced a "conflict of interest" in that "if they criticize the industry and suggest tighter regulations, they may become black sheep and lose lucrative consultantships." As for those economists working within the financial industry themselves, "one does not expect economists employed by real estate companies or by banks to be talking about housing and credit bubbles."[94]

A 2012 Economic Apology

Four years after the financial crisis broke, another leading economics journal, *The Journal of Economic Literature* (also published by the American Economic Association) published a survey article by MIT Sloan School economist Andrew Lo covering 21 leading books since 2008, about half by professional economists and the other half by economic journalists, all of them developing interpretations of the events and causes of the financial crisis.[95] The economics profession, as the article acknowledged, was now experiencing a crisis of confidence. Former Federal Reserve Chairman Alan Greenspan—holder of a PhD in economics from New York University—had been among the first to apologize in October 2008, confessing at a Congressional hearing that "those of us who had looked to the self-interest of leading institutions to protect shareholders' equity, myself included, are in a state of shocked disbelief."[96]

A key factor in the financial crisis was the collapse of the housing bubble and, as Lo wrote, it had to be admitted that "despite their eight-hundred year history, bubbles are still rather mysterious economic phenomena" for the members of the economics profession. Indeed, reflecting the traditional reluctance of economists to confront the existence of such "non-rational" economic phenomena, not only have economists been slow to study bubbles, but also surprisingly many have even expressed doubts that they really exist at all in contemporary economic circumstances (much of economic analysis has traditionally assumed "perfect information," thus implicitly ruling out bubbles). Economists have long portrayed the workings of competitive markets as efficient generators and consumers of in-

---

[94] Richard A. Posner, *A Failure of Capitalism* (Cambridge, MA; Harvard University Press, 2009), pp. 255, 259.

[95] Andrew W. Lo, "Reading about the Financial Crisis: A Twenty-One-Book Review," *Journal of Economic Literature* 50:1 (March 2012): 151-178.

[96] Quoted in Roger Lowenstein, *The End of Wall Street* (New York: Penguin Books, 2010), p. 285.

formation, but in the events leading up to the financial crisis, as Lo commented, it was undeniable that "the information-gathering function of the price mechanism was clearly awry" across the United States housing and financial markets, a fundamental challenge, as Greenspan recognized, to widely prevailing economic concepts.[97]

According to standard economic theory, countervailing forces of profit maximizing should normally work to correct market misperceptions of other parties—but, as one analyst put it, the financial crisis had shown how "markets can remain irrational a lot longer than you and I can remain solvent," exposing those who do have "rational" understandings to bankruptcy while waiting for the appropriate long run market corrections to actually occur. Contrary to the portrayals in economic models, the search for profits on Wall Street was not always a matter of careful calculation and deliberation; rather, some leading firms such as Bear Stearns had exhibited a "dysfunctional management and aggressive corporate culture—even by the standards of Wall Street."[98] Yet, the vast body of professional economic writings about the workings of markets in the United States had seldom said much about the importance of corporate culture, or even that American business cultural factors could significantly influence the workings of the wider American economic system.

As described in Lo's 2012 review article, the thinking and actions of American government officials were no less flawed than those found on Wall Street in leading up to the financial crisis. A host of "financial innovation[s] and a wave of financial deregulation, made possible in the new political climate, reinforced each other, leading to increased profits and a rapid expansion of the financial sector" from the 1980s onward. Sheila Bair, former chairman of the Federal Deposit Insurance Commission, finds that in the years before the financial crisis "it was because of industry pressure that capital standards were lowered, mortgage-lending restraints were blocked, and regulators were barred from regulating the derivatives market."[99]

Except for those who came from the financial community themselves, few federal officials, even in regulatory agencies such as the Securities and Exchange Commission, had a firm grasp of the actual detailed workings of financial markets in the 2000s. With such vast amounts of money at stake

---

[97] Lo, "Reading about the Financial Crisis," p. 170.

[98] Ibid., p. 168.

[99] Sheila Bair, *Bull by the Horns: Fighting to Save Main Street from Wall Street and Wall Street from Itself* (New York: Free Press, 2012), p. 356.

and ample funds available, Lo writes, "by the 1990s, the American financial structure was able to exert further influence on the political process in a number of ways: lobbying, campaign contributions, and providing official Washington with a cadre of finance professionals who had internalized much of the new, 'exciting' ethos of Wall Street."[100]

Business and government thus cooperated closely in overseeing the housing and financial market developments that finally produced the financial crisis and the Great Recession. Government regulation (or often the lack of such) exerted a powerful influence on business behaviour, and business involvement in government decision-making exerted a powerful influence on the actions of government regulators. Lo laments the "renewed regulatory capture by America's new masters of the universe that set the stage for the boom and bust cycles of the late 1990s and onward."[101]

Again, Lo sees cultural factors as critical in all this. Indeed, the decline in ethical standards on Wall Street was perhaps worse than elsewhere, exhibiting a "separation of business norms in the financial sector from those [prevalent] in the real economy." There was "a systemic problem of consolidation and influence [in financial markets], not merely of a small number of large financial institutions, but of an entire financial subculture" that then extensively interacted with its government financial counterparts.[102] This kind of close interaction between Wall Street and the federal government is to some extent unavoidable and even desirable, given the centrality of financial markets to the basic workings of the national economic system and the rapid pace of financial innovation, and increasing complexity of the financial markets in the 1980s and 1990s (developments which were often poorly understood not only by government regulators but also by some top executives of Wall Street firms who failed to grasp what even their own lower-level technical people were doing).

As Lo sums up his review in 2012 of leading books offering explanations of the financial crisis, "there is still significant disagreement [including among professional economists] as to what the underlying causes of the crisis were, and even less agreement as to what to do about it." Perhaps even "more disconcerting for most economists;... we can't even agree on all the facts. Did [Wall Street] CEOs [irrationally] take too much risk, or were they acting [rationally] as they were incentivized to act?" In offering

---

[100] Lo, "Reading about the Financial Crisis," p. 163.
[101] Ibid., p. 163.
[102] Ibid., p. 163.

public explanations of the financial crisis, Lo laments, a critical "mistake was quoted as fact by a number of well-known legal scholars, economists, and top policy advisors," including Columbia University economist Joseph Stiglitz (winner of the Nobel prize in economics in 2001).[103]

For professional economists who had long sought to analyze the workings of a broadly rational, predictable, and scientifically understandable economic system, it all amounted to "a terribly frustrating state of affairs." Lo was concerned that the damage to the prestige and reputation of the economics profession might be lasting. There was a real danger for professional economists, Lo suggested, in that they might now be "more likely to be thought of as [modern-day] astrologers, making pronouncements and predictions without any basis in fact or empirical evidence."[104]

Few economists today are happy with the record of the economics profession between 2000 and 2015 in understanding the forces at work in the American economy. Yet, while there has been some adjustment, including a new level of attention given to behavioural economics by scholars such as Daniel Kahneman (the 2011 Nobel prize winner in economics), there is little evidence of any significant movement for basic reform within the economics profession as a whole.[105] The same professional habits of thought largely prevail, the same institutional structures of professional economics remain little altered, much the same emphasis on modelling and quantitative analytical methods is maintained in professional publications. *The American Economic Review* is still unreadable without considerable mathematical and statistical background. Professional economic leadership originates in the United States in about 10 top university economics departments (with four of them, Harvard, Princeton, MIT, and Chicago especially influential), partially supplemented by about 10 to 20 lesser ranking departments.

Unlike the free market, where firms can actually go bankrupt, the academic world exhibits a greater institutional conservatism in America (as some wags have said, knowledge advances in the university world one dead professor at a time). The world of professional economics is perhaps better understood in religious terms; professional thinking changes in

[103] Ibid., p. 173, 176. On the role of Stiglitz, see William D. Cohan, "How We Got the Crash Wrong: Leverage Was Not the Problem, Incentives Were, and Still Are," *The Atlantic* (June 2012).

[104] Lo, "Reading about the Financial Crisis," p. 173.

[105] Daniel Kahneman, *Thinking, Fast and Slow* (New York: Farrar, Straus and Giroux, 2011).

American economics at about the same pace as the Roman Catholic Church revises its teachings (a very few extraordinary moments such as Vatican II aside).

Many economists, however, no doubt will make principled arguments for resisting hasty major changes in their profession. They might suggest that the financial crisis was simply a rare and exceptional set of events. Radically new forces emerged in the 1980s and 1990s in the American economic system, particularly the financial sector, and economists were admittedly slow to recognize and explore them. But economists should not overreact to such sudden transformational economic change. Most of the time, it may be reasonable to think, the traditional methods of analysis of professional economics may well prove adequate to the task. Such is the hope at least of economic religion.

Conclusion

The conceptual framework that economists and financial analysts inherited from the twentieth century in the 2000s proved inadequate to the task of foreseeing the collapse of the housing bubble, recognizing the potential for its far ranging macroeconomic consequences, and then dealing with the great recession and other troubling developments in the aftermath of the crisis. In this essay, I have suggested that a longstanding failure to address the ethical foundations of financial markets was an important contributing factor to the inadequacies of professional economic and financial methods of understanding.

A necessary reconceptualization, however, has yet to occur. When Wall Street banks must past stress tests administered by the Federal Reserve, and must seek approval for dividend payments and other key bank actions from the Federal Reserve, these banks are no longer private in any traditional sense that economic theory would have recognized. But what are they? In some respects one might say that since the financial crisis, we have witnessed a *de facto* partial nationalization of the financial sector in the United States—although perhaps it will not be permanent. But for now anyway, what kinds of goals and motives will drive the workings of our new quasi-private, quasi-public financial sector? The goal there is neither to maximize private "profit" nor "the public interest." The field of anthropology—including the study of the workings of culture and religion—may prove as useful as traditional economics in seeking answers.

Much the same might be said of the credit rating agencies which are formally private, but actually perform vital public functions—and since the financial crisis have been under increasing public scrutiny for this reason. In another example, efforts to rethink the future of Fannie Mae and Freddie Mac are complicated by the fact that these half private, half government agencies do not fit any standard concept of textbook economics. The salaries of the chief executive officers of Fannie Mae and Freddie Mac, for example, are greater than any officially federal executive including President Obama (although low by Wall Street standards). How are we to think about their proper compensation? We have little conceptual basis in standard economic thinking on which to proceed. Yet, the students of economics still learn the old textbook versions which are then elaborated with increasing technical complexity and sophistication as undergraduates advance to graduate school and to economic faculty status.

In short, bringing ethics and religion into economics must be part of a wider basic rethinking of the cultural and institutional realities of American "markets." Economic theory itself needs to be reformulated at some fundamental level. For many members of the economics profession, this will be challenging to say the least. Among the potentially radical consequences for the study of economic events in society, some theologians—if they can master sufficient understanding of core economic facts and other realities—might become important contributors to the contemporary economic discussion. As suggested by his most important pronouncements addressing the workings of the economic system, Pope Francis appears to be determined to enter this discussion.[106] Economists, for their part, may have to take up the close study of the workings and content of religion as they affect economic matters, as many of them may be surprised to hear.

---

[106] Encyclical Letter, *Laudato Si*, of the Holy Father Francis, *On Care for Our Common Home* (June 2015); Apostolic Exhortation, *Evangelii Gaudium*, of the Holy Father Francis, To the Bishops, Clergy, Consecrated Persons and the Lay Faithful, On the Proclamation of the Gospel in Today's World (November 2013).

A Partial Bibliography of the Financial Crisis

Bair, Sheila, *Bull By the Horns: Fighting to Save Main Street from Wall Street and Wall Street From Itself* (New York: Free Press, 2012).

Bernanke, Ben S., *The Federal Resource and the Financial Crisis* (Princeton, NJ: Princeton University Press, 2014).

Blanchard, Olivier, David Romer, Michael Spence, and Joseph Stiglitz, eds., *In the Wake of the Crisis: Leading Economists Reassess Economic Policy* (Cambridge, MA: MIT Press, 2012).

Blinder, Alan S., *After the Music Stopped: The Financial Crisis, the Response, and the Work Ahead* (New York: The Penguin Press, 2013).

Byrne, Janet, *The Occupy Handbook* (Boston: Back Bay Books, 2012)

Cassidy, John, *How Markets Fail: The Logic of Economic Calamities* (New York: Farrar, Straus and Giroux, 2009).

Davies, Howard, *The Financial Crisis: Who is to Blame?* (Malden, MA: Polity Press, 2010).

Cohan, William D., *House of Cards: A Tale of Hubris and Wretched Excess on Wall Street* (New York: Random House, 2009)

—. *Money and Power: How Goldman Sachs Came to Rule the World* (New York: Anchor Books, 2011).

The Financial Crisis Inquiry Report: Final Report of the National Commission on the Causes of the Financial and Economic Crisis in the United States (New York: Public Affairs, 2011).

Geithner, Timothy, *Stress Test: Reflections on Financial Crises* (New York: Crown, 2014).

Greenspan, Alan, *The Map and the Territory: Risk, Human Nature, and the Future of Forecasting* (New York: Penguin, 2013).

Johnson, Simon and James Kwak, *13 Bankers: The Wall Street Takeover and the Next Financial Meltdown* (New York: Random House, 2010).

Kaufman, Henry, *On Money and Markets: A Wall Street Memoir* (New York: McGraw-Hill, 2000).

Lewis, Michael, *The Big Short: Inside the Doomsday Machine* (New York: Norton, 2010).

Lo, Andrew W., “Reading about the Financial Crisis: A Twenty-One-Book Review,” *Journal of Economic Literature* 50:1 (March 2012).

Lowenstein, Roger, *The End of Wall Street* (New York: Penguin Books, 2010)

McLean, Bethany and Joe Nocera, *All the Devils are Here: The Hidden History of the Financial Crisis* (New York: Penguin, 2010).

Morgenstern, Gretchen and Joshua Rosner, *Reckless Endangerment: How Outsided Ambition, Greed and Corruption Led to Economic Armageddon* (New York: Times Books, 2011).

Paulson, Henry M. *On the Brink: Inside the Race to Stop the Collapse of the Global Financial System* (New York: Business Plus, 2010).

Posner, Richard, *A Failure of Capitalism* (Cambridge, MA: Harvard University Press, 2009).

Rajan, Raghuram, *Fault Lines: How Hidden Fractures Still Threaten the World Economy* (Princeton, NJ: Princeton University Press, 2010).

Roubini, Nouriel and Stephen Mihm, *Crisis Economics: A Crash Course in the History of Finance* (New York: Penguin Books, 2011).

Schiller, Robert J., *Finance and the Good Society* (Princeton, NJ: Princeton University Press, 2012).

Sorkin, Andrew Ross, *Too Big to Fail: The Inside Story of How Wall Street and Washington Fought to Save the Financial System—and Themselves* (New York: Penguin Books, 2010).

Stiglitz, Joseph, *Freefall: America, Free Markets, and the Sinking of the World Economy* (New York: Norton, 2010).

Tett, Gillian, *Fool's Gold: The Inside Story of J. P. Morgan and How Wall Street Greed Corrupted its Bold Dream and Created a Financial Disaster* (New York: Simon and Schuster, 2009).

Turner, Adair, *Economics after the Crisis: Objectives and Means* (Cambridge, MA: MIT Press, 2013).

Westbrook, David A., *Out of Crisis: Rethinking Our Financial Markets* (Boulder, CO: Paradigm Publishers, 2010).

Wolf, Martin, *The Shifts and the Shocks: What We've Learned—and Have Still to Learn—from the Financial Crisis* (New York: Penguin Press, 2014).

CHAPTER FOUR

GOD AND THE MARKETS: READING THE SIGNS OF THE TIMES

SUZANNE M. WILSON[1]

Catholic Theology and the "Signs of the Times"

One of the ways that we know God is by God's impact in our life and, as so many scripture stories reveal, God's impact is transformative, leading us more fully toward right relationship with God, self, others, and earth. So, when we approach the topic of God and the financial markets, we might ask: what transformation is needed today as a result of the way that financial markets have been functioning in the world? It is both a spiritual and an ethical question, and I will be delving into both fields as I engage the signs of the times in order to discern a Christian response to the financial markets of our day.

The theological concept of "reading the signs of the times" emerges from an understanding that God is at work in human history, that we human beings can come to a sense of God's activity in our lives, and that God desires that we will become attuned to, and cooperate with, divine action for transformation in the world. As such, it is a concept that is rooted in both contemplation and justice.

Scripturally, reading the signs of the times can be grounded in a statement that Jesus makes to the Pharisees and Sadducees in Matthew 16:4, "You know how to read the appearance of the sky, but you cannot read the signs of the times." In this story, the Pharisees and Sadducees are trying to test Jesus. They call for a sign from heaven; it seems that they want a grand performance that they can rip apart. Jesus is reminding them, and us,

---

[1] Suzanne M. Wilson is director of the Office for Systemic Justice for the Canadian Federation of the Sisters of St. Joseph.

that God is always present and acting in the ordinariness of our personal and collective lives. The spiritual task is to learn to recognize God's presence and activity.

In the Roman Catholic tradition, Pope John XXIII incorporated the term into modern Catholic social teaching. He used it to refer to the defining social movements of the age. In *Pacem in Terris*, written in the early sixties, he highlighted the women's movement, the movement for workers' rights and the breaking down of colonialism, as important signs of the times (*Pacem in Terris*, nos. 39-43, 1963). So, what do we have with these movements? On the surface, we have complex and imperfect socio-political movements that were creating both chaos and transformation. If we look a little deeper, we see that these movements contained transforming energies toward greater liberation and equality. Individuals and groups that had been pushed to the margins and silenced were now finding their voice, finding their power. And, if we look deeper still, especially with the gift of hindsight, we can see that these movements toward greater equality and respect for the dignity of all persons pointed to a deeper awareness that was emerging out of the collective unconsciousness of the human community. Not just as individuals, but as communities we were journeying toward a growing awareness of some of the biases that undergirded structures of oppression and exclusion in our society and in our world. Through these messy, loud, and sometimes violent social movements, we were waking up. Not all of us, and it was not a complete awakening to be sure, but it was happening nonetheless.

These were signs of the times. These were hints of God's presence and activity in the world. The challenge for people of faith was to see the hints, to see divine energies for healing, new life, and transformation, and to cooperate with these energies. Thus, reading the signs of the times is a deeply prophetic activity, focused on understanding what we are seeing when we look at current happenings in the world. It is also a contemplative activity, attuning us to divine presence in the midst of complex and mixed energies in the world. And it is about justice-making because the whole point of reading the signs of the times is to be able to work with these divine energies for transformation in the world.

The Second Vatican Council not only picked up this teaching around the signs of the times, but also brought it to the heart of the church's mission in the world, emphasizing that to carry forward the work of Christ in the world, the church has the "duty of scrutinizing the signs of the times and of interpreting them in the light of the gospel." (*Gaudium et Spes*, no. 4,1965). To put it another way: reading the signs of the times is an essential aspect of our efforts to cooperate with God in shaping the reign of God. It is a discernment that focuses on key contemporary events or movements, and identifies those elements that cohere with the gospels, and our Christian understandings of ourselves as persons and communities, as well as our understanding of critical ethical principles such as solidarity and the common good.

Signs of the Times in Our Time

The first step in reading the signs of the times is to study the context in which we live. What events are impacting our lives and all of earth community? How are they impacting people and earth community? How are people and all of earth community responding to these events? The second step has two critical and intertwined dynamics, requiring both contextual analysis and theological reflection. This step is done best in the context of a pluralistic dialogue, drawing in people from diverse social locations to ask critical questions. How are we to understand these events? Who has power? Who controls? Who decides? Who is left out? Who is included? How is the current situation influenced by past events? What cultural values are at play? What cultural assumptions are operating? What scriptural themes can help us to interpret this situation? How do biblical values compare and contrast with cultural values? Where do we see energies for healing, new life, and transformation? How is God present and acting in this context? The third step moves us from theological reflection to action, action that aims to transform injustice.

In identifying a focus on the financial crisis and its aftermath, this volume has already pinpointed a direction for our efforts to read the signs of the times. Likewise, the other essays in this book contribute varied analyses of the ways that turmoil in the financial markets is functioning in our lives. This reality offers me the freedom to focus sharply the arena for my reading of the signs of the times. I will work from my own social location, as someone who grew up in poverty, lives as a member of a Catholic religious order, and works at an Office for Systemic Justice, to focus on the question that I believe is, or at least should be, at the crux of our readings of the signs of the times: what transforming energy might be trying to emerge from our collective unconscious today? After a focused contextual analysis, I will move to a brief theological reflection and then explore possibilities for action.

Collective human consciousness evolves in response to what is happening in the world, so I begin with a summary of some key issues associated with the function of the financial markets in the world. Recently, the Occupy Movement hosted a global conversation intended to challenge the power that giant corporations in general, and big banks in particular, have amassed. The movement asserted that corporate giants have far too much control over government policy which they use to protect their power and profits at the expense of everyone else.

Now some years after the bailouts, the big banks have paid no penalties for the recklessness that caused the recession. Instead, they returned quickly to sky-high profit-making while citizens around the world were left to suffer joblessness, staggering debt, and brutal austerity measures. In a predictable scapegoating twist, people who were deceived and manipulated into taking bad loans are now blamed for trying to live beyond their means. To be sure, some people made some bad choices, but they were pushed and prodded to do so. Consider how, as the housing bubble grew, banks enlisted independent brokers, working on commission, to sign up borrowers to long, complex agreements. Bad choices were just a matter of time.

Big traders on the financial markets also have been manipulating the markets in deceptive ways. These traders, who are primarily affiliated with the major investment banks, enter the commodities markets "with enormous financial resources, enabling them to influence the ups and downs of market prices to an unprecedented degree."[2] Robert Pollin and James Heintz note that the overall level of futures market trading of crude oil contracts on the New York Mercantile Exchange in 2011 was 400% greater than it was in 2001 and 60% higher than it was in 2009. This increase cannot be accounted for simply by increases in the physical production of oil supplies because, even when these increases are taken into account, trading is still 300% greater today than it was in 2001, and 33% greater than 2009. The high-volume trading and the manipulation of prices are connected: "When [big traders such as those from major investment banks] come to hold dominant positions in the market, they also gain the power to move prices up or down through their own trading decisions.... When market prices are rising, they can buy large numbers of futures contracts, aiming to push prices further upward, then sell their contracts at market peaks."[3] It is an impact that is all the more disturbing when it af-

---

[2] Robert Pollin and James Heintz, "How Wall Street Speculation is Driving Up Gasoline Prices Today," *Political Economy Research Institute*, University of Massachusetts, Amherst, June 2011, p. 3.
[3] Ibid.

fects food commodities markets, leading to increased food prices, increased hunger, and increased deaths. Such traders can make enormous profits by manipulating the market, but this activity hurts ordinary people, most especially those already living in poverty.

And then there is the run-of-the-mill financial activity that simply reflects the unbridled profit-making at the heart of the financial system. When professional analysts and investment brokers carefully monitor the ups and downs of the market, they are also putting unrelenting pressure on corporate executives to maximize profitability and therefore shareholder wealth. In a related pattern, corporations seem reluctant to invest their wealth in productive expansion that would create jobs. This is so prevalent that, in August 2012, then Bank of Canada governor Mark Carney scolded corporate Canada because collectively, they are sitting on a $560 billion stack of cash—a pattern that has been going on for years.[4] Together these patterns indicate that the financial markets are not promoting the wellbeing of the productive economy as they were meant to do. For the most part, they are benefitting only the financial elites.

The focus on maximizing profitability has many other impacts as well. In this paper, I will focus on only two: the upward distribution of wealth, and the deterioration of earth's capacity to support and nurture life. I focus on these two because they help to highlight the interconnected nature of financial, economic, social, and environmental issues. Indeed, this interconnection is so significant that it is helpful to explore it before delving into the two aforementioned impacts of maximizing profitability.

Interconnection, Community, and the Economy

In June 2012, I was a delegate at Rio+20, the UN Conference on Sustainable Development. At the very core of this conference, there was a struggle over how to understand the relationship between the financial markets, economy, society, and environment. Corporations and governments tended to link the financial markets with the economy and then treat the economy, society, and environment as three separate spheres of influence. In this narrative, while it is important to pay attention to all three, sometimes trade-offs have to be made and, not surprisingly, in these trade-

[4] See how Jim Stanford traces the trend from 2000-2012: http://rabble.ca/columnists/2012/09/jim-standford-excerpts-caw-convention-document/, accessed Sept. 6, 2012.

offs the economy would always win.[5] However, many civil society groups at the conference were offering a very different kind of narrative. A dominant theme within the alternative approach might image these four systems as four concentric circles. The financial system is the smallest circle, embedded in the economy such that it is meant to serve the wellbeing of the productive economy. The economy, in its turn, needs to be understood as being embedded in society, serving the wellbeing of society. Society, likewise, is imaged as being embedded in earth community so that it is concerned with the wellbeing of all of earth community.[6] Finally, for people of faith, earth community is understood to be embedded in God, serving the Creator.

With this image, not only does earth community receive the attention that it warrants, but it is also clear that what happens in any circle impacts the others. All of these spheres are interconnected; a ripple in one affects the others. Indeed, that is the wisdom onto which the term "ecological justice" tries to hold: we need to be attentive to the ways that environment, society, and economy are relating to each other and impacting each other in order to work toward right relationship.

Within this context of interrelationship, I return now to two key patterns that emerge from the economy's narrow focus on maximizing profitability and channelling the flow of these profits to the most elite players in the financial markets: the upward distribution of wealth, and the deterioration of earth's capacity to support and nurture life. In particular, I want to highlight the impacts that these patterns have had on the wellbeing of our societies and on earth community as a whole.

First, the upward distribution of wealth is creating a growing gap between rich and poor, a pattern that is tearing at the fabric of society. As Wilkinson and Pickett note, "the quality of social relations in a society is built on material foundations [and] the scale of income difference has a powerful effect on how we relate to each other."[7] Their work indicates that the growing gap between rich and poor contributes to the fragmentation of society by structuring social patterns of privilege and marginalization.

---

[5] For a more detailed look at the governmental narratives see the final report from the conference at http://www.uncsd.iisd.org/news/un-releases-final-report-of-rio20.
[6] See Oxfam International for an example of an interrelated approach: http://www.oxfam.org/en/grow/video/2012/introducing-doughnut-safe-and-just-space-humanity.
[7] Richard Wilkinson and Kate Pickett, *The Spirit Level: Why Equality is Better for Everyone* (London: Penguin Books, 2009, 2010), p. 4.

Such inequality has widespread impacts in society. Using internationally comparable data, Wilkinson and Pickett have demonstrated that a range of health and social problems are more prevalent in societies that have a wider gap between rich and poor. The affected areas of impact include higher levels of mental illness (including drug and alcohol addiction), infant mortality, obesity, teenage births, homicides, and imprisonment rates, as well as lower levels of trust, life expectancy, social mobility, and children's educational performance.[8] And the real kicker is that these impacts are worse for all levels of society, not just among those who are living with the lowest incomes.

Poverty is devastating because it is a relation between people that is characterized by social exclusion as well as by distinctions in power and status that create unequal access to limited resources and opportunities. As such, it tears apart the social fabric of a community.

A focus on endless profit-making also leads to endless growth of the economy. While growth of the economy is not necessarily a bad thing, it becomes a problem when economic growth in already-developed countries is based on the consumption of material goods. If, for instance, growth in developed countries were based primarily in the growth of services such as childcare or efforts to address poverty, it would not be a problem. However, such is not the case. This is why Tim Jackson, Economics Commissioner for the Sustainable Development Commission in the United Kingdom, is concerned about the way that the structure of our financial and economic system relies on continued growth.[9] Structures that dictate that we must consume ever higher levels of material goods ignore the reality that we live on a finite planet and blindly lead us toward earth devastation.

The system that encourages so many people in North America to keep buying is complex. We can buy material goods at bargain prices because land, water, and workers are being exploited throughout the extraction, production, distribution, and retail phases of the process, and these real costs are being externalized such that companies do not have to address the impacts, but societies do.

It is a multi-layered economic system, but the financial markets are at its core and little will change until this core changes. As the system works right now, there is a necessary connection between growth and jobs be-

---

[8] Wilkinson and Pickett, *Spirit Level*, p. 19.

[9] Tim Jackson, *Prosperity Without Growth: Economics for a Finite Planet* (London, UK: Earthscan, 2009), p. 76.

cause the gains from increased productivity go to managers and shareholders with very little going to labour. As a result, the total number of jobs will decrease and unemployment will increase if the economy is not growing at a rate that at least equals the increase in productivity. If the system worked differently, gains in productivity could create greater time for workers to devote to personal development, family life, and community building.[10]

Earth systems are expected to support this endless growth, as we defy logic in the pursuit of perpetual growth on a finite planet. In the process, air, rivers, and lakes are polluted, fish stocks are depleted, drinking water is contaminated, soil is degraded, forests are stripped, the many systems that stabilize our climate are thrown out of balance, and species are made extinct.

This focus on systems and how they are functioning is important. When we understand how the financial crisis is intertwined with so many of the crises of our day, including economic, social, and environmental crises, it is easier to see that, at a deeper level we are talking about a crisis of civilization, a crisis of values. However, this is not to suggest that we can turn things around simply by becoming more virtuous individuals. Certainly, it is good to encourage ourselves to be virtuous, to buy less and live more simply, but we also need to be aware that everything in the system is working against this transformation.

The structures in our current economic model have globalized greed as well as incredibly distorted patterns of consumption in which a few consume far too much while the majority does not have enough. The spiritual and justice-based task is to create social and economic structures and systems that will globalize compassion and justice.

By paying attention to links between the financial and economic system, we can see how the addictive dynamics of globalized capitalism have contributed to a system in which corporations seek the highest possible profits, consumers demand the lowest possible price for goods, and societies and bio-regions pay the ultimate price. We can also see how the financial crisis is intertwined with so many of the crises of our day, including economic, social, climate change, food, and energy crises.

---

[10] David Korten, *Agenda for a New Economy*, (San Francisco: Berrett-Koehler 2009), p. 70.

The Role of Faith Communities

This struggle over how we understand the relationship between the financial markets, economy, society, and environment points to a critical role for faith communities in our time. Indeed, I am offering that this question of how we will understand these relationships is at the crux of engaging the financial markets as a sign of the times. I want to use the lens of the evolution of consciousness to explore this further. In particular, I want to return to that notion of identifying the healing and transforming energies that seem to be emerging from the collective unconscious into consciousness in our own day.

Authors who study the evolution of consciousness emphasize that our consciousness evolves in response to what is happening in the world and that we are living in a time when we human beings are able to choose consciously to nurture the evolution of our consciousness by acting from the highest value system that we are able to recognize.[11] Such conscious choices stretch us. They transform us, both individually and collectively.

Given this, I think it is helpful to consider the Occupy Movement, which also came into being in response to what was happening in the world, and in the financial markets in particular. It was a spontaneous movement, without a solid enough footing to take hold, but it gained enough resonance around the world that it cannot and should not be ignored. The Occupy Movement was criticized for its lack of focus but, collectively, the group was pointing to elements of a new vision for society, a new way of understanding the relationship between earth, society, and economy. At the heart of this vision was the value of solidarity. It was not just talked about; to a significant degree, it was lived. And, in the living, questions were raised for everyone. Will we choose consciously to enter into new ways of being in relationship, ways that may lead to transformation of ourselves and our society?

Some called this vision unrealistic, too idealistic. Certainly it is incomplete, but it seems to me that the ideals of such a movement have power because they are symbols that help us to remember (to be one-with) the transforming energies that emanate from similar movements in our foundational scripture stories. For instance, there are themes in the Occupy

[11] See Don Edward Beck and Christopher C. Cowan, *Spiral Dynamics* (Oxford: Blackwell Publishers, 1996). Also Ken Wilber, *The Integral Vision* (Boston, MA: Shambala Publications, 2007).

Movement that resonate well with the Exodus story, a journey into both an alternative consciousness and an alternative kind of community.

In this biblical story, God inserts God's self, that is, divine energies, into the wilderness experiences, thereby drawing a motley group of slaves into deeper consciousness and deeper community; a deepening that continues until we see the formation of an alternative kind of society that is meant to be rooted in solidarity. It is a journey that highlights the importance of integrating justice and contemplation in our lives, and one that points to a critical role for faith communities as we seek to respond to what God may be doing in the world today.

In the Exodus story we learn that God is what God does. And we learn that what God does is to care for us with faithful love by drawing us into relationships of justice and compassion. It is a story about slaves who know the experience of being excluded from the benefits of the Egyptian empire's social and economic systems. As slaves, they have learned that the powerful take what they want from others, hoarding as much wealth as they can, and creating scarcity for others as a result. They can only wonder what will happen to them in the wilderness if they continue to live by these patterns.

Through their wilderness experiences, and most especially through the gathering of the manna, the people learn new patterns for living together. They are learning to take only what they need and nothing more. Their eyes are opened to the ways that they create scarcity in the midst of abundance by refusing to recognize when they have enough. With a contemplative consciousness, they learn what it is that God wants them to learn in these experiences: God is caring for them by drawing them into new ways of being in relationship with each other and the goods of the earth.

The people slowly begin to see that they are interconnected. If they take only what they need, there is enough for everyone. If they take more than that, not only does the food rot, but the social fabric of the groups rots as well. A new rhythm is established in which the challenges of the wilderness, which serve as the current context for their lives, along with the challenges of being in relationship with each other, create a back and forth flow between insights into new ways of creating authentic community, on the one hand, and movement into deeper relationship with God on the other.

The Occupy movement, along with other responses to the crises of our time, such as the re-energizing of unions, the incredible network of NGOs that are collaborating to address interconnected justice issues and to work against the 'divide and conquer' approach of governments, and multi-faith groups working together on poverty issues, suggest that a deeper sense of solidarity and interconnectedness is trying to emerge from our collective unconscious.

If this is true, then faith communities need to be stepping, consciously and intentionally, into this emerging energy field. And we need to do so with a focus on both contemplation and justice, working collaboratively with specially chosen partners to bring concrete actions for solidarity into existence and simultaneously opening to the contemplative graces that can draw us into deeper consciousness, both individually and collectively. In what remains, I want to explore why the integration of contemplation and justice is so critical for creating the deep transformation that is so needed in the world.

Carl Jung's studies of the human psyche tell us that the unconscious is the creative source of all that evolves into the conscious mind; it is the raw material out of which our conscious minds develop; the source of human capacity for orderly thought, reasoning, human awareness, and feeling.[12] Every capacity of our functioning consciousness was first contained in the unconscious and then found its way to the conscious level.

The indwelling God, too, reaches out to us through our unconscious. We know that contemplative prayer and practice open us to the flow of psychic material and meaning from the unconscious. Through the process of learning to rest in God, beyond thoughts, feelings, associations, stories, or inner dramas, we are moved to a deeper consciousness as material in the unconscious is loosened. This is psychic material that the defence mechanisms of our childhood and our socialization process previously kept out of our awareness: unhealthy ways of relating, old wounds, or areas of our life that have remained undeveloped. Over time, we learn that God is powerfully present in that which we have tried to exclude from consciousness, and we are awakened to the reality that God is also powerfully present in relationships with those whom we have tried to exclude from our lives.

Contemplative consciousness might be imaged as a still, sacred space in which we interact with a divine presence that lures us ever deeper within. This space connects us to our complete self while, simultaneously, uniting us more fully with God, earth, and others. Contemplative conscious-

[12] See Carl G. Jung, *Memories, Dreams and Reflections* (New York: Pantheon Books, 1963), *Man and His Symbols* (Garden City, NY: Doubleday, 1964).

ness opens us to the interconnected whole of reality. Here we are awakened to our communion with God and, through God, all others.

Ken Wilber suggests that most of our problems emerge from our lack of awareness of the way that ego-consciousness creates boundaries.[13] As I develop a sense of self, I draw a boundary line between what is me and what is not. I link my identity with what is inside the boundary and disidentify with anything that is not. One problem with boundaries is that they always create their opposite; it is not possible to identify an inside without also identifying an outside, no pleasure without pain, no good without evil. The ensuing conflicts between the opposites potentially become the site of battles, with the intensity of the battle being dependent upon how strictly I maintain the boundary line. We have already seen how the boundaries created between self, society, economics, and environment contributed to harmful patterns of relationship.

In itself, there is nothing wrong with boundary making, as long as we realize that the boundary is a construction of our consciousness. Indeed, boundary-making is an important tool, enabling us to create elaborate means of sorting and classifying, which have led to a great deal of technological progress in society. However, to the extent that we are not aware, these boundaries function in an illusory way, creating a distorted sense of relationship.

Only a separate self, who mentally constructs borders to divide myself from others, can look at the abundance that surrounds us with both a greed that wants to hoard it and a fear that there won't be enough. Only a society that is filled with people who see themselves as separate selves-with-borders can take the abundance that surrounds us and then go about forming social and economic structures that create scarcity for some and extravagance for others (maximizing profit, shopping wherever can get the best bargain no matter what harm is done to the environment, or what the working conditions of the people who made the product).

These assumptions create both fear and a sense of rivalry in us, and they blind us to our deeper, truer identity which is rooted in our communion with God and all others in earth community—the identity that we rediscover through contemplative prayer and practice. We need to learn to recognize and quiet the inner patterns of thinking and feeling into which we've been socialized if we are to become attuned to God's still silent

[13] Ken Wilber, *No Boundary* (Boston, MA: Shambala Publications, 1979), pp. 2-29.

voice, which is much deeper within us. As we learn to journey into the sacred stillness, a deeper contemplative consciousness (a more unified consciousness) develops within us, and we intuit that there is so much more to us than we had ever realized. We become aware that we are more fully one with God, earth, and each other than we had ever imagined and, at the same time, completely distinct and unique.

Contemplative consciousness also draws us into a profound inner integrative process in which we become aware of our complicity with the oppressive systems in the world as we touch the values, assumptions, and biases that lie in the unconscious. In North America, our addictive patterns of consumption reveal one of the many ways that we are complicit with oppressive systems. Therefore, if faith communities want to nurture a deepening sense of solidarity in our culture, we need to deepen our awareness of how the system functions and how we are caught in it. We also need to begin the work of transforming these systems. We need to do the work of justice.

Certainly, everyone needs access to the basic goods and opportunities of a society. However, our consumer culture promotes the illusion that inner states such as satisfaction, security, prestige, or happiness are things that can be purchased. Even when our consumer goods fail to give us the desired inner states, we assume that this is because we do not have enough, an assumption that appears to operate no matter how much one has. Furthermore, because we are unconsciously seeking such inner states, it can be tempting to conclude that widespread inner transformation is all that is needed to bring about a change in this consumer culture. But this is one of many aspects of life in which we need to be attentive to both the personal and the social, the conscious and the unconscious.

Patterns of addiction have made their way into our policies and institutions in ways that undermine movement toward inner transformation. If we consider the five essential characteristics of addiction that Gerald May identifies in personal addictions (tolerance, withdrawal symptoms, self-deception, loss of willpower and distortion of attention), not only is it apparent that these signs are applicable to our consumer culture, but we can see paths of connection between personal and societal patterns of addiction.[14]

---

[14] Gerald May, *Addiction and Grace* (New York, NY: HarperCollins, 1988), pp. 25-30.

Tolerance refers to the pattern of wanting or needing more of an addictive behaviour in order to feel satisfied. It is readily apparent when we realize that, on average, a person in the U.S. consumes twice as much as they did fifty years ago, and I dare say that this would also be true of Canada.[15] Likewise, the societal linking of our identity with our consumption, through endless advertising that insists that we must have and wear certain things to be successful and admired, goes a long way toward creating a withdrawal-type of stress for the many who are not able to consume at such levels.

At the same time, the consumer culture is rife with self-deception. Consider again how we are encouraged to increase endlessly our consumption, even though the earth cannot possibly sustain such patterns. In the past three decades, one-third of the planet's resources, its 'natural wealth,' has been consumed.[16] We are not only ignoring the reality of living on a finite planet, we are ignoring the equally troubling reality that many of us are over-consuming in a world where millions upon millions of people still do not have access to the bare necessities of life.

In addition, our cultural lifestyle has become so busy and stress-filled that people easily feel overwhelmed. The very complexity of the economic system tends to drain us of the willpower that we need to begin to make changes, just as it undermines our attentiveness to destructive patterns by hiding much of the harm that is caused, whether by the pollution and human rights abuses that too often result from resource extraction, or the environmental degradation that is linked to the disposal of consumer goods.

Even at a cursory glance, we can get a sense of the addictive character of our consumer culture and recognize that societal change requires a systemic approach. We are left with a tension between the personal and the social. Individual choices to consume less are significant because they can play a role in stimulating awareness of the addictive nature of our consumer culture and point us toward new possibilities. However, the transformation of this culture, including its social and economic institutions, will not come about simply through these individual choices. Nor is it a simple matter of inner transformation on a mass scale leading to transformation of

---

[15] Betsy Taylor and David Tilford, "Why Consumption Matters," in *The Consumer Society Reader*, ed. Juliet Schor and Douglas Holt (New York: New Press, 2000), p. 467.

[16] Paul Hawken, Amory Lovins and L. Hunter Lovins, *Natural Capitalism* (New York, NY: Little, Brown and Company, 1999), p. 4.

policies and institutions. Even while I grow in awareness of some of my addictive patterns, and become more attuned to what needs to change in wider systems, I will continue to be affected by a counter-force that fuels my addictive tendencies as I keep interacting with the wider social and economic systems. The system itself needs to be addressed and transformed, alongside graced efforts to transform ourselves as one part of a wider system.

So, faith communities can nurture the emergence of greater solidarity and interconnectedness (deeper consciousness and deeper community) by deepening awareness of how social, cultural, and economic systems are functioning in our lives. At the same time, faith communities might encourage dialogue on the idea of limiting the degree of inequality in our societies.

Given the devastating social impacts of the growing gap between rich and poor, many of us would agree that there need to be limits to inequality. However, as Herman Daly, an ecological economist observes, "there is not a God-given definition of what the limits of inequality should be."[17] Nonetheless, he also notes that "universities, civil services, and the military seem to manage with a factor of 10 to 20 [that is, a pay scale in which the maximum incomes are 10 to 20 times higher than the minimum]. As a first step, could we not try to lower the overall range to a factor of, say, one hundred?"[18] Likewise, we can nurture solidarity by joining with other groups to protect bio-regions through the adoption of protective environmental regulations. Joining with others to work for such change also helps to transform us, as individuals and groups, particularly as we begin to see our complicity with harmful social and economic patterns.

The patterns of consciousness and community are intertwined. By exploring these connections, as I have been doing in this paper, we expose points of intersection between the conscious and the unconscious, as well as between the personal and the collective. At such points of intersection, there is great potential for transformation of our choices and actions because we create a doorway that enables an interactive dynamic between our own personal transformation and transformation in ecological, social, religious, cultural, and economic spheres. This interaction can function in a more life-giving way as we come to recognize our personal complicity

---

[17] Herman Daly, *Beyond Growth: The Economics of Sustainable Development* (Boston, MA: Beacon Press, 1996), p. 210. See also Herman Daly, *A Steady State Economy*, London: Sustainable Development Commission, April, 2008.
[18] Ibid., p. 210.

with the injustice that is happening in the world. That is, as we learn to see the many different ways that we have been formed into patterns of fear and scarcity, rivalry and exclusion, we have a graced doorway through which we can work for transformation of these patterns on a systemic level. Similarly, our interaction with social and economic issues, such as the role of the financial markets, can activate a deeper awareness of how the same patterns are operating within us.

It is easy to talk about change when others are the ones who need to change. It is tempting to focus only on the players in the financial markets, or those who got into mortgages they could not handle, in order to decide what they did wrong, how they need to change. But, if we do not identify how we are complicit in these wider social patterns, very little will change over the long term. Instead, we will find that we are caught in collective patterns of shadow projection, blaming others for patterns in which we all participate, creating new forms of exclusion and oppression. As Ann Ulanov notes, this is yet another place where the personal becomes social. After we project unwanted inner traits onto another, "this live bit of shadow menaces us from the outside. This other person or other group carries part of ourselves and we feel compelled to manage them, restrict them, and eliminate them. Thus bloom the ugliness of prejudice, discrimination, persecution and oppression."[19]

Instead, if faith communities were to host on-going dialogues about solidarity and taxes, we would be entering the rich and dangerous territory of our own unconscious assumptions about fear and scarcity, rivalry and exclusion. One need only mention the phrase "raise taxes" to evoke strong, negative reaction. And yet, this discussion holds all kinds of potential for creating the kind of solidarity that we see in scripture, and the kind of solidarity that was proposed by the Occupy movement in response to the excesses of the financial markets. This is territory that affects us all. Such dialogues would take us to the intersection of the conscious and the unconscious, the personal and the social. It is just one example of the territory that we must travel if we are to engage in deep social and economic transformation.

I have been suggesting that a deepening sense of solidarity and interconnectedness is at the crux of the signs of our times; it is an energy that is trying to emerge from the collective unconscious into our consciousness. If this emergence is to reach fruition, our efforts to read and engage the

---

[19] Ann Belford Ulanov, *The Unshuttered Heart* (Nashville, TN: Abingdon Press, 2007), p. 140.

signs of our times need to be grounded in an integration of contemplation and justice. Together, these dynamics teach us that God is powerfully present in that which we try to exclude, whether we are excluding something from our consciousness, excluding people from the basic goods of our society, or excluding regions of the earth from our concern. In this integration, we also discover that points of intersection between the conscious and the unconscious, as well as the personal and the collective, are intense points of transformation. To the degree that we can acknowledge our complicity in the systemic patterns that need to change, we can tap a graced energy for on-going transformation of our self and the world.

CHAPTER FIVE

FROM FINANCIAL CRISIS TO ECONOMIC JUSTICE THROUGH MONETARY REFORM: IMPLICATIONS FOR PUBLIC THEOLOGY

GEORGE H. CROWELL[1]

The 2008 global financial crisis was a brutal shock, especially to many who were economically vulnerable. But in fact, the money system in capitalist nations before 2008 had long been highly damaging. There has been so little public awareness of its abusive dynamics in recent decades, however, and we have become so accustomed to them, that we take them for granted as normal and acceptable. An earlier generation thought differently. In the United States, for instance, banking services were stabilized by legislation in reaction to the devastating impact of the Great Depression, primarily by the 1933 Glass-Steagall Act which separated speculative investment banking from the conservative insurance business, and from retail banking—basically deposit-taking and mortgage lending. Deposit insurance was another stabilizing factor. As we shall see shortly, the abandonment of such regulatory limitations on the banking sector in more recent history played a large part in the crisis of 2008. Between the 1929-1933 Great Depression and the 2008 Great Recession, the United States had about a dozen "recessions" (no longer labelled as "depressions"), but economists reassured us that these were merely routine, unavoidable expressions of the "business cycle." The crisis of 2008 was especially severe, and as such, needs to be examined carefully. Of crucial importance in this connection is the monetary system. Accordingly, the primary focus of this

[1] George H. Crowell, Th.D., taught Social Ethics in the Religious Studies Department, University of Windsor, 1968-1996. This chapter is a revised and supplemented version of a paper, "The Money System—From Austerity and Devastation to Justice and Sustainability," that was delivered at the conference on "Money-Creation in a Finite World" organized by Dr. John B. Cobb, Jr. through the Center for Process Studies at Claremont Theological School, April 10, 2012.

paper is to explain how harmful our little-understood, routine money system already was, and continues to be now, amidst on-going and growing abuses since the 2008 financial meltdown. But first some brief comments about that meltdown, and then about the relevance of monetary issues for public theology.

The 2008 Crisis

Fallout from the 2008 global financial crisis continues. Unemployment and under-employment remain high in many global economies. Millions of people globally have lost their homes, and millions more carry the financial burdens of homes worth less than they paid for them. Inequality of income and wealth continue to widen. The austerity agenda, justified by governments' indebtedness, is bringing privatizations and cutbacks to public services. It is now well known that the meltdown resulted from questionable and even fraudulent practices by powerful banking institutions with global reach, and that the bail-out occasioned by those practices not only failed to help the victims, but on the contrary enabled the perpetrators to add rich bonuses to their already bloated salaries. Meantime, no prominent bankers have been prosecuted,[2] and indeed, they continue their abusive practices with ever-new twists. Through the chicanery of interest-rate swaps, cities like Detroit are now being driven to insolvency. Wealthy bondholders are seizing remaining city assets while long-time city workers are losing their pensions.[3]

The financial crisis of 2008 and these continuing abuses were made possible largely by the 1999 repeal of the Glass-Steagall Act in the United States, and by similar measures elsewhere. Armies of well-paid lobbyists played a key role in bringing about this repeal, and they now pressure legislators ever more intensely to provide even more advantages to speculative investment banking, and to prevent any enactment of new restraining regulations,[4] especially for their immense volume of derivatives gam-

---

[2] This may change. See the Reuters column, "Holder Now Says: 'None Too Big To Jail,'" *Reader Supported News*, May 5, 2014—or it may not change. See Elias Isquith, "Matt Taibbi: 'It's Total Moral Surrender,'" *Reader Supported News*, May 19, 2014. http://readersupportednews.org/.

[3] Ellen Brown, "The Global Banking Game is Rigged, and the FDIC is Suing," *The Web of Debt Blog*, April 13, 2014. http://ellenbrown.com/.

[4] Daniel Wagner, The Center for Public Integrity, "Meet the Banking Caucus, Wall Street's Secret Weapon in Washington," *Reader Supported News*, May 5, 2014. http://readersupportednews.org/.

bling—likely more than 1,200 *trillion* U.S. dollars' worth in the global economy.[5] Recognizing the peril of this lucrative but hazardous business, the Bank for International Settlements, the centre of power for global private banking located in Basel, Switzerland, gained approval at the 2011 meeting of the G20 nations for a strategy to protect banks from collapse. This is the "bail-in" regime which allows major banks on the verge of failure to take over the assets of their clients—including our deposits—despite the dismal failure of the banking sector to reform! This is the strategy that was applied to Cyprus in March 2013. It was also a strategy that was made fully explicit in Canada's 2013 Federal Budget.[6] We have been told that our bank deposits remain safely insured, but we have not been told to what extent. The Canada Deposit Insurance Corporation, as of April 30, 2013 had only $2.6 billion of assets to insure $665 billion of deposits in Canada[7]—paltry protection in case a 2008-type financial meltdown should occur. The U.S. situation is similar. The Federal Deposit Insurance Corporation in 2013 had about $25 billion in assets to insure more than $9 trillion of bank deposits in the United States.[8] The types of financial exploitation which brought on the 2008 crisis thus continue to render our economic future dangerously unstable.

Charles Pierce vividly characterizes our current financial predicament:

> ...there is no pile of money anywhere in the country [U.S.], no matter how large or small, and no matter how vital to the people who were depending upon it, to which the grifters in the financial services "industry" do not feel entitled as fuel for their unquenchable greed. They will destroy lives because they have contempt for those lives. They will wreck people because those people are wreckable, and they will do it laughing.[9]

This attitude is rampant not just from a failure of personal morality, as is usually said, but primarily because it has become institutionalized. The

---

[5] Ellen Brown, "The Armageddon Looting Machine: The Looming Mass Destruction From Derivatives," *The Web of Debt Blog*, September 17, 2013: http://ellenbrown.com/.

[6] Jerry Ackerman and George Crowell, "Depositors Beware: Cyprus-style bank 'bail-ins' now also approved for Canada," *CCPA Monitor* (July/August 2013), 40.

[7] Information obtained from phoning 1-800-461-2342, the number given on the CDIC website.

[8] Ellen Brown, *The Public Banking Solution* (Baton Rouge, LA,: Third Millennium Press, 2013), 9.

[9] Charles Pierce, "Wall Street Predators Launch Secret War on American Retirements," *Reader Supported News*, September 30, 2013: http://readersupportednews.org/.

problem pervades the higher reaches of our dominant financial institutions, which are so powerful that governments so far have been afraid to rein them in.

This is a primary factor of our present situation that public theology must be prepared to confront. The Christian faith, thankfully, has a vast store of wisdom from its long tradition that can be applied to specific current social issues. Mentioned briefly here are some insights that are relevant to the sort of financial crisis that we now face.

Biblical Resources for Public Theology Concerning Financial Crises

When dealing with the 2008 financial meltdown, its precedents and continuing consequences, one of the primary resources for public theology is the biblical tradition which presents keen insights about similar financial crises that people have confronted in the ancient past—especially resulting from the use of debt as an instrument of oppression. As monetary reformer Michael Hudson, Professor of Economics at the University of Missouri-Kansas City, points out in a remarkable essay, recent scholars have overlooked or played down this part of the biblical tradition, considering it inappropriate for modern economic conditions. But Hudson calls attention to a core body of law central to both Old and New Testaments which clearly recognizes how debt can be exploited by creditors to increase their wealth and power while bringing devastating impoverishment to the economically vulnerable, along with inequalities that destroy community.[10]

Especially through the work of biblical compilers of the sixth and fifth centuries B.C.E., this body of law was codified primarily in Exodus, Leviticus, and Deuteronomy. The early prophets Amos, Hosea, and Isaiah had inveighed against abuses resulting from indebtedness. But after the rediscovery of an early Deuteronomic document in the temple during the reign of the Hebrew king, Josiah, in 610 B.C.E., and as a result of the chastening influence of the Babylonian exile from 586 to 538 B.C.E., this concern for the destructive impact of debt was more systematically codified and publicized. The Persian conquerors who overthrew the Babylonian empire in 538 B.C.E. allowed subject peoples, including the Israelites, to return to their homelands, and later allowed Nehemiah in 444 B.C.E. to lead in re-

[10] Michael Hudson, *The Lost Tradition of Biblical Debt Cancellations* (New York: Henry George School of Social Science, 1993). A list of biblical passages dealing with the debt issue appears in pp. 54-67.

building the temple. Integral to this project was the re-emphasis by Nehemiah and Ezra of obligations under their sacred covenant with God to prevent indebtedness from becoming an instrument of oppression.

This core body of written law was placed in the context of stories that established the very identity of the people of Israel who had been forced into slavery in Egypt. According to tradition, God responded to their distress through the exodus, the mighty acts by which he rescued his chosen people by freeing them from slavery in Egypt, bringing them to a land where they had a sacred obligation to establish a community where everyone was to be treated compassionately, and where such slavery was never again to be tolerated. The heart of this narrative tradition was repeatedly reiterated through such formulae as: "I am the Lord your God who brought you out of the land of Egypt, out of the house of bondage" (e.g., Ex. 20:2; Deut. 5:6), or, "Remember that you were a slave in Egypt and diligently observe these statutes" (Deut. 16:12; 15:15; 24:18, 22). The exodus memory is still stressed annually in Jewish tradition through celebration of the Passover.

Through this narrative tradition and through obligations that were spelled out in detail, the people were admonished never to take advantage of those who were experiencing economic distress by forcing them into debt. There is throughout this code of law frequent and vivid recognition of abuses that can occur when the rich lend to the poor who have been forced into borrowing as a result of misfortune—such as loss of crops or family members. Those who were more prosperous were urged ideally to assist the economically vulnerable—especially widows, orphans and aliens—through outright gifts of charity. But limits to generosity were recognized, so loans were permitted provided interest was not charged (e.g., Ex. 22:25; Deut. 23:19; Ps. 15:5). But while interest charges were forbidden, allowance was made for collateral on the principal of loans. Security or collateral for the lender could be provided in the form of land or even pledges of personal servitude from the borrower—despite the pervasive Old Testament revulsion against slavery. It was recognized that allowing for collateral could open the door to the whole range of abuses resulting from indebtedness. Therefore a remedy was prescribed. Every seven years all debts were to be cancelled. Land was to be returned to its original owners, and those in debt bondage were to be freed (Deut. 15:1-18 2). Special emphasis was given to this requirement after seven seven-year periods had passed in what was known as the Jubilee Year (Lev. 25:8-24). After a time when these requirements had been neglected, Nehemiah called together the people, reminded them of their obligation not to force the poor into debt, and browbeat them into a sweeping public debt cancellation (Neh. 5:1-13). The importance of this obligation, which must have been all too frequently violated, is apparent from the emphasis on divinely imposed penalties for violations (e.g., Jer. 34:8-2). The outrage that is expressed in such passages is analogous to the outrage that is appropriate for public theology to proclaim against the fraudulent behaviour of financial institutions today.

Concern for the impact of indebtedness continues in the New Testament. Jesus early in his ministry, according to the Gospel of Luke (4:18-19), chose to read in the synagogue from the book of Isaiah (61:1-2): "The Spirit of the Lord is upon me, because he has anointed me to preach good news to the poor. He has sent me to proclaim release to the captives and recovering of sight to the blind, to set at liberty those who are oppressed, to proclaim the acceptable year of the Lord." From this passage it is evident that Jesus saw his ministry as including freeing people from debt bondage, and calling for observance of the Jubilee year. Through the parable of the unmerciful servant, he referred forcefully to the obligation of creditors to forgive debtors (Matt. 18:23-35). Jesus risked his life in order to dramatize his concern for economic justice by driving the money changers from the temple, an act described in all four Gospels, and so disruptive to the money masters of his day that they surely played a key role in seeking his crucifixion. This act was more than an assault on the problem of debt, but was also an attack on other kinds of fraudulent, exploitive money manipulation—similar to types that are rampant in our own time. The basic biblical insight is that debt can be used as an instrument of exploitation that concentrates wealth in the hands of a few who, recognizing that their privileges are insecure, turn ever more to ruthless repression to maintain their power.

Public theology, which seeks among other things to enhance the moral fervour of the churches and their commitment to work for social justice, needs to draw on insights and convictions expressed in the biblical tradition regarding the injustices of that time and the struggles to achieve justice. But it also has responsibility to analyze the specific dynamics of comparable current injustices of our own day. In the following pages I attempt to contribute to an understanding of our present money system—both its abuses based largely in oppressive use of indebtedness, and the advantages that could come from remedies that are available.

The Routine Functioning of our Money System

Our daily lives are presently dominated by a money system which is extremely damaging because it forces us into debt. We are well aware of far-reaching social injustices and environmental devastation that plague our common life. But very few of us have any idea of the major role that our money system plays in contributing to these problems. Even among the many civil society organizations working valiantly for social justice and environmental protection, there is hardly any awareness of the damaging impact of our prevailing money system. Thus their efforts for needed change are often inappropriate and usually insufficient.

We deal constantly with money in our daily lives, and yet very few people understand the basic dynamics of our money system which operate below the level of our awareness. From much experience in Western capitalist nations, it is apparent that those who make it their business to understand money systems in order to use them to their benefit take advantage of our ignorance. Our ignorance, in short, makes us vulnerable to exploitation. So there is a considerable amount of bad news to encounter at this point. But there is also some remarkably good news! Knowledge and understanding could open possibilities for people to access extraordinary financial resources for creative social change.

It is my task here to attempt to explain clearly and concisely the workings of our money system, a system which has an incredibly powerful impact on our daily lives. Apart from the gross, not yet remedied abuses which brought on the present Great Recession, I will describe how the *routine functioning of our money system* works constantly to our detriment. However, I will also indicate how our money system could be transformed to become a potent instrument for creative social and environmental change. I will also stress the relevance of monetary reform for enabling us to overcome the little-questioned universal commitment to unlimited, unsustainable economic growth in our finite global ecological system.

Let me note to begin with that I am indebted to many highly expert and committed monetary reformers for my comments here, and recently especially to Ellen Brown, author of the astonishingly informative 2008 book on the dynamics of money systems, *The Web of Debt*, to her 2013 book, *The Public Bank Solution*, to the ever-increasing collection of articles on her website, www.webofdebt.com, and to her leadership through the Public Banking Institute, in the growing movement for state-owned banks in the United States.[11] I am also indebted to John Cobb who, since I contacted him around 1995 to discuss the chapter on money systems added to the second (1994) edition of his extraordinary book co-authored with Herman Daly, *For the Common Good*, has encouraged me in my work on this issue.[12]

The Current Austerity Agenda

Faced with disturbingly growing deficits and debts, governments all over the capitalist world are now imposing painful austerity measures on economies and populations. Millions of people, particularly in those communities and economies most severely impacted, lost their livelihoods and homes as a result of the Great Recession, and now such government support services as have been available—unemployment insurance, welfare payments, medical care, education, pensions, etc.—are under attack. Expenditures for environmental protection are also slated for reduction although increases are urgently needed. We are told that cuts are unavoidable. According to the prevailing wisdom, there are only two possibilities: either cutting government spending, or raising taxes. Almost inexplicably, there is no serious consideration of raising taxes even on the obscenely rich, many of whom have accumulated vast wealth as a result of the financial meltdown which they helped to engineer. So governments are propagandizing conscientious citizens, with considerable success, to accept cuts to valued public services in order to rein in alleged excessive government spending. Consideration of any kind of debt cancellation is out of the question. Our public indebtedness is being used as an instrument of oppression, and we are told that there is no viable economic alternative to austerity. We are being hoodwinked into believing that such oppression is necessary and legitimate.

We should, I suggest, be working insistently to have taxes on the rich raised promptly and substantially. Such action is needed not only to increase government income for maintaining and improving valuable public services, but also to reduce the ever-growing, disruptive disparity between

---

[11] Ellen Hodgson Brown, *Web of Debt: The Shocking Truth about Our Money System and How We Can Break Free* (3rd ed., Baton Rouge, La: Third Millennium Press, 2008); and Brown, *The Public Bank Solution: From Austerity to Prosperity* (Baton Rouge, La: Third Millennium Press, 2013).

[12] Herman E. Daly and John B. Cobb, Jr., *For the Common Good: Redirecting the Economy Toward Community, the Environment, and a Sustainable Future* (2nd ed., Boston: Beacon Press, 1994).

the rich and poor. Policy reforms like these feature prominently in the arguments of those seeking social change. But we need to recognize that a more just tax system can only partially reduce the much more basic, and very damaging impact of our money system. It is the latter question of the money system that needs special attention in our time.

Almost all discussion of public finance is confined to fiscal policy, the management of income and spending. We are all familiar with such fiscal policy from our own experience with the economics of personal and family life. So this narrow, limited, public discussion appears to express eminent good sense. But, beyond our awareness, and almost entirely excluded from public discussion, is the enormously powerful dynamic of monetary policy which goes far beyond mere fiscal policy. This is our primary concern here. But before I move into this crucial area, let me first mention that the economics of our public life, the economics of government, even in the limited area of fiscal policy, are radically different from family or business economics. When in the family or in business we run up burdensome debts, it is sensible and effective to cut spending. But it is not so straightforward a matter in our public life. When a government lays off public servants, it saves paying their salaries, but it loses the taxes they pay, and also the taxes of others who are no longer supported by their spending. The whole economy is driven down. Conversely if a government hires new employees, it receives their tax payments and the taxes of the others whom their spending supports. But even an enlightened and just government fiscal policy is woefully inadequate for meeting public needs. Even more crucial is monetary policy which could be reformed to overcome our problems with debt. So let us proceed to explore, in a non-technical way, the dynamics of our little-understood money system.

What is Money?

We are all well aware that money has always been a medium of exchange, a means for facilitating economic activity far more conveniently and efficiently than is possible through barter of goods and services. We are generally not sufficiently aware that modern money systems, with good reason, are no longer connected with gold or silver, or with any other specific commodity. Much past human experience has proven that attempts to connect money with some commodity, such as gold, whether directly through gold coins or indirectly by backing paper money with the promise to pay gold on demand, fail to provide a reliable medium of exchange. The value of gold or other commodities fluctuates too frequently to provide for a stable money supply, and can be too easily manipulated to our disadvantage by banks and speculators. Moreover, with growing global populations and expanding economic activity, supplies of gold cannot keep pace with needs for new money.

We are all familiar with cash, the paper bills and metal coins that are printed or minted by governments, and that we can carry for use in small-scale everyday transactions. The materials which governments use for manufacturing cash are worth much less than the money values that they represent. Cash, however, is only a small portion of the total money stock—well under 5% in most nations. We are also familiar with the fact that a far greater volume of economic activity, especially large-scale transactions, has long taken place through the use of cheques, by which people assign to others money that they have deposited in banks. In recent years, the use of cheques has been supplemented by electronic transfers, and by the use of credit cards and debit cards, further reducing the need for cash.

Almost all the huge volume of money transactions around the world takes place through banks. It is possible for people to carry on economic activity using only cash without ever making any use of banks, and this is undoubtedly the case with a vast number of desperately poor people, when they have access to cash at all. But people even of very modest means who receive or write cheques or who use credit or debit cards must necessarily work through banks. Their money is safer if deposited with banks, of course, and banks allow clients to withdraw cash even from deposits that have been made in the form of cheques. With a recognition of the small proportion of our money supply represented by cash, and of the dominant role that banks play in our money systems, a modicum of reflection makes us aware that most of our money supply now consists of records in computers controlled by banks. As bank clients, we usually have access to duplicate records printed out on paper. The question thus arises: Whence all this non-cash, computer-entry money, which can be exchanged through writing cheques and also through instructions conveyed by computers? What is the source of our money supply? This is a really crucial question.

The surprising answer is at the crux of what we need to know about our money system.

Where Does Money Come From?

It is widely assumed that our money supply is provided by national governments. This is not the case. In Western capitalist societies, almost all our money supply—about 97%—is created by privately owned, profit-oriented *commercial banks* in their process of making loans. It is widely assumed that banks lend the money of depositors, and, quite reasonably, profit from the spread between the interest they pay to depositors and the interest they charge borrowers. This also is not the case, and it is important to understand this fact. When a commercial bank has determined that a borrower has provided satisfactory collateral—a home perhaps, or a car—it issues a loan by providing the borrower with a deposit in the amount of the loan. What this means is that the private bank, through the simple act of making an entry in a computer of any desirable size, effectively *creates new money out of nothing*! With their goal of gaining profit, the banks, of course, charge interest on the loans they make. Governments have authorized commercial banks to exercise this extraordinary power, lending at interest money they have created out of nothing, and giving them the right to take over the collateral, the property of the borrower, in case the loan is not repaid.[13]

Is this not an obvious injustice? Privately owned banks, after all, do not lend the hard-earned money of depositors, or even their own hard-earned money. Yet, as soon as they make a loan, they are able to count the money they have, in effect, created *ex nihilo* as *their own*, and thus they are able to demand repayment with interest on that money. When the economy is expanding, the banks create and lend money freely, collecting interest, and when the economy is in decline they take over the collateral of borrowers—as they have recently been ruthlessly doing in the United States, seizing the homes of millions of people. Unlike the rest of us, the banks are in a position to profit whether the economy is expanding or contracting.

Most of us are well aware, from much direct experience, that banks have the power to decide whether they will lend us money, and, in case we are unable to pay them on schedule, they can foreclose on our property. When we recognize in addition, however, that banks create out of nothing the money that they lend, the imbalance of power and its resulting injustices become shockingly obvious.

But this is not the whole story. There are major additional problems arising from our money system with vast implications that remain overlooked and little understood.

[13] See www.positivemoney.org/how-money-works/proof-that-banks-create-money/.

The Far-Reaching Central Problem of Our Current Money System

Here is the fundamental reality, the key dynamic which makes our money system so extremely damaging. *When the banks, in their normal process of making loans, create money out of nothing, they create the principal for their loans, but they do not create the interest that they require to be paid.* Nearly all our money supply, the life-blood of our economy, the money upon which we all depend for our daily economic transactions, has been created as principal for loans, carrying with it the requirement that non-existent money for interest be paid on it. Almost our entire money supply is, therefore, debt-money. This perverse debt-money system has little-recognized, ruinous consequences. These can be enumerated as follows:

1. Competition. Each borrower is forced into competition with all other borrowers, including corporations and governments, to gain control over enough money, which has been created only as principal, in order to make regular loan repayments of both principal and interest. Borrowers must compete not only with each other for this money, but also with other participants in the economy who owe nothing, and who also depend upon this very same limited money supply. Where can borrowers obtain money to pay the interest? Ultimately from further borrowing at further interest—a process that obviously cannot possibly be sustained indefinitely. Without our full awareness, this competition for limited funds can become intense, subtly undermining impulses toward community, charity, and cooperation. Increasingly apparent now, moreover, are growing pressures by powerful corporations and governments to cut the wages of workers, who are now losing ground in this highly competitive power struggle.

2. Inflation. Businesses are often heavily dependent upon borrowing. In order to meet their many expenses, including interest payments as well as pressure to gain profits, they naturally do all they can to push up prices. Where money for interest payments is non-existent, inflationary pressure is driven not by *excessive* money in the economy, but largely by the *scarcity* of money. In so far as they can, workers push back for higher wages. The more inflation occurs, the more all participants in the economy strive to increase their share of income. The lack of money for interest payments is not the only factor here, but it plays a highly significant role in promoting inflation.

3. Recession. Where there is a lack of money available for interest payments, inevitably some borrowers are driven to default on their loans.

As growing numbers of defaults reinforce each other, increasingly cascading downward, recession looms. The banks reinforce this trend. In times of recession, banks decrease their lending, and concentrate on taking over the collateral of borrowers. When better-situated borrowers nevertheless succeed in paying off their loans, the banks take the repaid principal out of existence, and reduce new loans, thus diminishing the amount of money in circulation, and increasing the difficulties of borrowers. Money they receive in interest payments the banks get to keep as their own. But even this money remains part of the debt-money supply for which all money-users compete. Economists frequently refer to the "business cycle," which they see as the normal expansion and contraction of capitalist economies, but they fail to explain that it is *our debt-money system* which makes this cycle inevitable.

4. *Inequality.* As the banks collect interest payments on money originally created only as principal, and as they foreclose on the property of delinquent borrowers, wealth becomes increasingly concentrated in the hands of a privileged few, while many people, those who are more economically vulnerable, are increasingly impoverished. The Occupy Movement brilliantly highlighted the socially debilitating growth of disparities between the obscenely rich and the tragically poor. It would be helpful now if Occupy and other organizations working for social justice and environmental protection would identify and publicize the extent to which this disparity is rooted in our destructive debt-money system.

5. *No Money Without Debt.* In our money system, we cannot pay off our debts without reducing our money supply, for the simple reason that when the principal of loans is repaid, that money goes out of existence. Unless new borrowing then occurs—whether by individuals, or businesses, or governments—new money is not created. The truth is therefore that if we all exercised the virtue of thrift and paid off our debts, there would paradoxically be almost no money left. To put this into political perspective, if the United States government paid off its immense debt ($17.7 trillion at the time of writing), the result would not be financial liberation but devastation of the U.S. economy and much of the global economy as well—no debt, no money. How can austerity be anything but unjust in a system like this?

6. *Unsustainable Growth.* In efforts to meet the relentless, impossibly out-of-reach, interest-payment demands of our money system—which include *compounding* interest, exponentially growing interest demands, rising to impossible heights—both businesses and governments constantly press for unlimited economic growth largely through ever-increasing ex-

ploitation of our environment, essentially ignoring the depredations imposed on our planet's finite environmental life-support systems. While our money system is not the only factor promoting the dream of unlimited economic growth, this overwhelming, ignored problem of endless growth cannot be overcome as long as our present money system prevails, and as long as we are kept in the dark about how it functions. Economic growth will invariably be presented as a key solution to economic difficulties that arise from our debt-money system. Moreover, wealthy economic interests, including the most powerful banks, will continue to invest huge sums in highly destructive exploitation of environmental resources, as for example, in the Alberta tar sands, in ever more devastating weapons for war, and in the most ruthless form of environmental destruction of all—war itself.

7. Government borrowing. We come now to one of the most shocking, but most readily understandable consequences of our money system. Without having mastered other complexities of our money system, anyone can readily grasp this aspect. Governments in capitalist nations are prone to running huge and growing deficits and debts, and are at the same time forcing austerity upon their citizens, because they borrow from private banks and other money-lenders, and pay them interest. In Canada, for instance, governments at all levels put out some $60 billion each year for interest payments. The United States, at the federal government level alone in fiscal year 2013, made interest payments of $415.7 billion. In fiscal years 1988 through 2013, the U.S. government spent a staggering $8.7 *trillion* on interest payments (www.treasurydirect.gov). At present, interest rates are unusually low. When or if Western economies start to expand, however, our central banks will surely push interest rates up, allegedly to fight inflation, and even without higher debts, interest payments could rise rapidly. Here, however, is the startling reality: Such immense interest payments are *not necessary*! Just as private banks, with authorization from the very governments which are paying them interest, can create money out of nothing for lending, so governments themselves can create *interest-free money* out of nothing for public benefit. This urgently needed change is an essential, potent source of hope for the human future.

From Bank-Created Money to Government-Created Money

What emerges from this simple discussion is that the power to create money out of nothing is awesome. The startling fact is that whoever gets to benefit from the first use of newly created money gets something for nothing. The process is essentially the same as that by which counterfeiters print and successfully pass off cash. The question that arises is why, at the end of the day, we ought to trust commercial banks to exercise on a massive scale this same power. Counterfeiters have to cope with disadvantages, of course, that the banks avoid. They face difficult challenges in preparing convincing facsimiles of modern cash, and they run the risk of being caught and punished. Commercial banks, on the other hand, can legally, with the ease of making a computer entry, create any desired quantity of money. It is not an immense stretch to say that our banks can access money more easily than it could be picked off trees. People frequently say, "There is no such thing as a free lunch." Few have any idea what vast, endless "free lunches" are available to commercial banks.

Who, we need to ask at this point, *ought* to benefit from the power to create new money? From an ethical perspective it is clear who *should* benefit, is it not? Money is needed by all of us in order to facilitate economic activity. The need for money arises from the entire community. Therefore ought we not *all* to share appropriately in the benefit available from newly created money? The problem is not the sheer fact that money is created out of nothing. The problem arises from who benefits. It is fundamental to the cause of monetary reform to insist that the process of money creation should be brought under democratic control, so as to improve the lot of the many rather than of the few. It is entirely possible for our governments, who are, after all, elected by citizens, to take over at least in part, if not in full, the power to create money, and to use it for public benefit. Indeed, it has been said that this is the most powerful of all the economic tools available to governments. Furthermore, it is crucial to realize that, even in the *recent* past, governments have exercised this power on behalf of citizens, and they could do so again.

Strategic, progressive tax policy is, of course, also a powerful instrument for good, and is especially needed now to reduce the disparities between rich and poor. But even high taxes on the rich do not compensate adequately for the destructive impact of our debt-money system which functions largely beyond the tax system. We urgently need the remedy of government-created money. Not only could the destructive dynamics of our present money system be overcome in this way, but also with it, enormous transformative opportunities would become available. Through creating their own interest-free money, governments could avoid austerity measures, could rebuild decaying infrastructure, could maintain and improve valuable social programs, could create good full-time employment, could eliminate poverty, and could invest in restoring our environment, while at the same time steadily reducing government debts.

In the case of infrastructure, it would be especially appropriate for interest-free money to be lent to all levels of government as needed. At present, governments borrow at interest for such projects, and pay for them two or three times over. Interest-free loans would make it possible for them to pay for the projects just once out of tax income over the lifetime of each project—perhaps 30 to 50 years. This would free large amounts of tax funds for current program spending.

There is another astonishing possibility. When additional new money is needed in the economy, as in the present Great Recession, governments could simply spend money into existence as a free benefit for public use. Whether government-created money is spent or lent into existence, these measures put debt-free money into the economy, making possible great reductions of the far-reaching problems resulting from our present destructive debt-money system.

These possibilities are not simply a matter of hypothetical speculation. Between 1938 and 1974, the publicly owned Bank of Canada was used to create, essentially interest-free, a large proportion of the money in the Canadian economy. This policy played a key role in getting Canada out of the Great Depression and through World War II. It was also then used, rather remarkably, to build up infrastructure and social programs during some thirty post-war years, bringing with it the most prosperous period in Canadian history. The Canadian federal government, yielding to intense pressure from the banks, after 1974 quietly but steadily, behind the scenes, reduced its beneficial use of the Bank of Canada, and borrowed increasingly at interest from private banks and other private money-lenders, making it necessary also for provincial and municipal governments to do the same. Canadians live with the result now, in high annual interest payments on government debt, and in various jurisdictions the painful effects of an austerity agenda. They could, however, return to using the Bank of Canada for its originally mandated purpose of creating money for public benefit.

Whether the context is Canada or abroad, making use of government-created money could provide enormous financial resources for environmental protection and restoration, making possible constructive progress towards the hitherto "impossible" goals of reversing global warming, saving endangered species, promoting locally supported organic agriculture, enabling reforestation, conserving soil, deploying environmentally benign energy systems, cleaning up pollution, and much more. Ambitious initiatives never considered before could be made financially possible. Both social and environmental welfare measures could be funded abundantly. It should be noted that social justice and environmental improvement need to go together. Situations where people are desperately poor, while the rich focus on their own benefit and ignore the poor, or give attention to repressive measures to keep the poor under control, are far from conducive to a proper concern for our stunningly beautiful, incredibly complex, life-supporting, planetary ecological system.

But how about the fact, the possibility, the problem, that the sort of economy visualized here, with abundant government-created money stimulating new economic activity, could bring unsustainable economic growth in our finite ecological system? The work of monetary reform must include attention to developing the sort of economic growth that would protect, preserve, and improve our environment rather than degrading it. Let us be clear that shifting from a debt-money system to a debt-free money system would by no means automatically guarantee that government spending would be designated for social or environmental welfare. Having money creation under government control is not, then, a panacea. While monetary policy reform is a *necessary* condition for most of the entire range of social problems we face, it is not a *sufficient* condition. Far-reaching desirable changes would be made possible, but a profound public commitment to benevolent social and environmental ends would be required for them to be implemented. There is already available from the work of many civil society organizations and universities rich information about the work that needs to be done. Monetary reform could finance this work. But the spending must be wisely allocated, and the commitment to do so must be mandated by a committed and aroused public. This would, crucially, require a much more effective democracy than we now have. Any campaign for the sort of monetary reform advocated here is a struggle for the democratization of our money system, and such a campaign would have to be integrated with the wider struggle for greater democracy.

The obstacles against monetary change are enormous. Intense, even ferocious resistance would certainly come from the global banking system which understands full well that its enormous power is concentrated in its monopoly over the creation of money out of nothing. There is a centuries-long, sordid history of struggle by bankers against any government attempts to control money-creation for public benefit. The banks have it easy right now. They can present themselves as kindly and helpful, despite all their recent crimes, because we, the people, have so little understanding of how they really operate. These days, all they have to do in response to any suggestion for the sort of monetary reform we call for is to say that it would be inflationary. They remind us of the hyperinflation in Germany during the 1920s, and speak contemptuously of governments' madly "printing" huge quantities of inflationary money. Almost everybody falls for this, and thus the argument ends. Therefore money reformers—hopefully all of us—need to be prepared to refute these claims. So just a few final comments in response could be useful.

The Inflation Issue

We need to recognize that it is indeed possible for governments creating their own money to produce too much, thus causing inflation. We need to be fully aware of this, and to recognize the dangers, but first we need to emphasize how damaging our *current* bank-created debt-money itself has long been. It has, after all, its own record of promoting steady, on-going inflation. Inflationary pressures are built into its very genes. It is a startling fact about our current system that on average about 40% of the price of all the goods in our society is the result of accumulating interest expenses. This is a potent inflationary pressure that could be reduced if interest-free money became available.[14]

There is, in fact, evidence to indicate that when governments have controlled their own money-creation, they have managed their economies with very little inflation, as Canada did, for instance, between 1938 and 1974. The record shows that hyperinflations, including even that of Germany after World War I, were not driven by government irresponsibility, but by wealthy speculators, including private banks, manipulating national currencies to their own advantage.[15] The circumstances of Germany in the context of the impossible conditions imposed by the Treaty of Versailles are in any case exceptional, and can scarcely constitute an argument against the democratization of monetary policy under normal political and economic circumstances.

The task of monetary reform must nevertheless include arrangements for managing the money system to prevent either inflation or deflation.

---

[14] See Margrit Kennedy, "A Changing Money System," www.converge.org.nz/evenz/money.pdf, as recommended by Ellen Brown in "Time for an Economic Bill of Rights," Nov. 9, 2011 on her website, http://ellenbrown.com/.

[15] Ellen Brown, *The Web of Debt* (Baton Rouge, LA: Third Millennium Press, 2008), 237-247.

The National Emergency Employment Defense Act (NEEDACT) introduced into the United States Congress by Representative Dennis Kucinich in 2011 (based on the work of the American Monetary Institute headed by Stephen Zarlenga) proposed a Monetary Authority, charged with responsible management of the money supply. Public-spirited experts would be needed to bear this responsibility. But we must also fully expect that banking interests would inevitably strive mightily to gain control of such an agency, so as to use it for private benefit rather than the public good. In order to prevent such a travesty, we would need a public well informed about the issues at stake, not only to bring about monetary reform, but also to remain on guard to protect a democratically controlled money system—much as in Canada or the United Kingdom, for instance, an engaged public guards its public medical system. And we need our trusted civil society organizations, which have long been working devotedly across the entire range of social and environmental issues, to recognize the urgent need for monetary reform, and to include, as a key part of their mandate, the promotion and maintenance of a benevolent, government-operated money system.

Implications for Public Theology

Those who work in the area of public theology take on, among other things, the responsibility of publicizing injustices and calling for needed social change. This is a key educational task, and some people legitimately specialize in this area. But obviously education is not enough. The work of public theology needs to extend to campaigning for the needed changes.

In Canada the needed change in the routine workings of our money system is clear. We still have a publicly owned central bank, the Bank of Canada. Established in 1934, it was nationalized in 1938 under the leadership of Prime Minister William Lyon Mackenzie King, who summed up the issues at stake in 1935 in a radio address by saying:

> Once a nation parts with the control of its currency and credit, it matters not who makes that nation's laws. Usury, once in control, will wreck any nation. Until the control of the issue of currency and credit is restored to government and recognized as its most conspicuous and sacred responsibility, all talk of the sovereignty of Parliament and of democracy is idle and futile.

The reference to "usury" is striking: can one imagine that present political leadership would be so bold or so visionary in view of the challenges we face? Before nationalization of the Bank of Canada in 1938, however,

Canada had indeed experienced the dire circumstances described by King, and unfortunately, as the Bank of Canada's original mandate was gradually abandoned, Canadians have experienced the same sort of consequences once more. They thus need to recall and to affirm their own remarkable history of having used the Bank of Canada so successfully for public benefit between 1938 and 1974. Canada needs a movement to restore the Bank of Canada to its original mandate.

After it had become apparent that the Bank of Canada was becoming increasingly misused, a group of activists, including economists, in 1986 founded the Committee on Monetary and Economic Reform (COMER, www.comer.org), which has been working steadily for a return to the original mandate of the Bank of Canada. In 2011, COMER brought a lawsuit against the federal government of Canada to achieve that goal. This lawsuit, a remarkable effort for a small voluntary association, is on-going. But overall, COMER has had only limited impact, and is unlikely to be successful without much more substantial support from the public at large and from the great array of activist organizations that would all benefit from the government funding that could be provided through monetary reform.

Canadians who work from the perspective of public theology with concern for monetary reform need, I would suggest, to make common cause with COMER. Eleven church groups in Canada support KAIROS as their organization concentrating on work for social justice. My suggestion would be that they commission KAIROS to take on the monetary issue. This would be a significant step toward inducing the whole range of social justice and environmental organizations in Canada, including labour, to pressure for the monetary reform which could benefit all their various causes.

In the United States also, the American Monetary Institute (AMI), mentioned above, has been working for monetary reform at the federal level. Given the fact that the U.S. central bank, the Federal Reserve, is owned by a consortium of major privately owned banks, the task taken on by the AMI appears insurmountably difficult. The Public Banking Institute, founded by Ellen Brown, has taken a different tack. It has generated considerable momentum in its work to establish public banks at the state and local level. In the United Kingdom, Positive Money (www.positivemoney.org) under the dynamic leadership of Ben Dyson, is also campaigning hard for monetary reform. Opportunities for public theology to support work for monetary reform abound.

Conclusion

It is especially appropriate for public theology to deal with the dynamics of money systems, recognizing their capacities for ill and for good. The most basic sources for public theology in the biblical tradition focus heavily on the oppressive consequences of unrelieved debt, and on the urgent need for prohibition of interest-taking, and for periodic cancellation of debt. This tradition is especially relevant for our own day because our current money system immerses us in debt with widespread, ongoing, damaging consequences, as has been explained above. The dynamics of our debt-money system are less readily understandable, and therefore more insidious than the workings of money systems in biblical times. However, our current system has its own forms of debt-bondage—consider, for example, the oppressive burden of student debt. Except for the unattractive option of bankruptcy, the biblical solution of direct debt cancellation is not available to us. But monetary reform is available to us, through a movement that leads to shifting power to create money out of nothing from private banks to institutions under public control, for public benefit. This has creative possibilities that exceed mere debt cancellation. So potentially catastrophic are the dangers of another financial meltdown comparable to that of 2008, and so far-reaching are the potential benefits from changes in our present money system, that work in the area of monetary reform provides, I suggest, a worthy challenge for public theology.

CHAPTER SIX

THE TWILIGHT OF NEOLIBERALISM: OPPORTUNITY FOR A NEW CHRISTIAN LEFT?

BILL BLAIKIE[1]

Inequality is the Issue

In talking about a twilight for neoliberalism, I first feel compelled to begin with an acknowledgment of Michael Harrington, the great American democratic socialist, who wrote a book called *The Twilight of Capitalism*.[2] The particular risk that I run here is that of hoping that the "twilight" to which I am referring proves more real, or at least more immediate, than it did in the case of Harrington. For ironically, Harrington published this book in 1977, just before capitalism launched itself into a whole new phase of global expansion. Subsequent history has been characterized by unprecedented free market fundamentalism and a form of ideological triumphalism that has seemed for a while to leave all historic and contemporary critiques in its wake.

I would also note, without extensive commentary, that Harrington, who started out in the Catholic worker movement but later became an atheist, wrote another book just a few years later entitled, *The Politics at God's Funeral*,[3] in which, despite the insightfulness of much of the book, he got the future badly wrong. In 1983, the continuing relevance and intensity of

---

[1] Bill Blaikie, is a United Church of Canada Minister and a retired Canadian politician. Having served as a New Democratic Party Member of Parliament for Winnipeg Elmwood for 29 years (1979-2008), Blaikie is something of a fixture in Canadian pubic life. He is presently Director of the Knowles-Woodsworth Centre for Theology and Public Policy at the University of Winnipeg.

[2] Michael Harrington, *The Twilight of Capitalism* (New York: Simon and Schuster, 1976).

[3] Michael Harrington, *The Politics at God's Funeral: The Spiritual Crisis of Western Civilization* (New York: Holt, Rinehart, and Winston, 1983).

religion's role in the world of the 21st Century would have been hard to discern, especially among those who may have subscribed to the secular narrative about religion's impending disappearance.

My goal in this essay is, nonetheless, to speculate on what objective conditions may now exist for exposing the idolatry of the last thirty-five years, and returning to a more critical view of capitalism, on the part of citizens in general—and more specifically, on the part of the Christian community. It is basic to my argument that the financial crisis of 2008 in itself was not enough, or to be more precise, that it was not the objective condition for this change of mind, even though it was certainly a combination of the neoliberal ethos and whatever more ordinary ethical lapses may have combined on that occasion to produce it. The on-going objective condition required, rather, a condition, which preceded and now supersedes the financial crisis, is the reality of growing economic inequality. This is an inequality made all the more egregious, no doubt, by the way that citizens have been unequally called upon to save the powerful from their own market excesses, when no such urgency as yet attaches to the plight and solvency of those at the other end of the income scale. It is this question of inequality that I will refer to primarily in what follows.

The intransigence of ever-growing inequality, within countries and between countries, converges with the limits to globalization, the collapse of the Washington Consensus imposed on so many countries, along with limits to other factors which have helped to mask the ultimate frailty of the neoliberal model as a guide to human flourishing. To this would have to be added the growing identification of capitalism in the free trade era with our inability to save ourselves from the worst aspects of climate change, as Naomi Klein argues extensively in her new book, *This Changes Everything: Capitalism vs. the Climate*.[4]

In this convergence, I believe, there may be a new opening for the left in general and for the Christian left in particular. The opportunity thus presented, however, also represents a challenge. For even those who have, at times, questioned the dominance of the neoliberal paradigm of the past forty years have, very often, shared enough elements of the paradigm as to confuse the issue. Thus there needs to be a willingness to probe a bit more honestly into how even those who have publicly opposed what has happened during this time, have nevertheless also supported it in crucial re-

[4] Naomi Klein, *This Changes Everything: Capitalism vs. the Climate* (New York: Simon & Schuster), 2014.

spects. The job of transcending the paradigm will be a challenge for everyone, including those of us on the left, instead of just the usual culprits.

The Idolatry of the Market

It has been a time of great idolatry, as so many were led to believe that the market was not a human creation, but a force unto itself that should be respected and left to its own devices, in a way that even Adam Smith might find questionable. As Cambridge Professor Ha-Joon Chang says in his recent book, *23 Things They Don't Tell you About Capitalism*[5]:

> The free market doesn't exist. Every market has some rules and boundaries that restrict freedom of choice. A market looks free only because we so unconditionally accept its underlying restrictions that we fail to see them. How 'free' a market is cannot be objectively defined. It is a political definition.

Yet, as Chang also points out, neatly summarizing the experience of someone like myself who practiced left-wing politics for thirty-two of the years we are talking about:

> So, when free market economists say that a certain regulation should not be introduced because it would restrict the freedom of a certain market, they are merely expressing a political opinion that they reject the rights that are to be defended by the proposed law. Their ideological cloak is to pretend that their politics is not really political, but rather is an objective economic truth, while other people's politics is political. However, they are as politically motivated as their opponents. Breaking away from the illusion of market objectivity is the first step towards understanding capitalism.[6]

In my view, the way the market was objectified and elevated, from one false god among many in the human political pantheon that it used to be, to the preeminent false god of the neoliberal era of globalization and free trade, as if the market existed and acted outside of our collective acquiescence to it, or worship of it, as the case may be, is an open and shut case of idolatry. It represented a false image of what it means to be human, graven on the face of our understanding of political economy, and it fostered and promoted a false image of competition as the law that rules humanity instead of the laws of love and justice, which we find witnessed to in the biblical tradition.

---

[5] Ha-Joon Chang, *23 Things They Don't Tell You about Capitalism* (New York: Bloomsbury Press, 2011), p. 1.
[6] Ibid., pp. 1-2.

To use the language of "idolatry" at this point may seem to some to be excessive, but I contend that it is very illuminating. The very nature of idolatry involves humans granting god-like status or powers to something that they themselves have created, and forgetting that those supposedly god-like powers are not independent or objective, but rather, derive from the powers humans themselves grant. When we deny our own participation in reality, in this case, when we treat the market as if it is not a human creation, we are engaging in idolatrous behaviour. Some would act as if the market cannot be changed, modified, regulated, or even eliminated where necessary in some sectors of our life, as we did with health care through Medicare. When we act in this way we are forgetting that it is we ourselves who melted the gold to make this particular golden calf, or if not we ourselves, then those whom we and our neighbours have chosen to elect. For the irony, of course, is that this world in which we are said to have no choice but the market, has been the deliberate and preferred choice of those who sought to create the political environment of recent decades.

This is most obviously seen in the events and circumstances that led to the beginning of the period we are talking about, in the election of Ronald Reagan in the United States, and of Margaret Thatcher in the United Kingdom. What began with them, however, ultimately morphed into a global capitalist phenomenon that was enhanced by the collapse of the communist world, and the subsequent triumphalist ideological conclusions drawn about free market capitalism. This has subsequently been enhanced by the participation in the same system, for a while at any rate, by post-Soviet Russia, a Communist run state capitalist China, and also by the abject surrender of most of those on the liberal-left of the political spectrum in the traditionally democratic West. World leaders like Clinton and Blair, and in Canada, Jean Chrétien, refused to stand up to the corporate elite who were enjoying their new opportunities, as one analyst put it, "to use the integrating world economy in order to slip the leash of social regulation" that had been built up in the "golden age of capitalism" from 1945 to 1973.[7]

The last thirty years have been an occasion for idolatry, but not surprisingly, have also been a time of growing injustice. The injustice I am referring to is the injustice of greater and greater inequality, a radical ine-

[7] Jeff Faux, *The Global Class War: How America's Bipartisan Elite Lost Our Future - and What It Will Take to Win It Back* (Hoboken, N.J.: John Wiley & Sons, 2010), ch. 4.

quality. Jim Wallis of the Sojourner's Christian community in Washington D.C. talks about extreme inequality in his latest book, *On God's Side*.[8] The book title refers to the fact that in the arena of faith and politics, too much effort often goes into arguments about whose political side God is on, and not enough effort or reflection is devoted into figuring out how to actually be on God's side.

In any event, the general direction taken in the biblical tradition is clear. God does take sides, the side of the poor and powerless, and the wrath of the prophets is often directed at those who enjoy the inequality of their riches while ignoring the needs of the vulnerable at the other end of the inequality graph. One of the earliest of such prophets was of course Amos, who according to biblical scholar Walter Brueggemann, protested against the self-indulgent economy of the urban elites.[9] Those who oppress the poor and crush the needy are promised by Amos that the time will come when they will be taken away with hooks, as indeed they were a generation later when the Assyrians took them into exile. Unlike those who confuse being prophetic with prophesying, I will not speculate as to who the Assyrians in our time will be!

Of course, it is not just that so-called free markets create, accumulate, and exaggerate levels of inequality, as Thomas Piketty from the Paris School of Economics has argued exhaustively in his recent massive book, *Capital in the 21st Century*.[10] That would be bad enough, and I will talk more about this aspect of the matter shortly. What is worse is that the ideology of free markets has also involved a comprehensively reductionist way of thinking about life that should be of concern to all of us. The idea of the market, which is an abstraction that used to know its place, and that used to be kept in its place, has become so comprehensive and ubiquitous that it threatens to crowd out and supplant all other ways of thinking about what it means to be human and to be a fully human community.

In other words, markets are one thing, and still debatable as to their appropriate scope and nature, but the marketization of reality, and the *a priori* presumption in favour of the market approach is quite another. Many would argue that the market mentality subversively but inexorably

---

[8] Jim Wallis, *On God's Side: What Religion Forgets and Politics Hasn't Learned about Serving the Common Good* (Grand Rapids: Brazos Press, 2013).

[9] Walter Brueggemann, "Amos' Intercessory Formula," *Vetus Testamentum* (XIX, 1969): 385-99.

[10] Thomas Piketty, *Capital in the Twenty-first Century*, trans. Arthur Goldhammer (Cambridge, Mass.: Belknap Press, 2014).

eats away at the moral framework that is so necessary to healthy relationships in families, communities, and between individuals. Following the prophet Amos, and Walter Brueggemann, we might well say that the power of empire in our day, deeply committed as it is to a market ideology in which there is no sustaining social fabric, offers to humans only a dehumanizing competition for goods. In this sense, Margaret Thatcher's famous statement that there is "no such thing as society" is a self-fulfilling effect of the neoliberal ideology. You cannot preserve, or now rebuild, what you don't think is even there.

As John Kenneth Galbraith said in one of his final books, *A Journey through Economic Time*,[11] the time we are talking about was not a matter of unsuccessful policy, or unintended consequences. He cites Ronald Reagan as an example of someone who had a clear policy that accomplished in large part what it set out to do, which was to eliminate internal and external threats to the ongoing economic security and accumulating prosperity of what Galbraith called "the comfortably rewarded," right up to the "admittedly rich." A key domestic threat was the power of taxation, particularly progressive taxation, and the possibility that it might be used on behalf of those outside the favoured community. Galbraith characterizes Reagan's policy as one in which the poor were, to the greatest extent possible, removed from the public conscience. The policy implication was that taxation on behalf of the poor should be banned, and taxation of the rich should be decreased (not to mention that unions should be busted, or put on notice). But of course, you cannot actually run for office on an official platform of favouring the rich and being against the poor, so no end of other arguments have to be generated, from stimulating the economy and innovation, to making much of certain academic theories divorced from the human realities of their consequences, foremost among them being from the Chicago school of economics led by Milton Friedman.

The Irony and Incoherence of Free Market Idolatry

Needless to say, throughout this period there has been a persistent, deadly irony: the rich have needed to be rich in order to be motivated, while also, of course, the poor have equally needed to stay poor in order for them also and equally to be motivated. The ideology of the unfettered marketplace thus provided the context in which the rich could grow richer without having to answer for the poor getting poorer.

---

[11] John Kenneth Galbraith, *A Journey through Economic Time: A Firsthand View* (Boston: Houghton Mifflin, 1994).

Another persistent irony has been the way in which so many Christians, in what has come to be known as the "Religious Right," signed up for the neoliberal political project. From a Christian standpoint, it seems simple to me. Is the market Lord, or is Jesus Lord? If Jesus is Lord, then the market isn't. If Jesus is Lord, then Christians at least have to argue for a way of regarding the market that puts it in its place, that treats it as something purely secondary, as a tool at best, rather than as an end in itself or as a "god" to be served. To put the matter another way: Is humanity made for the economy or is the economy made for humanity? The importance of the question, and of the answer given, has unfortunately been lost on the Religious Right. As Geoff Faux argues in his book *The Global Class War,* the organizing genius of the Republican Party in recent American politics has been to obscure the contradiction between the interests of social conservatives and those of corporate investors. Social conservatives wanted to use government to restrict the ability of people to pursue their hedonistic instincts, and instead to foster moral and religious "purity." Corporate investors, on the other hand, wanted government to create conditions under which precisely the same hedonistic instincts could be stimulated and commercialized. The two opposing value systems were compartmentalized, and in the ensuing mix, social conservatives brought energy and votes to Republican candidates, while the corporations and investors brought the money. And, you might say, the concoction was all washed down with a generous swig of hostility toward an imagined common enemy, the so-called "liberal elite." With apologies for another American example of what I mean, because there are Canadian and other international parallels to how the "culture wars" have distorted the class wars, I have found Thomas Frank's observations on Kansas marvellously instructive. As Frank puts it in his book, *What's the Matter with Kansas? How Conservatives Won the Heart of America*:

> When two female rock stars exchange a lascivious kiss on TV, Kansas goes haywire. Kansas screams for the heads of the liberal elite. Kansas comes running to the polls place, and Kansas cuts those rock stars' taxes.[12]

Christians in the social gospel tradition, by contrast, along with strong elements within the social teachings of the Catholic Church, would argue that the economy is itself a moral issue, that radical inequality is a moral issue, that the economy is not independent of God's will for the world, and that, on this basis, and given the gross disparities between rich and poor,

[12] Thomas Frank, *What's the Matter with Kansas? How Conservatives Won the Heart of America* (New York: Metropolitan Books, 2004), p. 249.

the current global order leaves a great deal to be desired. Jesus imagined a different world than the one that was dominant in his time, and to put it mildly, he was not popular with the authorities. The church is called to the same subversive imagining when we are told that the way things are is the only way they can be.

What I am saying is that the church needs to call attention to the fundamental injustices implicit in the global economic order, such as are being fostered by the World Trade Organization. Against the interests of the poor stand various regional and bilateral trade agreements that do not even recognize, let alone enforce core labour standards—while at the same time being very strict about protecting the interests of powerful global corporations. This dichotomy, by which inequality is made normative, represents a perverse moral hierarchy that should be of concern. It ought to be something of concern not just to those who see a challenge in it to the sovereignty of their God, or of their God's justice. It also ought to be a challenge to all those who, whatever their religious beliefs, cherish democracy, and who think that the powers of democratically elected governments to act in the public interest, for the common good, or to preserve the environment, should not be impeded by a corporate bill of rights that supersedes all other considerations. We cannot be content with an economic order designed to put so much money in the hands of the few that the very idea of democracy is mocked.

Even as I write, negotiations have concluded a further erosion of the ability of governments to act in the public interest, in the context of a proposed trade deal between Canada and the European Union that promises once again to privilege the profit strategies of (this time) European multinational corporations over government policies designed for the benefit of Canadians. Neither Canadian citizens nor Canadian Christians should be silent in face of these attempts to institutionalize the neoliberal order.

Radical Inequality

Turning now more explicitly to the issue of growing inequality—indeed, radical inequality—it should come as no surprise that to the extent that inequality is a measure or indicator of injustice, a time of great idolatry has also been a time when inequality has grown in leaps and bounds. But in Canada we now have a deliberate policy-driven lack of clarity about the reality of the lives of low-income Canadians. The worst fears of those who opposed the elimination of the compulsory long form census by the current Conservative government were realized last year with the release of the voluntary National Household Survey—a survey in which both the poor, and what the *Globe and Mail* called the "super rich," are known to be less likely to respond. Without comprehensive statistical information, based on survey results that could be compared to former surveys, we find ourselves placed by neoliberal policy in the position of conveniently lacking evidence about the problem of inequality. Is it not a grand coincidence that it is now impossible to tell, as a Canadian social analyst, whether the poor in this country are getting poorer? What data collection remains is far more fragmentary than what used to be provided by the compulsory census. Nevertheless, some data can still be parsed, as demonstrated by a recent report on wealth distribution in Canada by the Broadbent Institute that is based on Statistics Canada data. I will refer to this report shortly.

Despite this recent strategy of neoliberalism in its Canadian form to obfuscate and deny, the evidence had already accumulated. After only two decades of the three I am talking about, a major study by the Toronto Centre for Social Justice called attention to the inequalities that were already present by that time, as a result of the corporate backlash against the growing equality that had been characteristic of the post-war era, referred to sometimes as the Golden Age of capitalism, between 1945 and 1973. Similarly, in 2011, a Conference Board of Canada study showed that from 1980 to 2005, the earnings of the top twenty percent of the population in income distribution rose by 16.4%, that middle-income Canadians' incomes had stagnated, and that earnings for those in the bottom group had slid. Jim Stanford, for years the chief economist for the Canadian Auto Workers Union and subsequently for the newly formed UNIFOR, points out by contrast in his book *Economics for Everyone—A Short Guide to the Economics of Capitalism*, that the income share of the richest one percent in Canada declined steadily during the post-war golden age, only to recover dramatically since 1980.[13]

An American study conducted around the same time showed that the richest one percent in the U.S. had almost tripled their share of national income since 1978, taking two-thirds of the income gains generated in the whole economy lasting the previous decade. The top twenty-five hedge fund managers made one billion dollars *each* in 2009, which is precisely when millions of ordinary folk were losing their jobs and homes. In 1980, the average CEO in America made forty-two times the average income. By 2004 that has increased to four hundred and fifty-eight times the aver-

[13] Jim Stanford and Tony Biddle, *Economics for Everyone: A Short Guide to the Economics of Capitalism* (London: Pluto Press, 2008), p. 165.

age income. In Canada today, the richest one percent, which is less than 250,000 tax filers, capture some 17% of total Canadian income. At least their share has only doubled since the more egalitarian 1970s. But then, Canadian tax laws make it easier to hide income in offshore accounts than American law does, so who knows what the real picture is?

What we do know is that bonuses at the big six Canadian banks reached 8.9 billion dollars in 2010, the highest ever. As documented by the Canadian Centre For Policy Alternatives, the typical Canadian CEO makes as much by 2:30 pm on January 3rd as the average worker makes all year. Yet the rhetoric heard in political debate is often about the inappropriate desire of those with long-established, well-paid but still modestly paid jobs not to be "kicked down the ladder" by concession bargaining, anti-union activity, and hostility to the idea of a living wage. Or again, we hear much about the burden on the taxpayer of unionized public employees who want to maintain their standard of living, and very little about the unwillingness of governments to collect the revenues needed to have decent cities and decent jobs for those who work for those cities.

The Canadian Centre For Policy Alternatives has done research which shows that the poorest ten percent of family units have experienced a 28% decline in wealth in the past twenty years, while in that same period the top ten percent have experienced an increase of 122% in wealth. A recent report by Oxfam claims that the richest *85 people* in the world own more than the approximately 3.5 billion people who make up the bottom half of the global population. And very recently, the Broadbent Institute here in Canada published a study which showed that the wealthiest ten percent own almost half of all the wealth in Canada, with the bottom thirty percent owning less than 1%. Perhaps the use of the concept, the 1%, employed by the Occupy Movement, could have other uses in the inequality narrative. During the heyday of the Occupy Movement, I recall the Archbishop of York saying with respect to the encampment at St. Paul's Cathedral, and what he called the scandalously unfair society created by excesses in the financial sector, that, "It is hard to imagine a more powerful way of CEOs telling someone they are of little value than to pay them one-third of one percent of your salary."[14]

Study after study, then, shows the same reality, with no promise of change absent a significant political shift either back or forwards to at least

[14] John Sentamu, "Archbishop's Call to Re-establish a Fairer Society," April 5, 2011, at http://www.archbishopofyork.org/articles.php/2238/archbishops-call-to-re-establish-a-fairer-society.

some of the features of the golden age of capitalism. Yet this seems almost an insurmountable task in the context of what Robert Reich has called "supercapitalism," in his book of the same name.[15] Reich, an economist who served as Bill Clinton's Secretary of Labor, argues that supercapitalism has replaced what he calls the democratic capitalism of the golden age. In his view, despite what might have been thought by some at the time, we did have a planned economy, planned by a corporate elite that was less internally competitive, and given to a style of management that saw executives as people who were expected to be somewhat statesmanlike in their balancing of the interests of all stakeholders, and not just shareholders. The fruits of prosperity were to be broadly shared, as a matter of deliberate and intentional policy.

Reich argues that, starting in the 1970s, a combination of innovation, technological change, focus on shareholder value, and later, globalization, brought on an era of stiffer markets and an atmosphere of corporate competition that set loose an army of lobbyists, determined to change the established rules in favour of their various clients. With housing being the obvious exception, prices could not rise in such a competitive environment, and so costs had to go down, as he says, "[sucking] relative equality and stability as well as other social values out of the system."[16] Meantime, the new worldwide supply chains introduced by globalization mean that despite appearances to the contrary, formerly well paid North Americans and Europeans compete not with foreign companies, but with companies from their own country operating elsewhere to take advantage of primitive regulations, low taxes, and cheap labour.

The more interesting argument that Reich makes is that all these structural changes have resulted in a shift in consciousness that has seen our identity as citizens eroded in favour of our identity as investors and consumers, as we monitor our own stake in the stock market, or as more and more of us become unwilling stakeholders through the conversion of pension plans to defined contribution plans rather than defined benefit plans—all the while uncritically enjoying the low prices at Wal-Mart brought to us by low non-union wages at home and abroad.[17] All of this renders us even more personally and unambiguously powerless than we might otherwise be, even as the money generated by supercapitalism overwhelms our de-

---

[15] Robert B. Reich, *Supercapitalism: The Transformation of Business, Democracy, and Everyday Life* (New York: Vintage Books, 2007).

[16] Ibid., p. 51.

[17] Ibid., p. 101.

mocracies. Just and unjust causes are all rendered morally equivalent by being reduced in the political conversation to interests or interest groups, when it is clear that corporate lobbying vastly supersedes the capacity of labour, environmental, civil, and church groups to mount a similar presence in the corridors of power.

Reich's argument is part of a larger argument that I touched upon briefly in my own book, when I noted one of the philosophical ironies of the last thirty years.[18] For this has been a time in which the left has been winning the culture wars, whereas the right has won the economic battles—with both drawing on and partaking in their own way of an expanded liberal, individualist, or autonomous view of human life, in which personal choice is increasingly exercised over values in the one, and exercised also in the consumption of products and services in the other. The peculiar relationship between these two poles is articulated well in a comment by Stanley Hauerwas[19] on the work of philosopher Alasdair MacIntyre, wherein he observes that, "The conservative commitment to a way of life structured by a free market results in an individualism, and in particular a moral psychology, that is as antithetical to the tradition of the virtues as is liberalism."

The individualist ethos referred to above, when reduced to or integrated into a larger culture of the primacy of choice, may clash with what Hauerwas refers to as the virtues, but it also increasingly clashes with elements of good public policy making, as choice itself becomes the policy pinnacle rather than any particular choice or outcome. The Canadian philosopher George Grant saw this when he lamented before the neoliberal era even, the way in which the question of what is a right comes to precede the question of what is the good,[20] as did Charles Taylor, in *The Malaise of Modernity*, when he talked about the need for a moral horizon in a world where the freedom to choose can become a freedom without content.[21] All this, I suggest, is still relevant in a morally pluralistic culture in which normative language is thought suspect, as judgmental and intolerant—which of course it sometimes is, but not always inappropriately so.

---

[18] Bill Blaikie, *The Blaikie Report: An Insider's Look At Faith And Politics* (Toronto: United Church Publishing House, 2011), pp. 23ff.

[19] Stanley Hauerwas, *Working with Words: On Learning to Speak Christian* (Eugene, OR.: Cascade Books, 2011), p. 210.

[20] George Grant, *Technology and Empire: Perspectives on North America* (New York: House of Anansi Press, 2011).

[21] Charles Taylor, *The Malaise of Modernity* (Concord, Ont.: Anansi., 1991).

If, as is claimed by some economists, there is no natural upper limit to the real income of the one percent at the top of the tree, and no natural upper limit to the income gap between them and the rest, then at what point does this become an occasion for rage and political turmoil? At what point does it become an occasion, in particular, for the recovery of *prophetic* rage and for the rediscovery of normative moral language? Radical inequality is not just "unfortunate," or sociologically "interesting." It is an *outrage*, an *offence* against the democratic spirit and the common good. It is a sin against the intentions of God for humanity and for the human community, and it deserves the kind of prophetic energy and denunciation that was mustered in earlier times—not only as in the days of the prophet Amos, but more recently around issues like the Vietnam War and the Civil Rights Movement. Where today are the Berrigans and the Martin Luther Kings to lead people in righteous anger against the way that extreme inequality threatens the solidarity of the human community?

Growing inequality is therefore the "elephant in the room" that political and business leaders have not wanted to name, the scandal that politicians have wanted to hide, and the news from which media barons have sought to deflect attention, but which is now being named and exposed in many other ways. It is even coming to the fore in popular culture, as Rick Smith, the Executive Director of The Broadbent Institute, pointed out in a recent article in the *Toronto Star*.[22] Smith pointed, for instance, to the success of *Hunger Games* books and movies, in which a nightmare society is defined by deep inequality, and he speculated that if this is any indication, there is a genuine pop-cultural fascination with the implications of the gap between the rich and the poor.

Inequality is even being named by those who have long thought it their spiritual duty to defend capitalism from the "atheistic socialist hordes" and their social gospel fellow travellers. Just recently, an article was highlighted even on the conservative Canadian "Cardus Centre" blog, in which one of its senior fellows mused, if not about the incompatibility of Christianity with capitalism in principle, then at least about its incompatibility with contemporary capitalism, and the inequality it is causing. References to the

[22] Rick Smith, "As Inequality Grows, so Does the Will to Fight It," *Toronto Star*, September 11, 2014, Opinion/Commentary sec. http://www.thestar.com/opinion/commentary/2014/09/11/as_inequality_grows_so_does_the_will_to_fight_it.html/.

need for strong unions in the teachings of Pope Leo and the theology of Abraham Kuyper were also found in the piece.[23]

It has always been a mystery to me why so many who raise the "family values" banner are so keen on an economic model that requires more and more families to need multiple incomes and have so little time left for family, church, and community. Why do they oppose adequate child care policies, especially when studies show that good child care makes such a difference, not just for the child cared for, but for the other children of the family whose educational and life opportunities are often sacrificed or compromised to provide care for younger siblings? There are policies that can make a difference, and hopefully not just in helping individuals to cope or compete in the current reality. Speaking of families, one of the ways that the downward pressure on real wages in recent decades has been alleviated, indeed *masked* over the last thirty-five years, has been the massive influx of women into the labour market, and the proliferation of two-income families. This, along with idea that all we need is more education and training, is perhaps near the end of its course—although it continues to be the mantra of good and bad governments alike who for different reasons are not willing to name the systemic origins of the problems we face.

If, as theologian William Sloane Coffin[24] is reported to have said, hopelessness rationalizes and adapts, whereas hope criticizes and resists, we have had rather too much of hopeless rationalizing and adapting, and not nearly enough hopeful resistance, over recent decades. This error is something that happened on a massive scale when the so-called Third Way of Blair and Clinton formulated a surrender to neoliberalism, and capitulation to the idea that taxes are bad.[25] Such acts of hopelessness, I believe, were profoundly mistaken.

Another dimension of this surrender to hopelessness has been the widespread de-legitimation of government, which amounts to the virtual

---

[23] James K.A. Smith, "Church against State?" September 18, 2014. http://www.cardus.ca/columns/4295/.

[24] William Rankin, "Review of *Passion for the Possible*, by William Sloane Coffin, Jr.," *Anglican Theological Review* 76 (1994): 389. Cf. William Sloane Coffin, *The Collected Sermons of William Sloane Coffin: The Riverside Years* (Louisville, KY: Westminster John Knox Press, 2008).

[25] For more on the virtues of taxing fairly, spending wisely, and regulating on behalf of the environment, a good recent intervention can be found in a book by the former Clerk of the Privy Council in Canada, Alex Himmelfarb: Alex Himmelfarb and Jordan Himmelfarb, *Tax Is Not a Four Letter Word: A Different Take on Taxes in Canada* (Waterloo: Wilfred Laurier University Press, 2013).

demonization of the state in some contexts, and the attendant ceding of democratic control over the conditions of life to corporate forces, not least through widespread privatization. The delicious contradiction here, of course, is that an exception has been made for the *Chinese* state, in which case the welcome mat has been laid out in the form of thirty-year investment agreements, for instance, that enable state-owned Chinese companies to widen and deepen their involvement in the Canadian economy. Such actions, however, will have fateful repercussions down the line for the robust democracy that is necessary if prosperity is to be both greener and more wisely and widely shared. Indeed the proliferation of state capitalism, particularly of that by non-democratic states, within the larger permissive neoliberal global market, is one more aspect of neoliberalism's demise, and points to the need for a re-assertion of the power of governments to act in the national interest in the democratic world.

Yet, as Jim Stanford says in the wonderful little book to which I have already referred, "there is nothing inevitable about poverty, despite the seeming universality of neoliberalism,"[26]—or what Pope Francis a few years ago referred to as "wild economic liberalism."[27] According to Stanford, countries operating on the Nordic model that invest in social programs, labour market supports, and other proactive measures can generate higher wage jobs and achieve very low rates of poverty. We need to return to a similar vision, a vision of political economy which makes a proud place once again for a positive attitude towards income re-distribution through good social wages, and income pre-distribution through securing and defending good individual wages.

Is it too much to believe, to *hope*, indeed, that in the convergence of the ongoing objective reality and offence of radical inequality, with a new openness on the part of the Catholic community thanks to Pope Francis to issues outside the "culture war" box—and similar trends in the Evangelical community—that together with the mainline Protestant remnant, some consensus on the need for change will emerge within the religious community? Why, after all, should religious faith be associated in popular imagination so obviously with the politics of the right? For a profound social justice tradition is to be found in all major faiths, so that a new, prophetic, ecumenical, and indeed, multi-faith challenge to the worship of the market

[26] Stanford, *Economics for Everyone,* p. 170.

[27] Jorge Mario Bergoglio and Abraham Skorka, *On Heaven and Earth* (ET New York: Random House, 2013), 172. Cf. my comments at https://www.broadbentinstitute.ca/en/blog/pope-francis-and-catholicisms-long-ignored-progressive-tradition/.

might arise. This is a need for which, among others, the American Rabbi Michael Lerner has argued forcefully in his book, *The Left Hand of God*, and it is a possibility that I believe we should embrace.[28]

But I hasten to add that this won't be easy. It will involve standing up against the spirit of the age, the prevailing idolatry, the corporate powers and principalities, call it whatever we may. Yet I would like to believe that the church, in collaboration with others, is uniquely situated to challenge the spirit of the age with another and ultimately more powerful spirit, and in doing so to help create the political space for such a movement to occur.

---

[28] Michael Lerner, *The Left Hand of God: Taking Back Our Country from the Religious Right* (San Francisco: Harper, 2006).

CHAPTER SEVEN

ADDRESSING THE GLOBAL CRISIS OF ECONOMIC GROWTH: AN INESCAPABLE ETHICAL CHALLENGE

FREDERICK BIRD[1]

An Unavoidable Crisis

The world now faces an unavoidable and fundamental challenge with respect to economic growth.[2] Without economic growth, we condemn the third of all humans living below the poverty line to continued poverty. Without economic growth these people will continue to live lives that are typically 20 years shorter and filled with more malnutrition, ill health, and social conflict.[3] Without economic growth, the economies of many industrialized countries will continue to sputter, and tens of millions of their citizen will suffer from long periods of unemployment and underemployment. Without economic growth, globally we are likely to experience continued economic instability. However, if as a whole the global economy continues to grow as it has grown over the past 60 years, we place the earth and the inhabitants of the earth at great risk, as we deplete natural resources and pollute waterways and the earth's atmosphere at disastrous rates. Continuing economic growth threatens the earth's climate, endangers her forests and limited supplies of fresh water, and is using up the limited supply of arable land. Economic growth at once seems desirable and necessary, on the one hand, and dangerous and threatening, on the other hand.

---

[1] Frederick Bird is Research Professor in Political Science at the University of Waterloo, and Distinguished Professor Emeritus, Concordia University.

[2] A version of this paper was given at a conference on Religion and Development at Wilfred Laurier University in February, 2013.

[3] See Paul Collier, *The Bottom Billion: Why the Poorest Countries are Failing and What Can Be Done About It* (Oxford: Oxford University Press, 2007).

How shall we find the appropriate means of balancing the integral yet opposing characteristic features of economic growth? Are their viable ways to foster, limit, and reverse growth at the same time?

Economic growth has been valuable and good in many ways. Historically, it has functioned as the primary means for reducing and overcoming poverty. Hundreds of millions of people in China and India recently emerged out of poverty as the economies of these countries steadily expanded. Everywhere, economic growth has functioned to promote public education, improve health services, and raise standards of living. As economies expand, countries are better able to defend human rights.[4] Interestingly, during periods of economic growth, people tend to become more tolerant of diversity, more committed to freedom, and more inclined to resolve conflicts non-violently through negotiations and compromise.[5] In fact, there has been an often-cited correlation between economic development and the establishment of democratic political institutions.[6] Continued economic growth holds out the prospect that, as a whole, people living on earth will find ways of being able to meet their basic needs on a small planet as their population rises to over nine billion by the middle of the current century.

However, economic growth has been dangerous and destructive in many ways. As a result of economic growth, humans have significantly depleted a number of natural resources, from global fish stocks to arable lands, from a number of strategic minerals used in the production of metals to an assortment of rare earth minerals.[7] In several areas in most continents, the processes of economic growth have aggravated deforestation as well as desertification. The activities associated with economic growth have increased the pollution of streams and oceans. As a result of continued economic growth, global emissions levels have greatly increased the greenhouse gases in the atmosphere in ways that have irreversibly and adversely affected global climate. Economic growth has not only ill-

---

[4] Charles Holmes and Cass Sunstein, *The Cost of Rights: Why Liberty Depends on Taxes* (New York: W.W. Norton, 1997).

[5] Benjamin M. Friedman, *The Moral Consequences of Economic Growth* (New York: Vintage Books, Random House, 2005).

[6] Seymour Martin Lipset, "Some Social Requisites of Democracy: Economic Development and Political Legitimacy," *American Political Science Review* 53 (1959): 69-105; C. B. Macpherson, *The Life and Times of Liberal Democracy* (Oxford: Oxford University Press, 1977).

[7] Tim Jackson, *Prosperity Without Growth: Economics for a Finite Planet*(New York: Earthscan, 2009), p. 18.

affected natural environments; it has also had adverse impacts on social environments as well. Economic growth has been associated with aggravated inequalities between the most well-to-do groups and those who are least economically advantaged. Economic growth characteristically undermines often highly valued traditional ways of life. It often occasions unrealistic expectations. Based on current practices, it would, for example, require the resources of several more earths to make it possible for all people on earth to live with the standard of living like those living in North Atlantic countries.[8] Many people correspondingly view continued economic growth as a threat to the planet and its inhabitants.

Global economic growth has occasioned sharply opposing evaluations. It seems that we cannot now live without it and we cannot now live with it. Economic growth occasions an unavoidable dilemma. It presents us with conflicting views, both of which are very compelling on their own terms, which cannot be easily reconciled. This is not a crisis we can ignore, or hope that matters will be resolved by themselves over time. This crisis cannot be adequately addressed by invoking many of the most highly regarded global ethical standards such as those embodied in the Universal Declaration of Human Rights or corresponding UN conventions. This is not a crisis that can be easily resolved or resolved at all by fostering half-way compromises. For example, many people have expressed hope that this crisis might be resolved by finding ways of increasing the efficiency of productive processes and in this way relatively de-coupling economic growth from adverse environmental outcomes. However, these kinds of efficiencies are likely to raise standards of living and the corresponding consumption of resources especially as the world population increases to nine billion by mid-century. This crisis cannot be addressed by appealing either for the expansion of charity or for greater commitment to justice, as valuable as both are likely to be for addressing many other contemporary global issues.[9] Neither of these responses directly function to modify either the need and benefits of economic growth or its deleterious and destructive effects. Many have expressed confidence that humans will come upon technological discoveries that will, as similar discoveries have in the past, enable humans to limit their impact on the planet at the same time as

[8] Lester R. Brown, *Who Will Feed China? Wake-Up Call for a Small Planet* (New York: W. W. Norton, 1995).

[9] See Peter Singer, *The Life You Can Save: Acting Now to End World Poverty* (New York: Random House, 2009); Thomas Pogge, *World Poverty and Human Rights, Cosmopolitan Responsibilities and Reform*, 2nd ed. (Malden, MA: Polity Press, 2008).

their economies grow. One might point, for example, to how the discovery of irrigation, modern organized work places, and solar energy each have played this kind of role.[10] However, these kinds of discoveries often have had unanticipated negative impacts on environments and, more importantly, as a whole these kinds of inventions and their deployment in most ways only modify without fundamentally addressing the central crisis. This crisis cannot be resolved by retreating into alternative intentional communities dedicated to living simple exemplary lives.[11] While these kinds of communities have found ways of living prosperous and flourishing lives with little impact on the environment, these communities only provide an alternative for a few. Those involved hope that by setting these kinds of examples, many others will follow. In a world of nine billion, this seems highly unlikely. Finally, this crisis will not be resolved by imagining that humans are likely in any basic ways to change the kind of creatures we have been for the past hundred thousand years and more. We are not likely to become more humane and more willing to adopt long range views of our lives in any fundamental way.

How humans address this crisis will affect and be affected by how we hold and understand the basic values by which we orient their lives. This is a very intimate crisis precisely because it touches upon not only national and international policies, but also the ways we carry out our ordinary lives. Because faith communities and their modern secular equivalents have played such a large role in establishing the points of reference in terms of which people live, these communities of belief and commitment must find ways of taking this crisis seriously, and while respecting both horns of this dilemma, explore viable ways of helping humans to flourish while living within the ecological limits of the earth. As a whole, humans have let the genie of economic growth out of the bottle and we cannot now put this genie back. When comparing this crisis to other crises associated with economic growth, which I will discuss several paragraphs further along in this essay, this is unmistakably a truly global crisis both in the sense that it affects us all, and it affects how we live within the ecological limits of the earth. I refer to this global crisis as well as a spiritual crisis because it is unavoidable, deeply shapes how we live, and can only seriously be addressed by taking into account and ultimately engaging the values by which humans live.

---

[10] Bjorn Lomborg, *The Skeptical Environmentalist: Measuring the Real State of the World* (Cambridge: Cambridge University Press, 2001).

[11] See David C. Korton, *When Corporations Rule the World* (West Hartford, Conn.: Kumarian Press, 2005).

In the remainder of this essay I propose a way of thinking about and responding to this crisis that respects the imperatives and urgency associated each side of this dilemma. I phrase this approach in terms that I think can be rephrased in relation to the traditions of discourse associated with diverse faith communities and the modern secular equivalents. While these activities are inextricably interwoven, I argue that it is useful to distinguish between processes of production and consumption, and to examine the ways the present crisis calls for quite different imperatives with respect to each. However, before pursuing this line of argument, it is necessary to reflect further both on the characteristic features of economic growth and current debates on how best to gauge it.

Characteristic Features of Economic Growth

What do we mean by economic growth and why has economic growth come to be viewed as normative? By economic growth we refer to the continuing improvements in productive processes that have the effect of raising standards of living and fostering wider ranges of opportunities. By means of economic growth, people find means to make more effective use of human and natural resources so that they can produce more goods and services to address their wants and needs. Over time as humans have discovered and made use of fire, the wheel, domesticated animals, literacy, educational systems, steam engines, telephones, and complex organizations, they have correspondingly fostered economic growth and enhanced their capabilities to live the kinds of lives they have reason to want to live.[12] Overall the processes of economic growth have resulted in increases in the amount of wealth to which people have had access. While wealth may assume diverse forms from property holdings to savings, from good credit ratios to worthwhile investments, from assets in the form of education or social relations to currency, economic growth has been associated both with the growth of wealth and in the diversity of the forms it assumes. Typically, we think of economic growth both in relationship to advancements in production processes and increases in consumption capacities. In what follows, I will point out why it has become imperative to distinguish between these activities.

---

[12] I am both paraphrasing Amartya Sen's view of economic development defined in terms of enhanced human capabilities and using this view in a slightly different way than advocated by Amartya Sen, *Development as Freedom* (New York: Anchor Books, 1999).

Although we often refer to economic growth in general terms, the characteristic features differ markedly depending upon whether we are focusing on the changes associated with quite primitive economic growth, the expansion of commerce, or industrialization. In approximate terms, there have been phases in economic growth associated in broad terms with the introduction of simple horticulture, the development of agriculture, various enhancements of agriculture associated with irrigation and the utilization of more recent technologies, the introduction and expansion of commerce—first local and then more distant, early stages of industrialization, advanced industrialization, and the organization of economies associated with mass consumer societies.[13] Different factors have played decisive roles in relation to different phases of economic growth. A well-informed appreciation of the diverse but similar ways economies develop by passing through these kinds of phases is important for a number of reasons. In the process we are reminded, for example, that many current forms of development become possible because they presuppose and build upon prior developments. Advancements in commerce typically become more likely because of prior developments in agriculture. Industrialization typically becomes possible as a result of antecedent developments fostering economic growth in agriculture and commerce. Correspondingly, in so far as we are interested in fostering economic growth in underdeveloped areas, whether these be defined in relation to countries or regions within countries, then it becomes important to encourage forms of economic development that seem appropriate given the extent to which the area has already developed. In some cases, as with the widespread adoption of mobile phones in Africa, it is possible to introduce quite advanced forms of technology in otherwise under-developed areas. However, in other in-

[13] Cf. Karl Marx, "Forms Which Preceded Capitalist Production," *Grundrisse*, trans. Martin Nicolaus (London: Allen Lane, 1973), pp. 471-514; Karl Marx and Frederick Engels, *The German Ideology*, ed. C.J. Arthur (New York: International Publishers, 1947), Part One; W. W. Rostow, *Stages of Economic Growth* (Cambridge: Cambridge University Press, 1961); and Talcott Parsons, *The Evolution of Societies*, ed. Jackson Toby (Englewood Cliffs, N.J.: Prentice-Hall, 1977). All are outline overall views of economic development similar to this model. Max Weber's *General Economic History*, trans. Frank H. Knight (New York: Collier Books, 1961), provides a similar although much more complex overview. One might criticize all of these models for imposing too restricted views on much more complex historical processes, for assuming excessively linear causal connections, and for overlooking quite different ways in which economies have developed in different areas and eras. Nonetheless, in broad terms these models remind us that economic growth has assumed different forms and that subsequent processes of growth characteristically presuppose and build upon prior processes of growth.

stances, the construction of more advanced forms of mining and manufacturing in areas in which there has been little economic growth with respect to agriculture and commerce, leads to the creation of economic enclaves not well integrated into these areas and of little benefit to the larger population of these areas.

Industrialization represents a noteworthy and historically fairly recent phase of economic growth, introduced initially in northwestern Europe in the middle of the eighteenth century. What has been remarkable about industrialization has been the tremendous expansion of productive powers and the correspondingly greatly increased levels of consumption. As a result of industrialization, people have been able to live much longer, to produce noticeably more goods and services, to invest in much greater ranges of public services, and to eat better and to live more healthy lives.[14] Since the late eighteenth century, industrialization has spread unevenly around the world. Today some countries are much more industrialized than others. In the more than one hundred least developed countries, and sometimes in large areas of otherwise economically developed countries, there are at most only few traces of industrialization. Often when people discuss economic growth, they are referring to industrialization, which is really only the latest phase in a much longer process of development. In terms of the overall phases of economic development, what many underdeveloped areas could benefit most from would be growth in the form of advancements in agriculture and local commerce.

Overall, the process of economic growth is associated not just with increases in *per capita* income, but also and in many ways more importantly with the development of usable assets, capital resources in the broadest sense of the term. Capital refers to durable assets that can be employed to foster economic activities generally and income in particular. For example, financial capital refers to investments which firms can utilize to acquire or contract to utilize lands, operating spaces, and other factors of production. Human capital refers to investments in training and education by which people develop their skills and habits of work that enable them to contribute more to productive processes. Typically, we refer to capital assets as investments because these assets are brought into being by deliberate actions by people who hope that by means of their initiatives they will in

[14] See Ferdinand Braudel, *Civilization and Capitalism*, 3 vols. (New York: Harper and Row, 1980, 1982, and 1984); and Gregory Clark, *Farewell to Alms: A Brief Economic History of the World* (Princeton: Princeton University Press, 2007).

turn reap corresponding benefits.[15] We can, in addition, refer to productive assets or capital, which refer to the technological and organization initiatives, such as the introduction of turbines and modern managed businesses, that make economic activities processes more productive. Many people have also called attention to the decisive role in modern industrialized societies played by the presence or absence of social assets or capital.[16] Here the reference is to social webs of relationship and trust that allow people to collaborate with each other in spite of differences in background. Most importantly, for the purpose of this essay, we need to refer to the development of natural assets or natural capital. The natural environment clearly has value in itself apart from any ways in which humans might interact with it for their own benefit. However, the earth and its resources benefit humans and their economic activities both as a result of direct investments humans have made to utilize these resources, for example, by digging wells, cultivating lands, and mining minerals, and because of the diverse and manifold ecological services which the earth provides humans through the atmosphere, the ocean currents, biodiversity of species, and the like. In this essay I refer to direct investments as natural capital because as a result of the development of these assets, humans have found ways to make much more productive uses of the earth and its resources. Over time, humans have found many ways to utilize given natural resources—lands, minerals, and waterways—more effectively. As an integral aspect of the overall process of economic growth, humans have correspondingly found ways of expanding the extent of capital assets in the form of financial, productive, human, social, and natural capital. They have in the process found ways of utilizing human and natural resources more productively. Although the investments that have resulted in expanded capital assets have occurred over long periods of time, the pace of investment has greatly increased with industrialization.

The expansion of capital assets has greatly benefited from the development of corresponding infrastructures, that is, socially shared institutions and provisions that have facilitated the development of these assets.

---

[15] My discussion of capital here builds upon Herman E. Daly's discussion of the relationship between human and natural capital. See Herman E. Daly, *Beyond Growth: The Economics of Sustainable Development* (Boston: Beacon Press, 1996). I have developed this line of reasoning in a number of essays. See, e.g., Frederick Bird, "Rethinking the bottom line: International Business and Global Poverty," *Management and Organization: A Multidisciplinary Journal of Business,* 2 (2011): 109—120.

[16] On social capital, see Robert Putnam, *Making Democracy Work: Civic Traditions in Modern Italy* (Princeton: Princeton University Press, 1993).

While in many areas a goodly proportion of these infrastructures have been developed through direct public investments, some infrastructural provisions and institutions have been developed through private enterprise. These include physical infrastructures: roads, canals, railroads, communication networks, electricity grids, water systems, sewage systems, social infrastructures such as schools, health care clinics and services, public welfare services, and policing services, as well as economic infrastructures, including laws protecting property rights and contracts, banking systems allowing for creation and expansion of credit, and public and private systems of insurance to manage risks. Correspondingly, the process of economic growth has been typically marked by the development of infrastructures that both foster and embody diverse expressions of capital assets. Again, with industrialization, there has been a corresponding increase in the development of publicly useable infrastructures.

There has been much debate about what factors have played and are likely to play the most decisive role in fostering industrialization in the past and in the present.[17] Without attempting to resolve this ongoing discussion, we can note the important role played at different times and places by a number of distinct factors, including accessibility of new technologies and sources of energy; changes in the organizational forms by which people engage in manufacturing and commerce; modern institutions and processes; the construction of physical, social, and economic infrastructures; and cultivation of dispositions favouring thrift, hard work, and the effective and not wasteful use of resources.

Although we can observe the ways economies of societies have grown or have not grown, both in the present and in the past, the view that economic growth is a normative standard that should be pursued and honoured is a comparatively modern assumption. Over the long course of hu-

---

[17] See, for example, Clark, *Farewell to Alms,* Part Two; cf. also the debates occasioned by Max Weber's, *The Protestant Ethic and the Spirit of Capitalism*, trans. Talcott Parsons (New York: Charles Scribner's Sons, 1958). Weber's account is far more complex than most of his critics realize. He not only calls attention to the role of cultural factors—what he refers to as "Practical Ethical of Worldly Asceticism"—but also indicates the decisive role played by the development of commerce, changes in legal understandings and institutions [for which see Weber, *Economy and Society*, ed. Guenther Roth and Claus Wittich (Berkeley: University of California Press, 1978), Part Two, Chapter VIII], technological discoveries, and political developments. See also William Easterly, *The Elusive Quest for Growth: Economists' Adventures and Misadventures in the Tropics* (Cambridge, Mass.: MIT Press, 2002).

man history, people typically either believed that economies would continue to operate much as they had in the past or assumed they would change as a result of major interventions caused by conquests, disasters, and other acts of God. Some people were indeed able to increase their wealth as a result of good or bad fortune. Characteristically, people enhanced their wealth by locating sources—such as conquered peoples, slaves, mineral deposits, and valued items that they could exploit for trade—from which they could extract wealth. Typically, those with control over the means of violence used this means both to gain and protect their wealth.[18] In keeping with these taken-for-granted assumptions, faith communities in the past did not regard material progress as a valued goal. In response to the current crisis with regard to economic growth, many representatives of contemporary faith communities have invoked these traditional views, explored how small can indeed be beautiful, and called for an end to preoccupation with economic growth.[19]

However, in modern times economic growth has come to be widely viewed as a taken-for-granted normative standard. Economic growth is both expected and regarded as good. Most modern economic models treat economic growth as fundamental. Economies either grow or decline. Although people like Herman Daly have long advocated for a steady-state economics, they have been in a distinct minority.[20] Economists are not alone in viewing economic growth as normative. The assumption that economic growth is both possible and imperative grows out of a number of overlapping developments. These include the widely shared Enlightenment belief in progress as both the mark and goal of modernizing societies. Variously based on their high regard for triumphs of science, their broadly held adherence to humanism, and their corresponding commitment to civility, Enlightenment thinkers and those they influenced viewed progress as the characteristic feature of modern as opposed to traditional societies. Modern societies were correspondingly expected to economical-

---

[18] See Douglass C. North, John Joseph Wallis, and Barry R. Weingast, *Violence and Social Order: A Conceptual Framework for Interpreting Recorded Human History* (Cambridge: Cambridge University Press, 2008); Damon Acemoglu and James A. Robinson make a similar argument in *Why Nations Fail: The Origins of Power, Prosperity, and Poverty* (New York: Crown Publishers, 2012).

[19] See E.F. Schumacher, *Small Is Beautiful: a Study of Economics as If People Mattered* (London: Blond and Briggs, 1973).

[20] Herman E. Daly, *The Steady State* (London: W. H. Freeman and Co. Ltd, 1972); and Herman E. Daly, *Beyond Growth: The Economics of Sustainable Development* (Boston: The Beacon Press, 1996).

ly progress.[21] The view of economic growth as a normatively-valued process emerged as well as the by-product of efforts of diverse groups of people especially in Europe and North America to develop self-organizing (and often self-governing) associations in the form of religious communities, voluntary associations, business enterprises, as well associations of workers.[22] Furthermore, the processes of industrialization themselves rendered ideas about economic growth both credible and desirable. People witnessed dramatic changes in their own lives and those of others. Many people found themselves living much better than their ancestors. They experienced economic growth as good, and they expected their descendants to enjoy enhanced growth as well.

Once economic growth is viewed as being not only possible and desirable, but also imperative, then the lack of economic growth is viewed as a problem. Correspondingly, for centuries the life conditions we associate with poverty, namely higher rates of illness, higher rates of mortality, higher incidents of social violence, and lack of opportunities for education, were accepted as the expected lot. However, once economic growth became a normative standard, then poverty and these conditions came to be viewed as problematic, as conditions that could and should be ameliorated. Correspondingly, as normative assumptions regarding economic growth come to be widely held, modern reformers have formed local, national, and international organizations dedicated to working to enhance the conditions of those who are poor.

Before exploring useful ways of thinking about the global crisis of economic growth, it is important to consider five other challenges endemic to the process of economic growth. These challenges have been present

---

[21] The assumptions regarding progress and economic growth are taken for granted by thinkers as diverse as Locke, Smith, Hegel, Marx, Comte, Spenser, and Durkheim. On the importance and association of ideas of civility and humanism, and their association with expectations of social transformation and economic growth, see Steven Pinker, *The Better Angels of Our Nature: Why Violence Has Declined* (New York: Viking, 2011).

[22] North *et al.*, *Violence and Social Order*, call attention to the tremendous expansion of self-organizing associations in industrializing societies. The association between these self-organizing groups and commitment to efforts to foster economic enhancement was noticed both by Alexis de Tocqueville in *Democracy in America*(New York, Vintage Books, 1945) Vol. II (Book 2, chapter 4, 5, 6) and Max Weber, "The Protestant Sects and the Spirit of Capitalism," in *From Max Weber: Essays in Sociology*, eds. H. H. Gerth and C. Wright Mills (New York: Oxford University Press, 1946).

and have been discussed since the beginnings of industrialization two hundred and fifty years ago. How we think of these challenges will influence how in turn we address the larger issue. These five challenges are as follows: firstly, how do we best manage the often disruptive social correlates of economic growth and especially industrialization? Secondly, how do we foster the kinds of economic growth suitable for the economic and ecological conditions in which we find ourselves? Thirdly, how do we work to make sure that economic growth is inclusive and not exclusive? Fourthly, over time as humans have identified and further developed diverse capital assets—from natural assets to productive assets, how can we act to resist the ever-present inclination to exploit these assets as if they were forms of disposable income? And fifthly, how do we best measure economic growth?

The first challenge associated with growth is that, while it may occasion many benefits, economic growth has always been also a socially disruptive process. As a result of economic growth, old ways of life are left behind. Traditional customs are often forgotten or simply treated with diminished respect. Frequently, traditional structures of authority lose some of their legitimacy. Old patterns of power are frequently overcome as new centres of power emerge. Because most processes of economic growth foster increased horizontal as well as vertical mobility, kinship bonds are typically loosened. These changes characteristically occasion conflicts as some groups take quicker and greater advantage of these changes than others. While some people clearly benefit from processes of economic growth, others clearly do not. With industrialization, the pace of these changes often quickens. Moreover, while the process of industrialization greatly enhances the opportunities for increased wealth, it also introduces increased economic risks, connected with the loss of income and investments associated with work-related accidents, unemployment, retirement, bank failures, bankruptcy, and economic depressions. Correspondingly, economic growth has challenged societies to find effective and humane ways of responding to these disruptions and risks. For example, communities of faith have in many places developed funds and hostels to support those uprooted by these processes. In modern times states have developed a wide range of public social insurance and public welfare institutions, like deposit insurance for banks, workers' compensation plans, and relief programs to manage these risks. Whether these programs adequately address these disruptions and risks is an ongoing concern.

Secondly, as we have observed, economic growth typically assumes different forms associated broadly with different phases of economic development. Each phase is roughly associated with corresponding opportunities and limitations. Attempts to foster more advanced expressions of economic growth in less developed economies are likely to occasion frustration and disillusionment when these efforts fail and/or exacerbate local social relations. We can illustrate these abstract statements with some concrete examples. Thus, for instance, many of the investments from industrialized countries in developing areas have given rise to what observers have referred to as dual economies, as small pockets of externally oriented enterprises traded with foreign investors, while the remainder of the society pursued traditional patterns of exchange and production. In the process, inequalities between these sub-economies greatly increased, further aggravating social and political tensions between them. To make reference to another example, many developing areas have been unable to make effective use of particular forms of investments and aid because they have not yet been able, or had the opportunity, to develop the antecedent conditions—often the corresponding physical and social infrastructures—to make good use of these investments and aid.[23] To cite another kind of example, the extent of change differs with different phases of development. As countries industrialize, the pace and extent of growth is often quite steep and dramatic. As they become more fully industrialized, growth rates become slower. Thus, the growth rates of countries like Korea, Japan, and China have been extraordinarily high during the periods of rapid industrialization, and have slowed and will likely slow as they become more fully industrialized. Similarly, although their economies continue to grow, the pace of growth in the northern European countries, in the United States and Canada, and in Japan have slowed in recent decades in part simply because continued opportunities for increased growth seem to diminish as countries become more fully industrialized. The challenge these countries now face is to foster forms of economic growth that seem appropriate to their stage of economic development, forms that may well involve dramatically reduced extraction of non-renewable resources.

The third challenge associated with economic growth is finding fitting ways of working to make economic growth inclusive. Economic growth frequently benefits particular sectors of a society rather than the society as a whole. Firms in extractive industries have especially functioned in this manner. Because they have not been well integrated with the economies of host countries, these firms have often functioned to aggravate local ine-

---

[23] I have pursued these issues at much greater length in a paper on "Mining and Inclusive Wealth Development in Developing Countries," presented at the World Mining Conference held in Montreal, August 14, 2013.

qualities. They have often acted to create much wealth for the small number of people directly involved in managing these operations, inflated local retail markets because of the extra wealth they are able to spend, exacerbated exchange rates to the disadvantage of other exporters especially in agricultural sectors, and thereby occasioned what observers have often referred to as the so-called resource curse. In the process, the wealth created by the extractive processes functions not to foster the general economic growth of these countries, but only wealth for the small enclaves directly affected and the governing officials who endorse these projects.[24] Finding ways to foster inclusive economic growth is a general challenge, and not only a problem associated with the extractive industries.[25]

The fourth challenge associated with economic growth focuses on the ever-present temptation to utilize the wealth associated with capital assets—financial, productive, human, social, and/or natural capital—as if it were income. Assets, well invested and protected, help to produce streams of income and income generating economic activities. However, if these assets are exploited for short term gains or used abusively, as happens when lands are over-used, employees are over-worked, physical infrastructures are allowed to deteriorate, and/or financial investments are carelessly made, then the overall stock of capital assets will be correspondingly depleted. Businesses in the extractive industries in particular face the ongoing challenge of trying to find ways of pacing the process of extraction so that they do not too quickly exhaust the sources in which they have invested.

The fifth challenge associated with economic growth revolves around efforts to find suitable and practical ways of measuring economic growth. In practice, economic growth is frequently gauged by measuring gross domestic product on a *per capita* basis. This approach provides an approximate measure of *per capita* income. It is widely used to estimate how well countries are doing economically, the extent of poverty within countries, and rates of economic development. Although pervasively utilized, this approach to gauging economic growth has also been strongly criticized. It is a mis-measure, a number of observers have argued, because it provides an account of overall market activity, without taking account of the depre-

---

[24] Macartan Humphreys, Jeffrey D. Sachs, and Joseph E. Stiglitz, eds., *Escaping the Resource Curse* (New York: Columbia University Press, 2007).

[25] *Inclusive Wealth Report: Measuring Progress toward Sustainability* (IWR) (Cambridge: Cambridge University Press, 2012), a project sponsored by the United Nations University, The International Human Dimension Program on Global Environmental Change, and the United Nations Environmental Program.

ciation of assets and the non-market contribution to the overall economy by households and civil society organizations.[26] Amartya Sen has persuasively criticized GDP *per capita* as a way of estimating economic growth because this approach erroneously assumes that we should be measuring economic development in relation to money. Money is, he argues, just a means for obtaining what people really want, namely, the capacity to access a variety of valued goods and services including longer and healthier lives, more consumer products, desirable social relations, more and better education, and political participation. Sen refers to this approach as the human capabilities measure of economic performance.[27] Inspired in large part by Sen's capabilities model, the United Nations' Development Program has constructed a Human Development Index, which measures overall patterns of economic growth in relation to a number of indicators, including rates of longevity, infant mortality, educational achievement, literacy, as well as *per capita* income. While recognizing the practical utility of GDP/*per capita* as a fairly easily measured indicator of economic performance, these critics in turn seek fuller accounts of economic growth that more closely represent the relationship between income levels and human well-being.

From the perspective of environmentalists these measures are all flawed because they fail to take account of the impact of economic growth on the earth and its biosphere. A more accurate measure of economic growth should, therefore, include some reference to the ways economic activities deplete various kinds of renewable and non-renewable resources and in turn pollute lands, waters, and the atmosphere. A number of different measures have been developed to take account of environmental impacts, including ones gauging environmental and/or carbon footprints of economic activities as well as so called "green" measures of GDP, which subtract environmental costs from GDP figures. The European Council developed a multi-dimensional measure that includes a number of social, environmental, and economic indicators. What these approaches share in

---

[26] Joseph Stiglitz, Amartya Sen, and Jean-Paul Fitoussi, *Mis-Measuring Our Lives: Why GDP Doesn't Add Up: The Report by the Commission on the Measurement of Economic Performance and Social Progress* (New York: The New Press, 2010), chapter 1.

[27] Amartya Sen, *Development as Freedom*, Introduction and Chapter One. See also Stiglitz, Sen, and Fitoussi, *Mis-Measuring Our Lives,* Chapter Two. See also Martha C. Nussbaum, *Women and Human Development: The Capabilities Approach* (Cambridge: Cambridge University Press, 1999).

common is a commitment to gauge the overall sustainability of economic growth when environmental impacts are taken into account.[28]

The recent Report of the International Commission on the Measurement of Economic Performance and Social Progress argues that it is a mistake to attempt to gauge economic growth in relation to a single measure. As I have already indicated, I agree. The Commission proposes developing some kind of hybrid measure that variously attempts to look at levels of *per capita* income and consumption and takes account as well of the stocks of assets, including natural resources, which current generations are able to pass on to future generations. In this essay I propose using two different measures, one, to gauge in what ways and to what extent economic activity enhances the capacity of people to people to live the kinds of lives they want to live and, two, to gauge in what ways and to what extent economic activity productively utilizes natural and human resources. The first measures the outcome of economic growth on human well-being broadly understood. It indicates how we consume. The second measures how economic growth affects the stock of assets, that is, wealth broadly understood, that we bring into being through economic activity and pass on for posterity. It measures productivity, appropriately understood, as the effective use of both human and natural resources.

Addressing the Global Crisis of Economic Growth

If we are going to find a way of addressing the current global crisis with respect to economic growth, then we need to explore alternative ways of thinking about economic growth that encourage us to foster growth where it is needed, and while restraining growth as a whole and especially in areas where it is likely to have the most disastrous consequences.

As a guide for reflecting on this crisis, I propose modifying guidance that John Wesley proposed long ago in a sermon on "The Use of Money." In that sermon Wesley argued that money itself was neither inherently good nor bad. "In the present state of mankind, it is an excellent gift of God…food for the hungry, drink for the thirsty, raiment for the naked." People have used money to feed their greed and to exploit others. They have also used money to care for others, to feed the hungry and cloth those without clothes. Money could be viewed as a gift of God, which humans might use beneficially or adversely. In itself money was morally neutral.

---

[28] See Stiglitz, Sen, and Fitoussi, *Mis-Measuring Our Lives*, Chapter 3, for a review of a number of these measures.

What mattered, and mattered a lot, were the uses to which people put money. Wesley then proceeded to outline and explain three broad counsels regarding the responsible use of money. He urged his audiences to "gain all you can," "save all you can," and "give all you can." It is, of course important to look carefully at how he explained and interpreted these counsels. In relation to the first counsel about "gaining all you can," he spelled out a version of the work ethic, advising his listeners and readers to work hard, to respect other workers, to work safely, and to utilize resources effectively. "Lose no time…do it [your work] as well as possible…learn from the experiences of others." In relation to the second counsel about "saving all you can," he articulated what might best be described as a consumer ethic, emphasizing the importance of making effective use of what we have, minimizing waste, and fostering thrift. "Not to use it effectively is to throw it away." In relation to the third counsel about "giving all you can," he set forth what we might today call a communitarian ethic indicating that in so far as we had first properly cared for our families and we had the means, then we should act to support our neighbours and those in need. God has given us all we have. We should, he declared, use what we have to care for ourselves, our households, and our communities, and others in need not as proprietors but as stewards of God's gifts.[29]

In broad terms Wesley's counsel regarding the responsible uses of money serves well as an initial point of reference for thinking about the responsible uses of economic growth in relation to the current global crisis. Correspondingly, we begin by acknowledging that economic growth in itself is neither good nor bad: what matters is how we engage in economic growth. Following Wesley's lead, we start by advocating that we produce productively. Given the fact that human and natural resources are limited and that by mid-century more than nine billion people will be living on the earth, we are then appropriately counselled to make the most effective uses of these limited resources. Correspondingly, we might then re-interpret Wesley's second counsel to argue that we ought to consume these resources sustainably. Like Wesley, we can urge people not to abuse and waste these resources, but to act to conserve and use them with respect. Finally, while using the language of charity, Wesley's third counsel urges people to view their lives broadly in relation to others with whom they have been called upon to live. Extrapolating this counsel to our current

---

[29] John Wesley, "The Use of Money," *Forty-Four Sermons* (London: The Epworth Press, 1944). Interestingly, Weber quotes from this sermon to develop his argument about the character of the so-called Protestant Ethic.

complex globalized world, we might then argue that we are called upon to collaborate globally as we seek to address this crisis.[30]

In the remainder of this essay, I will elaborate on these three principles. I will explore their normative and practical significance for the current crisis. I will call attention both to the widely based support for each of these principles and their practical relevance. I will argue that all three of these principles are important and that, while it is useful to distinguish among them, they must be honoured as a whole. After all, the practices of producing inherently involve forms of consumption, and producers produce goods and services in large part in response to demands of consumers.[31] Nonetheless, at least with regard to finding useful ways of responding to the current global crisis with respect to economic growth, it is useful to distinguish between these practices. I will begin with the principle of consuming sustainably, because endorsement of this principle is so widespread.

Consuming Sustainably

There are natural limits to what humans can consume. There is only so much fresh water and arable land, and in some places there are today insufficient quantities of both for the numbers of people living in these areas. As more and more countries economically develop, humans are consuming structural metals, like iron, bauxite, copper, and nickel faster than they are being mined.[32] Although there are vast quantities of some minerals, there are limited supplies of many others. Although humans have continued to discover new sources of oil and gas, it costs much, much more to extract oil and gas from sources like tar sands and shale, and the supplies of these hydrocarbons still remain finite. The cost for oil has quadrupled over the past decade. This change has occurred in part because of the added expenses associated with extraction, and even more so because of the greatly increased demand for oil as countries like India, Brazil, and China

---

[30] Many would argue that we are called upon to see ourselves as human as members along with other living things of the larger community of life on the earth. See Peter G. Brown, *Ethics, Economic, and International Relations: Transparent Sovereignty in the Commonwealth of Life* (Edinburgh: Edinburgh University Press, 2000).

[31] For an interesting exploration of these inter-relationships, see Karl Marx, "Introduction," *Grundrisse*, pp. 88-111.

[32] Jackson, *Prosperity without Growth*, p. 75; Jeff Rubin, *The End of Growth* (Toronto: Random House, 2012), p. 221.

industrialize and as larger numbers of their citizens begin driving automobiles.

Because of the discovery of new sources of minerals and energy and because we have also discovered ways of utilizing these materials much more efficiently, in spite of the continued steep growth in human population, we have not yet reached the so-called physical limits to growth as soon as soon as authors of the 1972 *Limits to Growth* book predicted.[33] Nonetheless, those limits are real. There are finite mineral sources and mineral are a non-renewable resource. Although we have been able greatly to expand global food production, there are limits here as well. We are already exhausting some fish stocks. In many areas because of over-use, soil used for growing crops has been seriously degraded. We have significantly depleted limited global supplies of ground water, especially in some areas such as the Middle East, northern China, and central United States. All of these limits will become more challenging as the population of the earth rises to more than nine billion by the middle of the twentieth century. The demands for finite resources will increase both with the growth in population and as formerly under-developed countries industrialize and their citizens seek consumer goods and services associated with industrialized societies. More people will want to live in comfortable housing with plumbing, electrical services, and corresponding furnishings. They will want to buy their own cars. As a result of these steep increases in demand, prices are likely to rise, as they already have risen for oil and many other commodities. These trends may well aggravate the growing and troubling divide between economically advantaged and economically impoverished.

Much attention has been addressed to the ways economic growth over time has had an adverse impact on the earth's climate. Although estimates of this impact vary, among the scientific communities studying the climate, there is almost universal recognition that human economic activity has not only increased air pollution in some areas to dangerously unhealthy levels, but has also caused the overall temperature of the atmosphere to climb. As a result of the human-occasioned global warming, glaciers and snow packs have been melting near the earth's poles as well as in high mountains from the Rockies in North America to the Himalayas in Asia. Melting ice and snow reduce fresh water supplies in some areas and occasion fears that ocean levels will rise enough to threaten low-lying populated lands all over the world. Global warming as well seems to be

---

[33] Donella Meadows, Dennis Meadows, Jørgen Randers, and William W. Behrens III, *The Limits to Growth* (New York: Universe Books, 1972).

associated with changes in weather patterns, including increased drought in some locales and more violent storms in other locales.

In response to these diverse problems, a widespread consensus has emerged that humans must undertake economic activity in the future in ways differently than we have in the past. We can longer assume, as humans have frequently assumed for centuries, that there are unlimited supplies of land, water, air, and minerals, which we can draw upon to address our needs and wants and into which we can dump our waste and emissions. We have to find ways of living within the ecological limits of the earth. As we seek to measure economic activity, we must take account of how we are depleting or adversely altering the earth's resources. Increasingly aware of these concerns, in 1984 the United Nations mandated the creation of an international commission to look at the relations between economic activity and the environment. As a guide for thinking about economic growth, that commission, chaired by Gro Brundtland, former Prime Minister of Norway, proposed that economic activity be guided by the norm of sustainable development. The commission argued that businesses and countries could continue to pursue economic growth so long as current economic activities provided the opportunities, and did not compromise the capacities for subsequent generations to pursue corresponding patterns of growth.[34] Subsequently, the principle of sustainable development has been variously interpreted, sometimes strictly in ways that would greatly restrict the non-renewable extractive activities, and sometimes quite loosely focusing on the overall social and economic sustainability of societies and not just on limits of particular natural resources. For the purpose of this essay, I propose to interpret this norm strictly in relation to patterns of consumption, and then to gauge consumption patterns in relation to the earth's ecological limits. In so far as economic growth is associated as well with increases in the productive utilization of natural and human resources, I will be arguing for greater productivity. However, with respect to patterns of consumption, I argue that the relevant point of reference is not the continued well-being of humans, but rather the carrying capacity of the earth.

With respect to consuming sustainably, I will make four broad proposals to help address the current global crisis. These proposals are interrelated. There is no simple way of reducing consumption and rendering our consumer choices more responsible.

[34] World Commission on Environment and Development, *Our Common Future* (Oxford: Oxford University Press, 1987).

Firstly, we need to find ways of limiting certain adverse industrial activities that endanger the earth and its inhabitants either proximately or over the long term. Within this category we need to include a number of practices, including the excessive emissions of carbon dioxide and other gases, the pollution of streams and ground water by careless industrial practices, as well as current patterns of fertilizer use, because of the impact of this use on the water quality of streams and lakes. While there are certainly disagreements about the levels at which these activities become noxious or excessive, nonetheless, over the long term, all of these activities, and especially the emission of so-called greenhouse gases, must be restricted. There is a growing sense of urgency about this matter. Industrial practices also endanger the planet by the ways they have acted to waste valued but limited natural resources. These include the flaring of unused natural gases; the overuse and degradation of soils; the careless discarding of unmarketable fish catches; the exploitation of limited arable lands for non-agricultural uses; the enormous dumping of industrial wastes that might with a little extra effort be re-used, re-cycled, or restored; and the less than efficient use of non-renewable mineral and energy sources. This list is just suggestive. Many other specific examples of the wasteful industrial uses of the earth and its resources might be cited. In general, businesses aggravate the current crisis to the extent that they seek to augment their incomes primarily by finding and exploiting sites where they can extract wealth from given sources, whether these be poorly paid labourers, the excessive credibility of customers, increasingly depleted mineral sources, or over-cultivated lands. Douglass North and colleagues argue that over the centuries prior to industrialization, economic and political elites have typically adopted this kind of approach to wealth creation. With industrialization, businesses realize how more wealth can be created by developing diverse assets that can in turn be utilized as ongoing sources of income.[35] In any case, too many businesses are depleting the natural assets with which they work. There is a widespread and growing consensus that these patterns of industrial abuse and wasteful use are unsustainable, and that they have put the earth and the long term viability of the global economy at great risk.

---

[35] See North *et al.*, *Violence and Social Order*; see as well Acemoglu and Robinson, *Why Nations Fail*, who make a parallel argument. See also Jared Diamond, *Collapse: How Societies Choose to Fail or Succeed* (New York: Viking Press,2005), who observes the way in which agricultural practices in some areas operate essentially as a way of mining the fields.

Recognizing the imperative to bring about appropriate changes, some governments and some businesses have begun to initiate fitting responses. Many governments have enacted laws to prohibit or greatly reduce the flaring of gases, to eliminate or greatly limit noxious emissions, and in particular to reduce carbon emissions. They have introduced extra taxes and fines to encourage compliance. Given the extent and urgency of the problem, much more needs to be done. Nonetheless, many resist these kinds of changes because they argue that these kinds of changes are not economically feasible at least in the medium and short term. Introducing these kinds of changes will, they contend, further threaten to cause economic slowdowns. In spite of these arguments, many businesses have begun to acknowledge the importance of these imperatives. No doubt, in large part because consumers have asked for changes and because it can sometimes make economic sense, many businesses have found ways to make much more effective use of oil, gas, coal and other sources of energy, limit pollution, and reduce emissions. For example, as they have attempted to operate in ways that are safer, healthier, and environmentally less damaging, chemical producing firms through the internationally adopted, industry-wide Responsible Care programs have discovered that these initiatives actually foster the more efficient and therefore less costly use of chemical feed stock.[36] A number of the large petroleum extracting and retailing firms have been quite seriously repositioning themselves as energy companies, recognizing they can no longer put off not only the need to find and develop alternatives sources of energy, like solar power, but also the need to utilize all energy sources much more efficiently. In a recent publication, Royal Dutch Shell admitted that business as usual was no longer possible. Precisely because of the global crisis regarding economic growth, the world was likely to become more economically and political unstable. Therefore, it was important for firms like Shell to become far more flexible and far more responsible.[37]

Although these responses are not without merit, they seem far too timid. It may well be that we cannot expect greater response until we are forced to introduce drastic changes as a result of environmental and/or economic crises which current practices will inevitably occasion. Some

---

[36] See John Moffat, Francois Bregha, and Mary Jane Middelkoop, "Responsible Care: A Case Study of a Voluntary Environmental Initiative," in Kernaghan Webb ed., *Voluntary Codes: Private Governance, The Public Interest, and Innovation* (Carleton University: Carleton Research Unit for innovation, Science, and Environment, 2004).

[37] See Shell News Lens Scenarios, March, 2013.

observers foresee the beginning of these necessary changes in the recent greatly increased global prices for energy. The steep rise in energy prices, which will inevitably increase as the global demand for energy steadily expands, already is causing businesses and government to re-think their current practices and policies. They are more likely to buy locally, to work more assiduously to conserve energy, and to reduce waste.[38] In partial response to complaints that appropriate ecological responses are economically unfeasible, I have in this essay distinguished between the need to consume sustainably and to produce productively because some of the economic slowdown occasioned by managing industrial consumption in more ecologically responsible ways can be addressed by finding ways to employ workers and natural resources more effectively. However, I will explore this topic further along in this essay.

Secondly, in so far as possible, we need to find ways of reducing population growth. The rapid and extensive expansion in global population over the past century has put an enormous strain on the earth's carrying capacity. As the population of humans has grown, the number of people consuming finite human and natural resources has also grown. In many of the least developed countries, the steady growth in population means that their slowly growing economies are unable to provide food and basic supplies to meet the needs of their own people. Most of these countries import food. Because of their often still under-developed character, in many settings rural lands cannot provide the jobs, food, or sustenance needed by all the people born in these areas. Millions of these people every year move into the increasing large urban complexes. While it may well be that the affluent consume far more than those who are economically impoverished, nonetheless the steady growth in global population aggravates all of these problems. It is now hoped that later in the twenty-first century global population will reach a steady state of between nine and ten billion people. Still, if there were viable ways of reducing the population growth sooner and reaching a steady state with a smaller overall population size, then that would seem to be especially important. In fact, a viable solution to this problem seems to exist. It is not necessary to hope for wars and disease or to introduce draconian population control measures. Over time, two factors have played especially instrumental roles in reducing the birth rates. One, as economies grow and as standards of living improve, birth rates tend to fall. That is why some forms of economic growth seem important. Two, providing primary and secondary school education for girls has been particularly helpful. This education may be desirable on its own merit both

[38] See Rubin, *The End of Growth.*

as a way of providing humane opportunities for girls and as a way of augmenting at the national level the overall stock of human capital assets. In addition, as girls receive education, they become more aware of their opportunities and choices, and they gain modestly but decisively in their capacity to shape the contours of their own lives. Anyone seriously interested in limiting the consumption of natural and human resources, and thereby helping to address the current global crisis with respect to economic growth, should therefore work to increase the global educational opportunities for girls.[39]

Thirdly, in our households and personal lives we need to find ways of consuming less and consuming more responsibly. If, as the world population expands and more and more people seek to live middle class lives, we hope to reduce the overall consumption of limited natural resources, then we must explore ways to consume less. We need to revive traditional ideas about living simply. We need to develop ways of living fuller and happier lives that do not require us to consume more commodities, whether these assume the form of bigger houses, more clothes, greater use of personal means for transportation, or more entertainment. We must find ways of measuring our economic well-being not in relation to what we earn or buy, but in terms of the quality of our lives. Many different kinds of people have been making these kinds of arguments, such as Martha Nussbaum and Amartya Sen, when they argue that we should gauge economic well-being in relation to our capacity to realize certain basic human capabilities.[40] The challenge here is how to transition from current, deeply-embedded habits of mind and heart that are also incorporated in taken-for-granted economic assumptions and move towards these alternatives viewed not simply as acts of personal virtue, but as expressions of widely-shared public purpose. Many groups and individuals have indeed adopted standards associated with living more simply. However, if we hope to have even modest impact globally, we need to translate these ideals into public policies.

---

[39] See Abijit Banerjee and Esther Duflo, *Poor Economics: A Radical Rethinking of the Way to Fight Global Poverty* (New York: Public Affairs, 2011); Amartya Sen, *Development as Freedom*, chapter 4.

[40] See Martha Nussbaum, *Women and Human Development*; see also her earlier work, *The Therapy of Desire: Theory and Practice in Hellenistic Ethics* (Princeton: Princeton University Press, 1994), and Amartya Sen, *Development as Freedom*. A similar argument is made by the International Commission on the Measurement of Economic Performance and Social Progress, Stiglitz, Sen and Fitoussi, *Mis-Measuring Our Lives*, chapter 2; see also Jackson, *Prosperity Without Growth*, chapters 6 and 9.

We can take a couple of steps in this direction by instituting policies that encourage both the conserving, non-wasteful use of resources as well as thrift. We can move in this direction in part by building upon existing initiatives. For example, many communities now foster the recycling and re-using of items that were formerly thrown into the garbage by the public collections of used plastics, glass, metals, paper and cardboard, and compostable wastes. In many communities, thrift stores sell used furniture, clothing, and other household items, and public food programs dispense meals prepared by using unsold items from both grocery stores and restaurants. We can take more serious steps as the Danish did when they introduced a sales tax on automobiles equivalent to the cost of the vehicles.[41] This tax clearly discourages people from buying extra cars. Many countries have introduced hefty taxes on gasoline not only to pay for the upkeep of roads and the construction of public transit systems, but also to use gasoline with greater restraint. As fuel prices continue to rise, these kinds of policies are likely to attract greater support. Nonetheless, we have a long way to go considering the hundreds of millions of gallons of oil consumed every day. It may well be necessary measurably to raise the level of value-added and consumption taxes not only to generate more public revenues to address public debts and to improve degrading public infrastructures, but also to foster more conservative habits of consumption. In the industrialized nations, too many people have been living beyond their means. It would be very helpful, accordingly, to revive traditional views about the importance of thrift as a means of reducing household indebtedness, encouraging investments and savings, and also moderating excessive patterns of consumption.

These diverse efforts to foster reduced and more responsible patterns of individual and household consumption confront a major, not easily addressed challenge. People living in modern industrialized societies highly value consumption as an expression of their fundamental freedom of choice. Liberal societies treasure freedom of choice as this is expressed in our choices regarding where we might live, with whom we will live, where we will work, and how we will live. The latter is typically embodied in a series of consumer choices related to housing, leisure time, food, clothing, transportation, and lifestyle. The high valuation of consumer choice is further reinforced by the widely held economic assumption that the most effective means to overcome economic slowdowns is to encourage increases in consumer activity. As societies began to industrialize and they expanded their industrial capacity, it was typically assumed that economic

---

[41] Rubin, *The End of Growth,* chapter 6.

prosperity was best fostered by encouraging hard, skilful work, new ideas, and financial investments. In late and post-industrial societies, the critical factor has become consumption. It seems we can now produce more than enough goods and services. Correspondingly, the economy may languish if not enough people choose to purchase what we produce. Therefore, through skilful uses of advertisements, we need to encourage greater consumption.[42] If these means seem inadequate, then, it has been argued, we may need to reduce taxes so that people will be encouraged to buy more.[43] Furthermore, if this latter initiative still seems to be ineffective, then others have proposed that we encourage people to borrow more so they can consume more, as in the recent efforts to encourage low income families to buy houses they couldn't afford or others to make more credit card purchases.

It is clearly time to re-think the presumed priority which modern societies and modern economics have assigned to consumer choice. We may well need to revive the ancient traditions which encouraged us to exercise our freedom of choice in ways other than how we consume: through friendships, family life, patterns of thought, and leisure activities that we can pursue independent of consumer markets. We can also observe that how we consume has indeed become crucial for economic well-being, not in terms of the volume of what we consume, but in terms of the wisdom and restraint of our purchases as we recognize the possible adverse impact of our choices on the well-being of the earth, its climate, and its inhabitants. In relation to the recent financial crisis and great recession, we can further recognize the adverse consequences of the uses of dubious means to increase the volume of consumption. I have in mind here practices of fostering highly risky home loan arrangements and tax cuts, both of which

---

[42]Daniel Bell, *The Cultural Contradictions of Capitalism* (New York: Basic Books, 1976), analyzed how consumption had become the critical factor for modern industrialized economies. A similar argument, especially with regard to the increasingly importance of advertising, was made by John Kenneth Galbraith, *The Affluent Society* (Cambridge: The Riverside Press, 1958), chapters 10 and 11.

[43]See Irwin Garfinkel, Lee Rainwater, and Timothy Smeeding, *Wealth and Welfare States: Is America a Laggard or Leader* (New York: Oxford University Press, 2010); Molly C. Michelmore, *Tax and Spend: The Welfare State, Tax Politics, and the Limits of American Liberalism* (Philadelphia: The University of Pennsylvania Press, 2012); see also Bruce Bartlett, *The Benefit and the Burden: Tax Reform—Why We Need It and What It Will Take* (New York: Simon and Schuster, 2012). While the Kennedy/Johnson tax cut of 1964 seemed to foster economic growth in the USA through modest increases in spending, subsequent tax cuts introduced in the 1980s and 2000s did not have the same effect.

aggravated the crisis and excessively reduced the capacity of governments to respond to the crisis, and almost exclusively benefited the rich.

Fourthly, one strategy that will indeed help to foster sustainable consumption is to introduce reforms that will provide for a fairer allocation of economic opportunities both globally and within countries. With some notable exceptions, since the late 1970s economic inequalities have increased both internationally and domestically. Households with the highest incomes (1% or 5% or 10%) are earning more income and amassing greater wealth while the 40% or so of households with lowest incomes are becoming comparatively worse off. By standard income measures, overall global economic growth has slowed, except for dramatic economic growth in countries like China, India, Indonesia, and Brazil. The gap between the advantaged and disadvantaged has become wider with the exception of the economies of these same economically expanding countries. The gap has grown because many of the especially well-to-do have enjoyed higher incomes and lower taxes at the same time as the more impoverished groups have experienced much higher rates of un- and under-employment. For the purpose of this essay I am interested in analyzing the relationship between these economic disparities and overall patterns of consumption. Efforts to create economic opportunities for low income households will cause these households to increase their purchases but largely in modest ways. These efforts again in modest measures would increase overall demand in ways that would be good for the economy as a whole. Because these additions in purchases and demand would be small and incremental, there is little chance efforts to boost the economy by helping those least well off would adversely affect the environment. We can thereby both expand the economy and do so in ways that have little negative impact on the earth and its carrying capacity.

Producing Productively

Producing productively is as important for protecting the carrying capacity of the earth as consuming sustainably. Because we live on a planet with limited natural and human resources, it is vital that we find ways of utilizing these resources as effectively as possible. Producing productively aims to do just that. Accordingly, economic growth ought to be thought of and gauged in relation to the effective and therefore productive utilization of available resources. Most importantly, economic growth should not be measured in relation to income, which simply represents the current capacity to consume. Rather, economic growth is best measured in terms of the development of those institutions and provisions that make it possible to utilize resources more effectively and therefore more productively. This utilization in turn yields income in diverse forms. Economic growth then is most appropriately thought of as the further expansion of useable assets that facilitate the productive use of human and natural resources. From this perspective, economic growth takes place to the extent that people in a given generation are able to preserve, add to, and pass on to the next generation stocks of what I previously broadly described as capital assets, that can in turn be drawn upon and utilized to foster the effective utilization of resources and corresponding flows of income.[44]

This is a fairly abstract statement. I now need to explain and further elaborate on it. As a part of the overall processes of economic growth, humans have developed a wide range of useable assets, such as currencies, banking systems, educational services, mechanisms to access and deliver sources of energy, legal institutions, and insurance schemes. We can easily add to this list by making references to systems of credit, physical infrastructures, structures to supply potable water, property registries, and the like. As societies create and further develop these kinds of assets, they thereby greatly enhance their capacities to make effective use of limited natural and human resources. In the broadest terms these assets may all be referred to as capital assets, that is, as durable institutions and provisions designed over the long term to generate varied products, services, and incomes without directly diminishing the assets themselves so long as these assets are regularly maintained. In order to maintain these assets, it is important to invest in them regularly in appropriate ways, the forms of which depend on the character of the assets themselves.

For heuristic purposes, as I have already indicated, it is useful to distinguish between financial assets, productive assets, human assets, social assets, and natural asserts. In the following paragraph I will further elaborate upon my previous discussion. Financial assets include a wide range of institutions and provisions which allow for the creation and protection of financial wealth. These include the development of currencies, savings accounts, various financial instruments like credit systems and bonds and corporate shares, as well as public and private insurance systems. The value of financial assets inheres both in the arrangements to store wealth as well as the wealth that is thereby invested and protected. Productive assets in turn refer to organizational and technological arrangements by means of

[44] The Commission on the Measurement of Economic Performance and Social Progress makes a similar argument. See Stiglitz, Sen, and Fitouusi, *Mis-Measuring Our Lives*, chapter 3.

which people directly utilize natural and human resources to produce goods and services that meet human needs and wants. We would include within productive assets the domestication of animals, systems for irrigation, the development of a wide range of tools, the creation of workplaces, the development of meritocratic systems of administration, as well as modern systems of electronic communication. Human assets refer to all of those investments, including especially educational systems, which greatly increase the skills and capacities of humans to utilize other assets more effectively. Among other human assets, several that have played decisive roles in fostering economic productivity include a number of social skills as well as dispositions favouring hard work, thrift, and entrepreneurship. Social assets include the culturally cultivated capacities to trust others, to develop useable networks beyond kinship ties, and to community relations with diverse others. We might well include as social assets the expansion both of civil society organizations as well as public governmental bodies in so far as they all facilitate or foster social cooperation.[45]

In addition, economic growth has also been facilitated by the development of natural assets. To be sure, the earth has existed long before humans appeared on earth and will most likely exist long after humans no longer exist on earth, if not sooner then at least as the sun ages and the corresponding increase in solar heat and radiation make life on earth impossible. Obviously, the earth has value in itself quite apart from humans. From a biblical perspective, the earth was viewed as good by God without any reference to humans. An "Earth Ethic" may well call upon humans to care for and protect the earth simply because that is what the earth deserves. However, the language about economic assets is human-centred. So when we refer to natural assets, we are referring to ways in which the resources of the earth have become useable by humans in durable ways. The domestication of a number of animals as well as invention of agriculture represents useful examples of the way the earth and its resources have become assets for economic activity. The human uses of fire represent another useful and important example of a resource of the earth that has become a natural asset. Over time humans have learned how to extract water from the earth by drilling wells, diverting streams, catching rain in basins, and constructing dams across rivers. These examples point to an important norm with respect to all assets and natural assets in particular.

---

[45] North *et al.*, *Violence and Social Order*, call attention to the great expansion in the number and diversity of social organizations as the characteristic feature of modern industrial societies, characterized by what they refer to as open access social order.

Assets are best used if users fully respect the character of the asset and do not use up or otherwise degrade assets. While humans have long ago learned how to make water into a natural asset, in modern times they are both depleting and degrading this asset.

I have argued that economic growth consists in the creation and protection of human and natural assets, which in turn make it possible for humans to utilize human and natural resources more productively. However, whenever humans act to destroy, deplete, or degrade these diverse assets—as they do when they overwork labourers, pollute water supplies, or exhaust mineral resources—then their actions must be regarded as unproductive and value-destroying no matter how much income they may produce in the process.

Societies are more able to develop useable economic assets to the extent that they have constructed the corresponding physical, social, and economic infrastructures that both embody many of these assets and facilitate the creation and protection of others. As societies develop their physical infrastructures, they correspondingly create the conditions—roads, water systems, electricity grids, and the like—that facilitate the expansion of local commerce, the growth of local industry, even the construction of schools—concomitant with increasingly productive utilization of their human and natural resources. The expansion of social infrastructures has had corresponding consequences: as societies develop educational services, health services, and social insurance programs, they correspondingly strengthen human and social assets, which in turn foster economic growth. The development of economic infrastructures plays an equivalently instrumental role, by expanding credit, institutionalizing market exchanges, fostering commerce, and facilitating investments. In many respects, the best rough estimate of the extent and the ways in which developing countries are developing is to examine the degree to which they have been able to establish and to enlarge upon physical, social, and economic infrastructures.

Economic growth is thus best viewed as the process of asset development. As societies develop their economic capital assets, by increasing both the scope of these assets as well as the effectiveness of particular assets, they develop their ability to make more productive use of available resources and increase the accessibility of previously inaccessible resources. Understood in these terms, economic growth as the process of producing more productively remains a valuable objective for both developing and industrialized societies. Therefore, just as in response to the current global crisis regarding economic growth, it has become imperative to consume sustainably, so it has also become an imperative to produce productively. However, with regard to productivity, the agendas facing the developing and industrialized societies differ in important ways.

Before examining these distinct agendas, we need to discuss briefly how we might at least approximately measure economic growth defined as the productive development of economic assets. As the Commission on the Measurement of Economic Performance and Social Progress observed, we need to use several different indicators.[46] In general terms, we will need to gauge the extent and the ways societies have over selected periods of time established, further developed, maintained, and/or degraded the basic range of financial, productive, human, social, and natural assets associated with economic growth. We will, accordingly, be measuring productivity not just in relation to the extent to which given hours of labour are able to produce diverse goods and services whose economic value is measured by current market prices adjusted for purchasing power parity. This widely used measure of productivity ignores completely the extent to which we have found ways of using given quantities of natural assets more effectively or the extent to which we have depleted or degraded these assets. This approach to gauging productivity is far too narrow. It is a mismeasure of productivity, not only because it overlooks the development and uses of natural assets, but also because it overlooks as well the development and uses of productive, social, and financial assets. It is true that we will not be able to measure productivity as precisely as we might hope because we have adopted a broader more multi-dimensional understanding of productivity. Nevertheless, we can, as uses of the Human Development Index demonstrate, find some approximate measures that gauge various ways in which economic assets are being established, expanded, used effectively, and/or abused. We can, for example, in approximate terms measure the extent of credit available through local banks, the availability of fresh water, and the access to and extent of electrical energy. One of the benefits of using these kinds of multi-dimensional measures of economic growth is that we will be forced to recognize that economic growth as increases in the productive uses of natural and human resources is in fact a complex, multi-dimensional process.

Defined in relation to the development of economic assets and the productive uses of given resources, economic growth is an imperative for large parts of the world that remain under-developed. Economic growth becomes a means of reducing poverty that still afflicts at least one third of

[46] See Stiglitz, Sen, and Fitoussi, *Mis-Measuring Our Lives*, chapter 3.

all humans. Economic growth offers the promise for developing needed physical, social, and economic infrastructures. Understood as producing productively, economic growth offers prospects of establishing, developing, and utilizing limited natural and human assets more effectively.

There are a number of critical issues that we must address in order to foster fitting and effective patterns of economic growth in developing areas. We have already made passing reference to some of these.

First, it takes a long time for economies to grow, to establish and enlarge upon the economic assets—and the corresponding institutions and infrastructures—that constitute the basic building blocks of productive development. The economic arrangements associated with industrialization are best introduced in societies which have already found ways to make more effective use of resources through more modern methods of agriculture and have become more economically inter-connected through the expansion of local commerce. It is easier for firms to produce productively to the extent that they can utilize the economic assets embodied in developing corresponding physical, social, and economic infrastructures. Marx once wrote that "Men make their own history but they do not make it just as they please; they do not make it under circumstances chosen by themselves, but under circumstances directly encountered, given, and transmitted from the past."[47] Correspondingly, if we hope to foster modern forms of industrial life in developing countries, we need first to work at establishing their preconditions, which include working to develop more productive forms of agriculture, more effective forms of local commerce, and the infrastructures that facilitate these developments.

In contrast, many investors from industrialized countries and many of the economic and political elites in developing countries seem to be especially interested in fostering developments that generate much wealth in the short term for those involved. Often these ventures focus on the extraction of minerals and energy and/or growth of commodities for foreign markets. Typically, the enterprises involved, like businesses in old company towns, build infrastructures almost exclusively for their own uses rather than collaborating with local agents to develop larger, more encompassing road systems, electricity grids, water systems, as well as educational and health services. Both foreign investors and local elites seek to augment their power and wealth. As a result, while over the short term these ventures do generate streams of income for those involved, they often only

[47] Karl Marx, *The Eighteenth Brumaire of Louis Bonaparte* (New York: International Publishers, 1963), p. 15.

marginally help to establish and expand the economic assets associated with producing productively. To be sure, in many developing countries some of the wealth produced by these ventures has ended up in government revenues and some of these funds have been utilized to fund infrastructure projects. Many observers argue that local business and political elites in many underdeveloped countries typically form patrimonial alliances that generate incomes for those immediately involved but lead neither to the development of effective systems of public administration or anything like thriving business sectors.[48] Recently, a number of observers have criticized the failures of international aid programs to foster economic growth in developing countries.[49] One might make an equivalent critique of international investments in so far as in many areas billions of dollars invested have had only marginal impact on developing the broad range of economic assets integral to the increasingly productive utilization of limited natural and human resources.

If least developed countries are going to grow economically, then they must find ways of producing more productively. They need a different approach to economic growth, one that is much more oriented to developing economic assets broadly understood and the corresponding infrastructures. In the process, they need to strengthen effective systems of public administration, encourage and support the expansion of local businesses, stimulate local commerce, and foster the development of institutions that make these developments possible. Economic growth in this form is possible, as we can see from examples of development in places as different as South Korea, Chile, and Indonesia. However, as these examples well illustrate, recent economic growth in these countries benefitted from the prior development of diverse social, productive, and human assets and corresponding infrastructures. Before their recent and noteworthy periods of marked economic expansion, these countries had educational systems, comparatively reliable systems of public administration, many energetic local business enterprises, and modest but useable physical infrastructures.[50]

---

[48] See Antoinette Handley, *Business and the State in Africa* (Cambridge University Press, 2008).

[49] See William Easterly, *White Man's Burden: Why the West's Efforts to Aid the Rest Have Done So Much Ill and So Little Good* (New York: Penguin Press, 2006); and Dambisa Moyo, *Dead Aid* (New York: Farrar, Straus, and Giroux, 2009).

[50] See Sylvia Maxfield and Ben Ross Schneider eds., *Business and the State in Developing Countries* (Ithaca and London: Cornell University Press, 1997).

Second, in so far as possible, it is important to foster inclusive patterns of economic growth in developing countries rather than growth that assumes enclave-like forms. The issue here concerns the degree to which any investment, government program, or private enterprise broadly helps the society as a whole to develop or rather functions primarily to benefit particular groups. Often investments in developing countries have not been well-integrated into the economies of the host country. In part these enterprises remained isolated because they were developed to sell what they produced—copper, oil, cotton, tobacco, or coffee—on foreign markets and they used few local enterprises as suppliers. Many developing countries created export processing zones which, while they did offer employment opportunities for some workers and returns for a few local investors, played little or no role in developing economic assets and infrastructures for the host countries. In many cases, foreign investments were not integrated in local economies simply because physical and economic infrastructures of these countries remained under-developed. Both host countries and foreign investors are accordingly challenged to find ways in which foreign investments can become more fully integrated in local economies and thereby have greater impact on the development of economic assets in these countries. One strategy for helping to realize this goal would be to require foreign investors to partner with enterprises from the host country to develop at a regional or provincial level, and not simply at a site or local level, the several infrastructural services that foreign investors will require simply to do business. As a condition of doing business, foreign firms would be expected to collaborate with partners from the developing areas to construct on a wider scale the systems for providing electricity, water, transportation, garbage collection, health care, and security which they need in order to do business. In the process these ventures not only will produce income for investors and employees and taxes for governments, but also will work to establish and strengthen capital assets, broadly understood, that will in turn render the overall economy more productive.[51]

Third, efforts need to be made to limit the degree to which industrialized nations directly act to restrict the productive growth of developing

[51] I have developed this line of argument both in an essay on "Perspectives on Global Poverty," in Frederick Bird and Manuel Velasquez, eds., *Just Business Practices in a Diverse and Developing World* (Basingstoke: Palgrave-Macmillan, 2006), chapter 7, and in a more recent essay on "Mining and Inclusive Wealth Development," presented at the meetings of World Congress of Mining in Montreal, Canada, August, 2013.

areas. From this perspective, many developing countries suffer not just from the lack of development and not just from the legacy of past colonial practices. They suffer as well because of the ways they are currently impeded from productively developing their own financial, productive, human, social, and natural assets. I will review several noteworthy examples. For instance, by virtue of price supports and tax credits they offer to agricultural enterprises in their own countries, industrialized countries in the European Community, North America, and Japan act to frustrate the efforts of farming enterprises in many developing areas to sell their produce both at home and abroad. In many developing countries, agricultural sectors are correspondingly less developed than they might otherwise be. In addition, many international businesses operating in developing areas pay taxes much lower than they might be expected to pay because they have made abusive use of transfer pricing practices, related to services and products they have acquired from foreign branches of their own companies. Although mining operations in Chile have greatly expanded since the 1990s, and although these firms have extracted minerals worth billions of dollars, these firms have paid little or no taxes to the government of Chile because of their clever use of transfer pricing.[52] As a result the Chilean government simply has less revenue for upgrading the physical and social infrastructures of the country. Furthermore, to the extent that foreign enterprises invest in enclave-like projects in developing countries, they also correspondingly occasion and intensify inequalities in these countries in ways that aggravate social tensions and undermine social capital.

While continuing to be an urgent imperative, fostering the productive development of the economies of developing areas will not be easy. It will take much time. However, when we view economic growth as the development of capital assets, then at least we have a better sense of how we might most effectively proceed. In keeping with the principle of consuming sustainably, we remain focused on establishing, expanding, and protecting diverse human and natural assets.

The agenda for economic growth in the industrialized societies differs. We remain interested in producing productively. We maintain our focus

[52] Manuel Riesco, "Pay Your Taxes! Corporate Social Responsibility and the Mining Industry in Chile," in Manuel Riesco, Gustavo Lagos and Marcos Lima, *The "Pay Your Taxes" Debate: Perspectives on Corporate Taxation and Social Responsibility in the Chilean Mining Industry*, Draft Report Prepared for the United Nations Research Institute (Santiago, Chile, 2004), http://biblioteca.hegoa.ehu.es/system/ebooks/17341/original/Pay_your_taxes.pdf, pp. 14-54.

on cultivating, refining, and protecting capital assets. We continue to call attention to activities that seek to mine assets for current flows of income and thereby to deplete or degrade these assets, whether these are human or natural assets.

From the perspective of our model regarding the productive utilization of natural and human resources, two issues especially seem to call for concerted public attention. These issues are different but may be related in terms of how we choose to address them. One issue concerns the especially high rates of un- and under-employment, especially of young people. Although these rates have been climbing over the past three and half decades, they have become especially aggravated since the financial crisis of 2007-8.[53] In some countries un- and underemployment rates for young males have reached 50%.[54] Un- and underemployment is in part a social problem because of the way this condition affects those involved and the degree to which those affected act in ways that are damaging to others. For example, many of those who are unemployed or underemployed over long periods are more likely to fail to support their families and dependents, engage in antisocial behaviour, acquire what they want or need by illegal means, and/or become easy recruits for militant terrorists groups. However, from the perspective of our model of productive growth, those who suffer from high rates of un- and underemployment represent underutilized and degraded human assets. Effective labour markets ought to be able to help those seeking workers to find employees and for those seeking employment to find work. To be sure a small portion of those who lack regular full time work do so on account of normal imperfections in labour markets on account of the fact that job seekers lack skills for available positions, cannot easily move to places where there are job openings, or lack information about these opportunities. However, in the present case, to a considerable degree the high rates of unemployment and underemployment reflect the overall lack of demand. The current challenge then is to find ways of increasing demand for labour that are economically feasible, add to the productive capacity of society, and do so in ways that are sustainable in terms of finite natural and human resources.

The situation with respect to underemployment and unemployment seems like an irresolvable conundrum that must be addressed effectively

---

[53] See Naomi Klein, *No Logo* (London: HarperCollins, 1999), Part Three; see also "Generation Jobless: Youth Unemployment," *The Economist* (April 27, 2013), pp. 58—60.

[54] Un- and underemployment is, of course, not just a problem for industrialized countries. It is also a severe problem in many developing countries.

but cannot be easily resolved. It does not seem likely that we will be easily able to create new job opportunities by stimulating consumer purchasing any time soon. In any case, mindlessly fostering consumer spending by encouraging consumer borrowing not only represents a deeply flawed practice, but would also foster over-consumption in ways that deviate from our standards of sustainable consumption. Would it be possible to call upon governments to increase their indebtedness in order to stimulate the demand for more workers? While many would immediately object to this suggestion, we need to pause and reflect before we so quickly dismiss this idea. The governments in many industrialized countries have already been engaged in activities like this. In the United States, for example, the federal government has been effectively investing to stimulate job opportunities indirectly both through the Earned Income Tax Credit, which adds to the incomes of otherwise low paid workers, and the tax credit for mortgage interest payments, which indirectly works to subsidize the housing industry. The government subsidizes the agricultural industries with billions of dollars of price supports. The government also provides effective subsidies through the ways they undertake contracts for defence spending. Obviously many people overtly opposed to governments acting to increase demand for labour in practice avidly support policies that do just that. Moving people otherwise opposed to acknowledge their implicit support for these kinds of initiatives is not likely to be easy.

Much depends on what kinds of actions governments might undertake to stimulate increased demand for labour and how much these initiatives are likely to cost over time. Much depends on whether government actions facilitate genuine growth, as in the increasingly productive use of natural and human resources, or the facsimile of growth, like purchasing otherwise unaffordable housing by taking out loans only repayable if the market prices continue to rise and the increasing value of the purchase allows one to re-pay the loan. In relation to this question, it is instructive to compare two programs developed by the federal government in the United States during the depression of the 1930s. The better known of these was the Works Progress Administration (WPA), which funded all sorts of programs including municipal improvement projects and theatre groups. To qualify for these positions, applicants had to apply through local welfare offices and they were paid welfare wages. Although the WPA gave rise to many civic improvements, many felt it largely consisted in make work projects. The government also funded the Public Works Administration (PWA), which undertook a number of major construction projects especially involved in developing physical infrastructures in the form of electricity, water supplies, and roads for parts of the country, especially in rural areas, where these were missing. The PWA paid workers at going rates. In turn as these workers spent what they earned in local communities, they helped to revive the economies in these communities. The workers themselves and their communities in turn were able to make larger tax payments. Although the PWA cost the government more per worker, it had a much larger and more permanent impact on the economic growth of the country.[55] The PWA helped to build infrastructures and foster genuine growth, and the economic growth in turn eventually helped to pay off the cost of the initial investments.

If countries have any hope of addressing the problem occasioned by this huge oversupply of able-bodied adults looking for work, then they need to explore initiatives like the PWA. Responding to this crisis in a half-hearted way is likely to make matters worse by driving up public debts without producing genuine growth. As interesting and useful as the WPA was, it did not have anywhere near the equivalent impact. It did not strengthen the asset bases of society to anything like the same extent. It was what we might call a humanitarian initiative and an unusually creative one. It represented a far less effective instrument for stimulating an otherwise depressed economy. Accordingly, using as a point of reference our model of economic growth as asset development, we can then explore what kinds of initiatives might be undertaken to stimulate the demand for labour in ways that help build infrastructures and capital assets in sustainable ways. Interestingly, as we look for possible ways to address the under-development and under-utilization of labour, we confront a second major issue facing many industrialized societies, namely, the degradation and under-development of several different kinds of physical and social infrastructures.

In many industrial societies as the demand for their services increases, physical and social infrastructures are deteriorating. Road systems are overcrowded and not always well-maintained. User complaints increase. Many public school systems seem to be performing less well than they did in the past. Water systems are depleting limited sources. More demands are placed on healthcare services than they can address in a timely manner. Court systems grind along dispensing justice but doing so in ways that often waste the time of litigants and lawyers. Increasing numbers of elder-

---

[55] See John K. Galbraith assisted by G. G. Johnson, Jr., *The Economic Effects of the Federal Public Works Expenditures* (Washington, D.C.: National Resources Planning Board, U.S. Government Printing Office, 1940); and Donald S. Howard, *The W.P.A. and Federal Relief Policy* (New York: Russell Sage Foundation, 1943).

ly and handicapped people seem to need more services than are available. The overall quality of life seems to be deteriorating. At the same time, as we have already observed, diverse eco-systems from lakes and rivers to wetlands and marshes, from endangered species to over-used parklands call for increased care and attention. While industrialized countries may not now experience what are usually called economic depressions, one might make a case that their physical and social infrastructures are experiencing something like the equivalent of depression. They just are not working as well as they might.

It is possible to see how industrialized societies might benefit from economic growth both in general terms as the more effective utilization of limited natural and human resources as well as in specific forms designed to find employment opportunities for underemployed and unemployed adults looking for work, and to strengthen and invigorate social and physical infrastructures. Because we live in a world of limited resources, economic growth, understood as the process of asset development, remains a desirable objective for both developing and industrialized societies.

Collaborating Globally

In order to address responsibly the current global crisis with respect to economic growth, I have argued we should not look for a position midway between the current champions of economic growth and the champions who call for limits to growth or the end of growth. Rather, as I have indicated, we need to re-think the nature of economic growth in ways that allows us to respond effectively both to the most compelling arguments for restraint as well as to those arguments that favour economic growth in targeted areas redefined in terms of the development of durable and productive assets. I have argued that we cannot effectively address this crisis by favouring restraint in the industrialized world and by favouring development in the developing world. Rather, in so far as this is indeed a global crisis, then we need to consume limited natural and human resources sustainably in both developing and industrialized countries. Furthermore, in both developing and industrialized societies it is useful to encourage efforts to develop durable capital assets and to strengthen corresponding physical, social, and economic infrastructures, thereby utilizing natural and human resources more effectively. Overall, the current crisis calls for us seriously to re-think what we mean by economic growth, to recognize it as a multi-dimensional process, and to develop responses that at once foster both fundamental restraint because the resources of the earth and its inhabitants are limited, as well as efforts to utilize these resources more productively.

If we have any hope of addressing the current global crisis with respect to economic growth responsibly, then we must do so by collaborating globally. If we any have hope of restraining growth where it needs to be restrained by consuming sustainably while at the same time stimulating growth how and where it needs to be stimulated by producing productively, then we must find ways to foster broad global cooperation with respect to these pressing objectives. It is not enough to produce interesting and incisive analyses and/or to articulate eloquent and fact-laden warnings. For appropriate actions to take place, we need to engage in reciprocating conversations with people who are likely to disagree with us. We need to listen to and talk with both those sympathetic to our concerns and those likely to resist any meaningful efforts to address this crisis. At the same time as we work to develop realistic agendas to address these concerns in timely ways, we need to reach out globally to involve all relevant players in on-going conversations about these matters. These conversations must include those who are likely to have divergent interests and harbour distrust. We will not be able to address this crisis adequately with agreements just among democratic countries, or industrialized countries, or African countries, or Muslim countries. We won't be able to address this crisis if we are only able to reach understanding among trade unions and environmentalists, but not business enterprises or understandings among businesses and environmentalists that exclude representatives of labour.

If we are unable to collaborate globally to address this unavoidable crisis, then the crisis is likely to get much worse. Many will suffer from continuing poverty, from adverse climate change, from stalled economies, from increasingly high prices for energy and some minerals, from underemployment and degraded infrastructures, and from rising sea levels. Conflicts will become exacerbated between those fostering particular forms of economic growth as this furthers their interests and those opposing any forms of growth because of adverse impact on the planet.

We must work to make conversations about this crisis as inclusive as possible, so those with effective decision-making power, whether they are governments or businesses, faith communities or trade unions, not only voice their concerns, but also listen attentively to those who voice divergent views. Faith communities are especially challenged to educate themselves regarding this crisis and to participate in unfolding discussions fully because at base this is not just an economic crisis. It is a crisis that challenges our basic assumptions about how we as humans are expected to live our lives on this planet.

It may be impossible to reach any kind of lasting resolution regarding this global crisis, given the deeply held divergent views of a number of contemporary groups. Still, there are good reasons for hope. Eventually, the crisis may become so exacerbated, that it will be impossible to ignore. However, in that case, our responses are likely to be forced and the self-interests of those most powerful are likely to determine actions that are taken. It would be far better to find ways of responding before the current crisis becomes too severe. As I said, there are reasons to hope. People from diverse and differing backgrounds have at times found ways of reaching workable normative agreements to guide their interactions with respect to other global issues. In spite of the continuing resorting to the use of armed force, people from diverse nations have agreed to the Geneva Conventions regarding the rights of the wounded, prisoners, and civilians in situations of armed conflict. Although these conventions continue to be violated on occasion, as do all normative standards, they have also over time gained both in official endorsement and in practical application. Likewise, in spite of their disagreements, people from diverse nations have endorsed a number of declarations and covenants spelling out basic human rights. While support is not universal, still many who dissent from particular clauses, not only embrace the broader notion of human rights, but also have voiced their commitment to most of the rights invoked by these United Nations documents. We can point to a number of examples where people from diverse cultures and political persuasions have reached other normative agreements regarding global issues. Consider, for example, the agreements on trade of endangered species, the international ban on land mines, the Equator Principles which establish normative requirements with respect to how development projects funded by loans from a number of international banks ought to proceed, and the Kyoto agreement regarding emissions of greenhouse gases. Some of these agreements gained wider assent than others. All gained wide compliance from countries that otherwise differed on many issues. Elsewhere I have referred to these kinds of global agreements as examples of the practices of global ethics.[56] They represent examples of people from diverse backgrounds developing workable frameworks to address particular global problems in spite of deeply-held disagreements about other matters.

[56] Frederick Bird, Sumner Twiss, Kusumita Pedersen, Clark Miller, and Bruce Grelle (in process) *The Practice of Global Ethics*(a book manuscript under submission for publication).

What matters is that people concerned about the global crisis with respect to economic growth find ways of engaging in some kinds of serious conversations with each other. Whether they begin from the perspective of those who continue to view growth as imperative—whether as a means of overcoming economic slowdowns or as a means of alleviating poverty—or they begin from the orientation of those who point with alarm at the ways growth has adversely affected the earth, they need to enter into thoughtful dialogues. At the extremes, both groups have developed a range of arguments to how the concerns raised by their opponents ought to be dismissed or treated as comparatively of little importance. At both ends, proponents feel that their own arguments are not being taken as seriously as they ought to be taken and that too many people are being persuaded by others either because they have not really thought about these matters realistically or because it simply serves their self-interests. In the process, too many of those concerned have been engaging in by-passing monologues rather than genuinely reciprocating conversations. At the outset, what is required is that those concerned attempt to listen more attentively to others with whom they are inclined to differ and to see what elements of their opponents' arguments they might thoughtfully consider, and might in some instances propose ways of re-assessing to fit more closely with their own concerns. I doubt whether these kinds of conversations will be easy or will result in quick resolutions. However, over time they can be educational.

As they seek to engage globally in these kinds of reciprocating conversations, it is important to keep this point in mind. As we engage in these conversations, we are not simply trying to win debates. Hopefully, we are also trying to learn, to gain a better sense of what is happening and what is likely to happen. Therefore, it is very important that these conversations proceed on the basis of reliable information. It is important to seek out relevant analyses by trained investigators, who are studying the impacts of economic activities on social and natural environments, examining the viability of alternative energy sources, and exploring in particular and global ways how to consume more sustainably and how to produce more productively.[57]

This third basic principle, which I have referred to as collaborating globally, may be more important as a means of addressing the global crisis with respect to economic growth than the first two about consuming sustainably and producing productively. After all, any agreement or norma-

[57] Clark A. Miller and Paul N. Edwards, eds., *Changing the Atmosphere: Expert Knowledge and Environmental Governance* (Cambridge: MIT Press, 2001).

tive understanding worth anything must be one in which people from diverse nations, economic philosophies, political persuasions, and faith communities seek to reach by seriously conversing with each other.